The End of Economic Man?

Custom and Competition in Labour Markets

David Marsden
Lecturer in Industrial Relations
London School of Economics

WHEATSHEAF BOOKS

First published in Great Britain in 1986 by
WHEATSHEAF BOOKS LTD
A MEMBER OF THE HARVESTER PRESS PUBLISHING GROUP
Publisher: John Spiers
Director of Publications: Edward Elgar
16 Ship Street, Brighton, Sussex

British Library Cataloguing in Publication Data

Marsden, David W, 1950–
    The end of economic man? : custom and competition
    in labour markets.
    1. Labour supply
    I. Title
    31.12   HD5706
    ISBN 0–7450–0042–8

Typeset in (Times Roman 11/12 point) by Photo·Graphics,
Honiton, Devon
Printed and bound in Great Britain by
Biddles Ltd, Guildford and King's Lynn

THE HARVESTER PRESS PUBLISHING GROUP
The Harvester Group comprises Harvester Press Ltd (chiefly
publishing literature, fiction, philosophy, psychology, and science
and trade books); Harvester Press Microform Publications Ltd
(publishing in microform previously unpublished archives, scarce
printed sources, and indexes to these collections); Wheatsheaf
Books Ltd (chiefly publishing in economics, international politics,
sociology, women's stuidies and related social sciences); Certain
Records Ltd, and John Spiers Music Ltd (music publishing).

To my family and my friends

Contents

Contents

Acknowledgements

I should like to thank especially Professor F. Sellier who invited me to the Laboratoire d'Economie et de Sociologie du Travail where this work was begun, and who has encouraged me to persevere with it. I should also like to thank F. Eyraud, P. Ryan, J. J. Silvestre, as well as J. R. Crossley, S. Dex, R. F. Elliott, C. Johnston, D. Laussel, T. Nichols, M. J. Piore, W. Sengenberger, M. Vernières, P. Wiles, and my colleagues at the LSE, especially in the Department of Industrial Relations and in the Centre for Labour Economics.

1 Introduction

1.1. INTRODUCTION

The aim of this book is to take a critical look at some recent developments within economics which have sought to break away from the restrictive and unrealistic assumptions of perfect competition, and to grapple with some of the complexities of the institutional and social forces acting upon labour markets. Although the tone will be critical, students of sociology and industrial relations need to be aware of these developments, just as economists need to be aware of some of the limitations of this work.

The theoretical developments are also important to a wider audience. They represent an attempt to come to terms with some of the changing features of labour markets, particularly as a result of the extension of legislation and of collective bargaining in many countries during the 1960s and 1970s, as well as with some of the older, and still persistent, 'peculiarities' of labour that Marshall observed cause labour markets to behave differently from markets for other goods. This chapter begins by outlining these questions, and then begins to set out the case for a more multi-disciplinary approach to theory, research and policy analysis based more on the evidence and arguments of all three of these disciplines. It is argued that some of the characteristic postulates of economic theory which will emerge in the course of the book are obstacles to such a wider approach.

The final chapter seeks to build on the earlier ones, and proposes a view of labour markets in which occupational labour markets,[1] which come closest to those of the competitive model on account of the greater possibility they offer for labour mobility, are akin to public or collective goods such that where adequate provisions for their organisation and finance are lacking, internal labour markets[2] will be the norm. An occupational market may be defined

1

as relating to persons endowed with a particular skill or qualification, validated by a diploma or by the opinion of their peer group, and is often organised on collective lines. Competitive markets for skilled labour should be treated as institutional phenomena on a par with other institutions in labour markets, and not as representing a natural model towards which labour market organisation converges. The final chapter also attempts to trace out some of the implications for this reversal of perspective on labour markets, and to use it to explain some of the peculiarities of labour markets as compared to markets for other types of commodities. In addition, it removes a number of obstacles to cross-disciplinary research and policy analysis. In that chapter also, a certain number of types of labour market intermediate between occupational and internal labour markets will be analysed.

1.2. RECENT CHANGES IN LABOUR MARKET ORGANISATION

During the late 1960s and 1970s, there occurred a period of change in labour market organisation in many industrialised countries that was as dramatic as that of the emergence of widespread collective bargaining in the early twentieth century in several western European countries, or after the Wagner Act in the United States. In many countries, there was a big growth in labour legislation concerning both individual and collective rights. At the individual level there was increased protection against arbitrary dismissal, and acceptance of the principle that individual workers should be compensated for facilitating economic changes for example through redundancy, and at the collective level increased rights of consultation, information, and even negotiation over management decisions which could adversely affect employment. Examples of the former would be the British Redundancy Payments Act of 1965, and Employment Protection Acts of 1975 and 1978, or the Italian 1970 Workers' Statute. Increasing the powers of workers collectively, and extending their influence further into traditional management issues, were the 1972 German Works Constitution Act extending the powers of the works councils, the French legislation increasing the powers of the Enterprise Committees, the Swedish industrial democracy act (the MBL Act) not to mention the initiatives of the European Community in the area of industrial democracy which are yet to bear fruit. Moreover, collective bargaining also penetrated into new areas, as with the West German 'rationalisation agreements' of the early 1960s, and agreements on labour force reductions in both France and Italy in the middle to late 1960s. In Britain also productivity bargaining, despite its reputation as a loophole in incomes policies, has continued to thrive as many companies rely upon negotiation to introduce changed working patterns. Even in the United States, the recent crises in the automobile industry have led the companies to develop for the first time 'employee involvement' schemes which they had always vigorously opposed in the past.

Added to this is an increased awareness of the great effectiveness of the social organisation of the large Japanese firms whose emphasis upon internal labour markets for their core labour force stands in stark contrast to the conventional view of western occupational labour markets. Indeed, the contrast between the flexibility of Japanese labour in deployment between jobs in these internal labour markets contrasts with the much greater rigidity of job demarcations that arises from attachment to occupational labour markets. This interest in Japanese management methods can be measured in the number of management books on Japan, the number of visits by western production and personnel managers to Japanese firms, by the attempts to apply certain Japanese methods, such as 'quality circles', and the 'just-in-time' system for the elimination of intermediate stocks, and in the large number of joint ventures between western and Japanese firms, which although partly aimed at plugging gaps in the markets of the western firms, are also undertaken in the hope of benefiting from Japanese organisational expertise. Indeed, so extensive is the interest in

Japan, that some writers have begun to compare the 'Japanese revolution' in work and production organisation to the revolution in production methods introduced earlier this century by Taylor and Ford. The implications of these for the organisation of western labour markets and for our theories of how labour markets work have yet to be explored.

Moreover, the increased legislation and collective bargaining over major lay-offs in western labour markets have raised the cost of hiring and firing labour, so that western firms also appear to be placing a greater emphasis than before upon their internal labour markets. And this combined with the great interest among managers in Japanese techniques of manpower management may cause a move away from the traditional occupational labour markets of some western countries such as Britain.

In addition, the 1960s and 1970s have also seen increased state intervention in employment measures, and particularly in vocational training and retraining. Indeed, it may seem ironic that the British government which most espouses economic liberalism, and which abolished a number of the statutory bipartite industry training boards, should have undertaken the biggest, and potentially most far-reaching youth training programme any British government has ever embarked upon. Few European governments have refrained from extensive intervention in youth labour markets in recent years. To this one should add the impact of wage regulation, be it in the form of the French and Dutch minimum wages, or the British incomes policies, or the state-supported collective bargaining in Italy over the system of wage indexation.

Thus, in recent years it is hard to escape the conclusion that the labour market in most western countries now is subject to a wide range of external influences which may profoundly alter its behaviour. To understand how it functions under these new conditions, it is more important than ever to try to understand the interaction between conventional market and institutional and social pressures, and to do so we need explore ways in which the knowledge we have of labour markets from labour economics can be usefully combined with that of labour market institutions and group behaviour from industrial relations and from industrial sociology. This needs to be tackled at the level of understanding both how the processes covered by these disciplines interact, and how the concepts from these disciplines can be articulated with each other to form a coherent model.

1.3. LONGER-STANDING DOUBTS ABOUT THE PARALLEL BETWEEN LABOUR AND OTHER GOODS

In addition, it has long been recognised that labour markets differ from other markets in the economic system. Marshall recognised that labour differed from other commodities because workers are inseparable from the services they provide, and therefore carry their history, their culture and their social norms into their place of work. Keynes and Hicks also recognised that the employment relationship differs from other types of contractual relationship because of its frequently long and indeterminate duration which provides time for customs and norms, particularly those of 'fairness', to build up around it. Indeed, although most economists would probably agree with Reder that the framework of price theory should not be lightly cast aside, and that '*ad hoc*' exceptions should be treated as unsatisfactory, they would probably also accept that price theory has to be applied to the labour market with great caution. Several economists have attempted to develop economic theory in such a way as to take account of such influences, and to accommodate both the evidence that pressures of supply and demand, of competition, and of substitution are active in the labour market, and the equally powerful evidence, often from other disciplines, that custom, social norms, group pressures, and institutional rules are also active in shaping wage structures, labour mobility patterns, and other aspects of labour market behaviour.

There has been a long and often heated debate over the validity of economic theories of the labour market. The frequency with which wage claims are based on comparability, on established differentials, or on social justice, and the widespread justification of existing differentials by reference to custom or to the social status of a particular occupation, show that the arguments used in pay bargaining often reach far beyond the confines of labour markets. As any person acting as a mediator in pay disputes knows, moral arguments enter as often as does the availability of labour, and for the purposes of reaching a settlement, may often exert as powerful an influence on the outcome. Often also, the reasons people give for leaving jobs appear to have little to do with economic calculation. Many people's willingness to quit their jobs without having already found an alternative job even in periods of high unemployment would be surprising if everyone were continually weighing up the costs and benefits of remaining in their current job, and were seeking to maximise their lifetime earnings. The studies of labour mobility, discussed at various points in this book, also show that quite large differences in pay levels can persist between firms employing apparently similar labour in the same locality without any very strong tendency for workers to move from the lower- to the higher-paying firms. Such observations have led many to be sceptical about the relevance of economic theory to the study of labour markets, and have caused them to focus much more on organisational and institutional factors and social norms, factors often referred to by economists as 'sociological'. However, against this, one has to set the not inconsiderable body of evidence, mostly but not exclusively of an econometric nature, which provides at least some support for the mainstream economic theories of the labour market. Possibly one source of reconciliation between these divergent sets of observations lies in the frequently large unexplained residuals in econometric studies, and the number of exceptions to case study evidence.

1.4. SOME FINDINGS OF RECENT COMPARATIVE RESEARCH ON LABOUR MARKETS

The need for cross-disciplinary work on labour markets,

and to reassess economists' treatment of the social aspects of labour markets, is given a new urgency by the accumulating results of comparative research in different countries. This is begining to question a number of the standard models of the labour market which have served for a long time. For example, occupational labour markets have provided the basic model of the labour market in mainstream economic theory for many years, perhaps since Adam Smith. But key sectors of the Japanese economy function largely without such labour markets. There is keen competition to enter the large firm sector of employment, and there are low status labour markets in certain other sectors, and for temporary workers, but these are very different from the occupational labour markets of Britain or the United States. Indeed, even within western Europe, there is increasing evidence that the degree of reliance by firms upon internal and local labour markets varies considerably between countries, and that occupational labour markets, far from being a natural occurrence, depend heavily upon patterns of union organisation and upon national systems of vocational training. Another example would be the relationship between wage payments and effort and training. It may appear almost self-evident to European or American economists that there should be a close relation between these because of labour market pressures. But in Japanese firms, age stands out as a prime determinant of an individual's earnings, and for a great many workers, firms can rely upon non-pecuniary methods of motivation. Indeed, a strong interest is shown in these by western managers who believe such forms of payment may be more effective, particularly where the quality of output is important. A third example would be the different attitude of Japanese employers, not just in the large firm sector, to manpower reductions in the face of a decline in product demand.

If such practices were confined to Japanese business, then we could perhaps be content with the already difficult task of understanding western labour markets. But closer inspection of continental European countries and comparisons between Britain and the United States indicate a considerable variety in patterns of labour market organisation and of employer policies between these countries. Indeed, even within these countries there are important differences between sectors. Occupational labour markets appear to be more developed in Britain and West Germany than in France or Italy, and there is some indication that internal labour markets for manual workers may be more developed in the United States than in Britain. On the second comparison, earnings increase with age most in Japan, and least in Britain and West Germany, but they also increase a good deal with age in France, Italy, and the United States. Concerning lay-offs, there is increasing evidence that compared with some continental European countries, it is relatively easy for British employers to obtain redundancies, possibly because of a different pattern of labour market organisation, and different expectations that workers have of their employers. These comparisons could be multiplied many times over, and a number will be discussed, as will their implications for economic theory, throughout this book.

To understand these differences, and their implications for policy analysis, one needs to start from a recognition of the reality of the different institutional arrangements and the differences in motivation patterns.

1.5. THE NEED FOR A MULTI-DISCIPLINARY APPROACH TO LABOUR MARKET ANALYSIS

The problems arising from recent developments in labour legislation and collective bargaining, the longer-standing 'peculiarities' of labour noted by Marshall and many others, and some of the recent comparative research all point to the close relationship between competitive, institutional and normative forces on labour markets and the behaviour of employers, workers and their unions. Yet the high degree of specialisation among labour economists, industrial sociologists and industrial relations specialists means that people from each discipline often define their own research and policy problems in isolation. People in industrial sociology or industrial relations frequently complain about the narrow unrealistic models used by economists, but at the same time economists complain with some justification that the other two focus upon enterprise level relations or upon union behaviour as if labour markets did not exist.

It might be thought that what is needed is to bring together teams of specialists from these disciplines to deal, for example, with a specific policy problem. On occasions this has indeed been done, but often with only limited success. There might be several reasons for this besides those of personality and personal career orientation. First, such cooperation is often based on the premise that each discipline relates to a specific problem area of its own, and the skills of those engaged in each specialism are complimentary. But in fact this is only partly true. First, both the 'formalist' and the 'substantivist' definitions of the scope of economics, for example, cover the activities of trade unions, and the group pressures involved in informal workplace bargaining. Indeed, Becker, who is one of the current outstanding exponents of the modern formalist school within economics, would argue that these phenomena do indeed fall within the scope of economics and that the conceptual tools of economists are those most appropriate to their analysis. Equally, on the substantivist side, workplace relations and collective bargaining are very closely, although not exclusively, concerned with work and sharing its product. In a similar way, the definitions of the scope of sociology by Durkheim as the study of 'social facts', or by Weber as the study of 'social action' are also too all-embracing, and would also include people's choices and behaviour in markets, and in the workplace.

Secondly, it is only partly true that the specialists of each discipline bring different and complimentary skills, which can be brought together like those of engineers, designers and marketing specialists in the design of a new car, or those of different maintenance trades in repairing machinery. The amount of overlap between the objects of each of these social science disciplines means that there is a good deal of contested ground. The different disciplines make, to some extent, different predictions about human behaviour under similar circumstances, and stress different causes for observed patterns of behaviour. Because of the close relation between theories, or research programmes and the observations which they generate, each discipline bases its theories on different, but overlapping sets of evidence in relation to which it has shaped its key concepts. This indeed accentuates the problems arising out of this contested ground.

Had the problem of cross-disciplinary research simply been one of bringing together experts from different disciplines, this book could have been organised around research themes, contrasting the approaches, theories and evidence of each discipline in relation to a particular phenomenon, such as the action of social norms on labour markets or the behaviour of institutions in the labour market. After reading this book, it should be clear to the reader that such a plan would have failed because of the major differences in the way in which each of the disciplines defines its problems and directs its enquiry.

The consequence of this focus on different aspects of related problems is that one cannot really confront the theories from the three disciplines as competing in the way rival hypotheses compete within a research programme. They are more like theories from different research programmes or from different paradigms. They mostly compete indirectly by the logical implications which follow from their analysis. For example, while industrial relations specialists might have much that is of interest to say about custom and practice as they identify it, economists have relatively little of interest to say about the process as such, but what is interesting is the way in which they have tried to take account of its action upon the responsiveness of wage levels and working practices to more general economic pressures. Similarly, Becker's theory of discrimination in the labour market tells us very little about the nature of discrimination as such, and little that would enrich sociological or psychological theories, but it is extremely interesting as a theory of how it affects labour markets. Consequently, it was decided not to organise the book around a confrontation of these disciplines on particular questions.

1.6. THE APPROACH ADOPTED IN THIS BOOK

There are many different angles from which the question of cross-disciplinary work can be approached. Of the three disciplines mostly covered in this book, labour economics, industrial relations and industrial sociology, the first has the most fully developed core of theory, and contains the most systematic account of the working of labour markets. But being more systematic has tended to close off enquiry into aspects of labour markets which do not fit easily into its main body of theory. Thus labour economics has tended to be less eclectic than either industrial relations or industrial sociology. Consequently, the problem of cross-disciplinary work is posed more sharply in labour economics than in the other two disciplines, although the problem exists there as well. For this reason, the book will focus mostly on attempts by economists to deal with the influence of institutions and certain 'non-economic' forces on labour markets.

Rather than contrast what each of the three disciplines has to say about a particular problem, this book will instead examine a number of strategies used by economists to take account of factors influencing labour markets which do not belong to the conventional field of economics. This approach highlights some of the fundamental problems raised by cross-disciplinary research. Each discipline has developed its own core of theoretical concepts and its own rules of evidence, and has reshaped its theoretical core in the light of new empirical research. Each has specialised in a certain range of problems, which in reality are closely interrelated, but specialisation has meant that the central concepts of each of the three disciplines are to a fair degree incompatible one with another. One illustration of the degree of divergence, which is picked up later in this book, is the treatment of work group norms in the labour market. Economists commonly treat these as 'rigidities' in an otherwise freely adjusting system, whereas industrial relations specialists tend to stress the processes by which these norms change, and thus their flexibility. In relation to their own criteria both may be partly right, but if economists and

industrial relations specialists are to be able to work together
on common research and policy problems, there needs to
be some mutual adaptation of these criteria. These criteria
derive from the central core concepts of each discipline.
Thus the problem of cross-disciplinary work involves a
degree of adaptation of these core concepts, hence the
interest of this book in the strategies adopted by a number
of economists to analysis of these 'non-economic' influences
on labour markets. How have economists sought to adapt
the tools of economic analysis to these problems, and what
have been the limitations on this work? The limitations are
assessed in terms of empirical evidence drawn from the
other disciplines, although this cannot be an absolute criterion of their validity.

The reason for looking at strategies

The approach adopted has been to take different strategies
adopted by economists for introducing concepts and problems from industrial relations and sociology into economic
analysis. This is because the problem of extending the scope
of economics in these directions is in fact one of the construction of cross-disciplinary theory and explanation. This
involves two basic problems, and both derive from the fact
that concepts used in the social sciences to a greater or
lesser extent depend upon the theoretical matrix within
which they are developed, and continue to develop.

The first problem stems from the way the concepts used
to describe a phenomenon in a particular disciplinary theory
depend to a considerable degree upon related concepts in
the same theory. For example, the concepts of labour
supply, or of elasticity of demand, make little sense without
reference to a market for labour, and more generally to their
broader theoretical context in economic theory. Theories
consist of interrelated concepts which all help to define each
other, and this makes piecemeal borrowing of concepts from
another discipline problematic.

The second is that one should not confuse the terms of
everyday language with the technical terms of the social
sciences. The latter, when used carefully, help to organise
sets of fragmentary empirical observations into some kind

of coherent pattern, taking us beyond what can be reached with the concepts of ordinary language and everyday experience. Thus the theories and concepts in all three disciplines can lay claim to a degree of empirical support and of success in systematising our disparate sets of observations. As such, one can also say that most of the principal and tested concepts have a fair degree of empirical support.

The problem is that often the way such terms are used in one discipline cannot easily be reconciled with related terms in another discipline. The aim of much of this book is to examine strategies that have been used by economists to attempt such a reconciliation.

The types of strategy examined

Five strategies used to adapt concepts relating to the conventional area of another discipline are identified, and they fall into three broad types. The first type involves complete adaptation of the concept or complete redefinition of the problem so that it becomes fully consistent with the basic approach of economic theory. The third entails some reciprocal adaptation of concepts within economics. Intermediate between these two, the second type of strategy adapts the external concept fully to the main core of economic theory, but seeks to maintain a degree of specificity for the process described by the concept.

Chapter 2 corresponds to the first of these types. It examines cases in which labour economists have sought to integrate certain institutional forms completely into the framework of economic analysis by focusing on the functions served by these under conditions in which the full requirements of perfect markets could not be met. The intermediate type of strategy is dealt with in Chapter 3, in which the approach of Becker and of Lévy-Garboua had been to treat discrimination as a form of behaviour which departed from normal wealth-maximising behaviour and which had a non-economic status, but they reduced it to the status of a 'taste' in an individual's utility function, so that the normal calculus of economic theory could be applied.

The subsequent chapters deal with the third type of analysis in which there is some reciprocal adaptation of some of the central concepts of economic theory in order to accommodate the action of a social or an institutional process and identify three different strategies under this heading. Each takes a particular aspect of economic theories, namely the time component, the spatial component, and that concerning the types of actor involved. These are examined in turn. The first seeks to deal with the influence of social norms by articulating their action with that of the time component of economic processes. The second takes the spatial aspect of these processes looking at the structuring of labour markets, and the third takes the action of groups in labour markets by their impact in structuring the actors within labour markets.

1.7.　OUTLINE OF THE FIVE STRATEGIES

The first strategy examined seeks to explain fully the various institutional phenomena within labour markets without making any change in the basic framework of economic analysis. The cases analysed include theories about the nature of the labour contract, about the nature of the internal structure of firms, and notably the authority hierarchy, and about the labour market activities of trade unions. The first two sets of studies seek explicitly to analyse the labour contract and the authority structure in terms of the failure of two of the standard assumptions of perfect competition, namely full information and absence of uncertainty, particularly as concerned the fulfilment of contracts. The analysis of trade unions seeks to provide a microeconomic foundation for trade union activity.

The central aspects of the employment contract which the implicit contract and the hierarchy–contract theorists sought to explain were those of its duration, the conditions for lay-off, and the relative stability of wages compared with fluctuations in output. The relative fixity of wages combined with fluctuations in employment, and sometimes with legal or collectively negotiated terms for lay-offs, were widely observed in western industrialised labour markets, particularly during the period after the oil crisis.

The strategy in this case has been to define the problem purely in terms of the standard neo-classical model, making little or no adaptation of this core, but defining the institutional phenomenon purely in terms of its possible relation to this core. In calling 'implicit contract' theories of the labour contract 'insurance' theories, Stiglitz (1984) captures an important element since they treat the employment contract as embodying both a remuneration and an insurance element to cover against uncertainty and fluctuations in product markets.

Similarly, the model of the authority hierarchy in the firm proposed by Alchian and Demsetz treated this institutional fact purely as a response to the difficulties of monitoring the fulfilment of contracts, and according to their theory, lack of perfect information causes the observed institutional pattern. And again the phenomenon in question is fully adapted to fit the theoretical core of economics.

The second strategy is intermediate between fully adapting the external concept to the framework of economic theory, and adapting that framework itself. The strategy involves treating the particular phenomenon, in this case social norms (of which discrimination is a particular case), as the result of behaviour which is not wealth maximising although it still involves maximising behaviour—based on a utility function containing additional arguments. It thus maintains the standard calculus of utility maximisation, and makes no explicit change in the type of actor or in the type of space on which they move.

Despite recognising its non-monetary nature, Becker and Lévy-Garboua nevertheless considerably adapt the concept of discrimination in order to encompass it within the framework of optimisation. There being no explicit change in the apparatus of economic theory, there is a major implicit adaptation of the concepts of discrimination and of group norms. These imply the existence of relations between groups, one of which discriminates against the other and in favour of its own members, but this element disappears in Becker's and Lévy-Garboua's treatment.

Particularly in Becker's case, the wider interest of his analysis is that he sees discrimination as just one example, and an especially strong example, of the action of a social norm upon the labour market. Thus at one level his book is about the economics of discrimination, but at another it is about the economics of social norms and their effect upon decisions by labour market actors. That Becker's approach belongs to the second strategy is easily seen if one contrasts it with the 'statistical' theories of discrimination, according to which employers are optimising under conditions of imperfect information.

The third type of strategy involves adapting also the framework of economic analysis to varying degrees. A central feature of most social theories is that they contain a time component by which the various processes described within the theory are articulated. They also contain a spatial component which describes a set of conceptual locations between which these processes take place, and they contain a set of actors. These different components of a theory are all closely interelated. Movement on the spatial component requires some way of measuring time within the theory, and this time component is influenced by the way the spatial component is defined. Moreover, the concept of the 'actors' is influenced by both, as they are partly defined in terms of the processes they represent which are articulated in a theoretical time, and in terms of the way in which they can move upon the theoretical space.

If only one process is held to be at work in a particular theory, then the time component is fairly unimportant, but it becomes crucial if there is more than one, and they interact. A time component then has to be defined in order to define the cycles of action and reaction between these processes. Outside models of instantaneous adjustment with simultaneous determination of variables time becomes crucial.

The spatial element is also important. It plays a vital role in the interaction of different processes encompassed within a theory. Labour mobility between firms across the labour market is an obvious spatial component within economics, but in theoretical terms it need not be identified with geographical movement. Instead, its primary notion is that of movement between employers who might all be in the

same location. A person working from home can change
employers many times without changing physical location.
Other forms of spatial movement commonly recognised
within labour economics which do not imply geographical
movement include job mobility within the same firm, or
promotion to new jobs. In this case, movement to new
functions might lead one to contrast vertical and horizontal
movement in labour markets. Here the concept of space is
related to that of adjustment process, and just as economic
processes can be articulated through time, so they can be
articulated in a theoretical space.

That economic social theories specify actors may seem
rather obvious. But again there is a danger of translating
these too quickly into concrete terms. Actors within theories
are defined in terms of the kind of actions they can undertake within the context of the theory. Thus within economics
workers provide labour, and seek the most advantageous
terms compatible with other non-pecuniary objectives they
have. They are also attributed with certain powers, such as
leaving their present employer to search for job information,
or combining with other workers in pursuit of similar objectives. Thus one could regard them as defined, within the
theory, by certain behavioural rules and subject to certain
constraints. It is likewise for firms. A change in the scope
of action of such a theoretical actor can be achieved by
changing these rules, and thus altering that actor's con-
figuration.

Thus it is possible for the rules defining actors within the
theory to be related to those defining the space on which
they act, and to those defining the processes which interact
within the theoretically defined time.

The interrelation of all three elements can be illustrated
by an example from the game of chess. In chess, the actors
are defined not by their physical appearance, but by the
types of movement on the chess-board that each is allowed
to make. The king is additionally defined by certain moves
that he is not allowed to make (moving into 'check'), nor
must he be exposed to check by the moves of other pieces.
The space is defined by a set of rules expressed as constraints
on the moves which are possible from certain positions on

the board, but the rules defining the space can be changed, as is the case when people play 'cylindrical chess' in which moves normally restricted by the edge of the board can be continued from the corresponding square on the opposite side—as if the board were cylindrical in shape. Finally, the time component intervenes by the order of the moves. In chess, it is very simple.

Chess may be a rather limited model of the empirical world, but it is not a bad model of a theory as it illustrates the interdependence of time, space and actors, and it also illustrates the importance of rules in defining each of these, and how altering the rules can alter any one or all three of these components.

The first case to be dealt with is that of introducing the influence of the non-economic factor by treating it as a process active through time, and articulating it with other economic processes by playing on the time structure of processes within economic theory.

One of the best-known ways of articulating different processes in time within economics has been Marshall's distinction between the economic short and long periods. In the short period most of the variables of the long period are treated as fixed, in particular those affecting substitution between the main factors of production. Hicks' strategy for dealing with the influence of custom upon relative wages, one adopted by a large number of other writers, was to treat the processes generating customary differentials as active in the economic short period as the possibilities of substitution were limited, but as doomed in the economic long period. This periodisation was of course defined in terms of the processes required to alter some of these parameters, and only indirectly corresponded to physical time. The strong assumption about the social processes generating customary differentials was that they could be adequately contained in the economic short period. Thus there is a degree of mutual adaptation in this strategy, adapting the concept of custom to fit within the short period, and adapting economic theory by stressing the distinction between the short and long periods.

The second of these three strategies involves altering the

structure of the space on which labour market actors move. This idea is very explicit in the theories of labour market structure. The actors are not much changed, but the rules concerning the workers' scope for labour mobility between firms are altered either by specific rules restricting hiring and access, or by the impact of costs upon cost minimisation rules applied to employers, or of utility maximisation applied to workers. Within this approach, much of core of economic theory is again preserved by restricting the scope of action of social norms and of institutions by stressing the importance of production technique and its influence on work organisation and skill training. It is interesting that even Aglietta and Boyer maintained the importance of the constraints of production techniques over employers' decisions on the organisation of work, despite their position on monopolistic regulation of labour markets.

The third strategy is to specify differences in the organisation of the actors. Different types of actor are admitted into economic analysis on the assumption that their impact upon the rules defining the scope of markets is small. Unions are deemed to be acting upon pre-existing labour markets. Thus one might seek to build up models of union influence from a micro-economic foundation in the way Oswald suggests, and then trace union action from this. It is argued in the chapter devoted to this strategy that this degree of independence should not be assumed, and that actors both influence the space upon which they act (as in defining the scope of labour markets for example), and are influenced by that space. Thus the approaches discussed represent an adaptation of economic theory to cater for different types of actor, but they also place major constraints on the nature of the influence they exercise, and on the patterns of inter-action that can ensue.

1.8. SOME POSTULATES OF THE MAINSTREAM NEO-CLASSICAL MODEL OF THE LABOUR MARKET

There are a number of common postulates of mainstream

economic analysis of labour markets which will emerge as
obstacles to a broader cross-disciplinary approach through
the coming chapters, and it is perhaps worthwhile summarising them now.

Modern neo-classical economics is not a monolithic block
of theory, and it would be very difficult to identify a single
research programme even among neo-classical labour economists. Nevertheless, there are certain shared postulates,
often of an implicit nature, concerning methods and the
type of explanation used. Some of these can be obstacles
to a broader cross-disciplinary approach to labour markets,
and the purpose of this section is to outline these in prep-
aration for the chapters to follow. The most important of
these are: (i) the adoption of 'methodological individualism', (ii) the assumption of the logical priority of perfect
competition, (iii) the assumption that the labour market
contains large numbers of jobs in different firms requiring
similar skills and aptitudes which can be provided by local
labour markets, (iv) the treatment of the firm as a sort
of transmission mechanism between markets, and (v) the
assumption that technology is the key determinant of the
factor combinations between which firms may choose.

Methodological individualism is one of the key principles
underlying neo-classical models of the labour market, and
it states that the explanation of labour market processes
should be sought in the interaction of individual workers
and employers, each with their own sets of preferences.
Within each of their preference sets they are treated as
utility maximisers, although this is often simplified to treating them as wealth maximisers. Economic man is an individualistic utility maximiser, and indeed one of the main
arguments against the introduction of some kind of group
rationality arises out of the logical problems, such as the
Arrow or the Condorcet paradox concerning the aggre-
gation from individual to group preferences. According to
this paradox, aggregating sets of individual preferences,
which are all transitive at the individual level, can violate
transitivity at the aggregate level. On these lines, with this
model of individual choice, it is possible to show that there
is no such thing as a rational group.

The second postulate is that the competitive model of markets is logically prior to other types of market, in the sense that one should seek to explain why other forms of labour market organisation might develop out of competitive conditions, and how they can persist within a competitive economy. The application of this postulate can be seen in a number of cases. For example, considerable effort has gone into relaxing some of the very restrictive assumptions of the perfectly competitive labour market, such as the availability without cost of information about market conditions, alternative jobs and job applicants, and the absence of uncertainty in order to make the theory more applicable to actual problems such as unemployment or the nature of the employment relation. However, the method has been to examine the costs to labour market actors of efforts to improve their knowledge of available jobs, or to invest in new skills within the framework of an otherwise perfectly competitive labour market. Thus the centrality of competition as the fundamental explanatory principle is maintained. This of course is not to deny the important body of analysis of imperfect competition, but even there it is usually maintained that in an otherwise competitive system it will be limited.

The third assumption, which underlies the competitive model, is that the jobs in most firms can be done by a fairly large number of workers provided they have the appropriate skills. In its most extreme form of homogeneous labour, all jobs can be done by all workers, and in its more realistic model the labour market is divided into a number of occupational labour markets, such that an electrician's job in one firm involves the use of the same skills as in another. In this model, skills within an occupation are transferable between firms, otherwise the achievement of equilibrium by movements of labour towards higher-paying firms would be impossible. In the course of this book, a good deal of discussion will be given over to the question of job structures, and the problems arising out of these for our models of the labour market. In such a model of labour market structure, it is natural that the content of rational choice by individual workers seeking to maximise their net advantages should be centred upon searching for information about advantages in other firms (maintaining the possibility of changing employer), and on obtaining access to different occupational labour markets through investment in training.

Most neo-classical theorising on the labour market is based upon two main cases: labour markets for unskilled or casual labour, and occupational labour markets involving transferable skills. These types of labour market come closest to the competitive model, but they are not the only, nor even perhaps the most widespread, forms of labour market. In these two types of labour market, adjustment to changes in product markets or to changes in production methods takes place, in theory, primarily through the price mechanism, with changes in relative wages serving to direct labour to those uses in which its marginal value product is greatest.

The fourth postulate is that the firm can be treated as a transmission mechanism between markets, in this case between capital, labour and product markets. There has thus been an emphasis upon the coordinating function of managerial authority, and on general or transferable training. In the first case, managerial authority is seen primarily as playing a coordinating role, particularly because the labour contract is seen as one which is incompletely specified when workers are taken on, because the transaction costs of fully specifying all the tasks to be carried out *ex ante* would be too high. Hence the emphasis upon the role of information costs as a determinant of managerial structures, and the argument of some neo-classical writers that, from a formal point of view, it makes little difference whether it is the entrepreneur who hires the workers, or the workers who hire the services of the coordinator–entrepreneur.

In the second case, despite the early work of Mincer (1962) which showed the importance of on-the-job training in the United States economy, the implications of the firm's role in providing in-house training and work experience have on the whole been neglected, or it has been assumed that such experience is of equal benefit to all firms, and is thus transferable. The chief exceptions to this are the writings on company 'internal labour markets', and Okun's

(1981) attempt to trace out their macro-economic implications for inflation and unemployment, but despite attempts to explain their emergence as a result of optimisation under competitive conditions, as will be argued in Chapter 5, these writings take one outside the standard competitive model of labour markets, and in particular outside competitive equilibrium.

The fifth postulate is that technology is the chief link in the derived demand for labour as it determines the shape of firms' production functions, and the elasticities of substitution between different factors of production. Underlying the production function it is assumed that for each set of relative prices there is a technical blue print of production, and this determines the skills that will be required from the labour market. The content of these skills and the job contents are taken as technical data, dictated by the range of production techniques available.

When one reflects that the greater part of industrial relations and industrial sociology deals with group activities, the internal dynamics of organisations, social norms and the processes of rule making both within and outside the firm, it is easy to see that there is a considerable gap between the approaches to theory construction in these disciplines and in economics. This is not to ignore the considerable debate among sociologists over the merits and weaknesses of methodological individualism, and whether explanations of collective actions could be reduced to a set of statements about the actions of the individuals making up a particular collectivity, and the growth of mathematical sociology which has borrowed a certain amount from economics. But the debate about methodological individualism within sociology has remained much more abstract, as both sociologists and industrial relations specialists have continued working with concepts much more directly related to collectivities and groups and their norms in such a way that, mostly, the reducibility or otherwise of their concepts to statements about individuals has remained rather academic. In contrast, in economics, the tastes and choices of individual agents usually form the starting point of any economic reasoning.

Similarly, with their emphasis upon the idea of a job market and of transferable skills, there is a wide gap between labour market theories in the broad neo-classical tradition and much of the industrial relations literature on job regulation, and, with the emphasis on price theory within economics, there is also a gap between this and the issues of comparability and fairness in pay bargaining whose dynamics and origins are the bread-and-butter questions industrial relations specialists seek to understand.

1.9. TOWARDS AN ALTERNATIVE APPROACH

The final chapter, as mentioned, sketches out an alternative view of labour markets in which it is argued that the markets most likely to conform to the competitive model are those for labour with transferable skills, and those for unskilled labour, but the first of these, at least, depends upon a considerable institutional underpinning. The cost of such institutional support, and the problems of sharing its funding, often among private employers and workers, make it analogous to a public or collective good. By arguing that provision of in-house training within firms' internal labour markets is the main alternative, it is shown that unless the cost of occupational markets can be fairly equitably spread, firms will mostly rely upon their internal markets. Thus it could be argued that internal markets prevail if there is a failure to establish suitable occupational markets.

This has fairly important implications for labour market models because, except for unskilled markets, there is no justification for assuming that competitive labour markets should be the predominant form. Also, the ability of firms and workers (and sometimes the public authorities) to establish occupational markets may often itself depend upon the prevailing forms of group organisation. This of course runs counter to the logical primacy of the competitive model, and also, in practice, to methodological individualism.

This approach makes more room for a cross-disciplinary approach as institutional and normative influences take their place in labour market analysis with an equal logical status to that of supply and demand analysis, while leaving the precise balance between these in any one study as an empirical question. It does, however, raise some difficult methodological questions because to date each of the three disciplines has developed its own methodological canons fairly independently of the other two. Thus it is unlikely that the canons of one discipline can be applied to assess the degree of empirical support for a particular cross-disciplinary hypothesis. It is not easy, for example, to combine econometric evidence with case study evidence, especially if the former has had to forsake a number of the common assumptions, such as competitive markets, in its operationalisation. If one does, how should the results be evaluated? Some ideas are offered at the end of Chapter 8, but fuller development requires a separate study.

NOTES

1. Osterman (1982) has referred to such markets as 'craft' markets, but because this word has many connotations, it was felt better to speak of 'occupational' markets.
2. An internal labour market may be said to exist for a particular job if an employer regularly fills vacancies for that job from among his current employees, usually by upgrading or redeploying.

2 Labour Market Institutions and Economic Analysis

2.1. INTRODUCTION

A growing awareness of the institutional arrangements governing labour markets in recent years has led a number of economists to attempt to develop a micro-economic theory to explain their existence and their effects. Neo-classical economic theory teaches that if there is a fall in the demand for labour then wages will fall until employment levels are restored. But this is rarely observed in practice. Keynes and Hicks suggested that the reason for the stability of wage levels in the face of a fall in demand was the result of workers' beliefs about fair wage relativities. But such an explanation takes us outside the realm of mainstream micro-economic analysis. In recent years, it has been suggested that this downward inflexibility of wages is due to the nature of the employment contract, if not explicitly, then implicitly. Those taking this view then seek to explain why workers and employers should negotiate contracts which provide stable wages even though this may lead to lay-offs in a recession. Their aim is to explain this using the standard tools of micro-economics, and thus to show that there is no need to make *ad hoc* appeals to independent institutional or social pressures to explain why the predictions of economic theory appeared to fail.

The internal organisation of companies has provided a similar problem for mainstream economic theory. If the world is made up of a myriad freely contracting individuals, as is supposed in the purest versions of economic theory, why should the employment relation be one of sub-ordination to a hierarchy of authority? Another group of economists, taking their cue from Coase (1937), has sought to show that talk of authority and power is misplaced, and that hierarchical organisation within firms is to be explained either by difficulty of enforcing and coordinating a myriad of short-term contracts, or by the inherent difficulties of evaluating the productivity of individual workers when working as part of a complex team. This group of economists then argues that there is mutual benefit in the separation of supervision and execution of tasks.

Trade unions have also posed serious problems for mainstream economic analysis because of the difficulty of integrating their behaviour into the rest of micro-economics. Dunlop's suggestion that they be treated as monopoly suppliers of labour gave many valuable insights, but he provided no link between the choices of individual workers and union behaviour. For example, in choosing a wage level to aim at in negotiations, what combination of pay and jobs should a union select, as the greater the mark-up over competitive wage levels, the smaller the union's potential membership? Dunlop and others have suggested a number of alternative union objectives, but these seemed somewhat *ad hoc* in the absence of any strong micro-economic grounding.

These three examples have a common strand in their aim to show that some anomalies of economic theory apparently due to the influence of institutional pressures upon labour markets can, with sufficient ingenuity, be explained by the normal tools of micro-economic theory. On the whole, they follow Friedman's principle of parsimony, and eschew the institutionalist explanations as *ad hoc*.

The purpose of this chapter is not to contest the internal logic of these programmes, as this is the object of considerable debate and is undergoing further refinement. Instead it seeks to tackle the broader question of the validity of their treatment of institutional and social pressures on labour markets. Within their own framework, the methodological canons of parsimony and of the refusal to fall back on *ad hoc* explanations of what would otherwise be anomalies may be right, but it will be argued that recent successes have been achieved at the expense of a very narrow conception of the empirical phenomenon to be explained, and one which is not borne out by evidence from industrial relations and industrial sociology, and sometimes also from other areas within labour economics. In many respects, the problems to be explained have become stylised facts, rather than ones based on empirical observation.

One of the main criticisms to be developed in this chapter is that these approaches are unrealistic in two senses. The first is that they misrepresent the institutional and social processes at work surrounding the employment relationship, and secondly, that they mostly seek to explain only stylised descriptions of the institutions governing these relationships. The first would matter less if they were seeking to move from a small set of assumptions to explain the structure of labour market institutions as observed empirically. Then at least Friedman's justification of lack of realism of assumptions could be called upon. But mostly they are seeking to explain one aspect of a particular labour market institution taken in isolation—a stylised fact. In the case of the employment contract, it will be argued that they have confined their attention to contracts which provide for a fixed wage with a certain probability of lay-off, and ignore the very extensive joint regulation by workers' representatives and employers of the whole framework of such contracts, and the activities involved in their day-to-day application. This is not simply a question of a need for greater complexity, or for greater descriptive realism, but it will be argued that such processes are an integral part of employment relations and the employment contract, and cause it to be subject to a wide range of social and organisational pressures. This is not to deny that the provision of stable wages may be of considerable benefit to workers, but it is a different thing to say that wage insurance, for example, is the key process underlying employment contracts.

Descriptive simplicity in the assumptions used in a theoretical model has two practical advantages. It enables one to trace the logical implications of a set of propositions which might otherwise prove intractable, and it can force one to select what seem to be the most pertinent aspects of a process. Subsequently, the suitability of these choices is tested by the degree to which the predictions of such models correspond to empirical observations. This places a heavy burden upon the quality of the final empirical test, and then it is important that models explain empirical observations and not just stylised facts.

In addition, the validity of the assumptions is only partially justified by generating good predictions. The same outcome could in theory be derived from other sets of assumptions. The number of other such sets is reduced by Friedman's rule that the model's assumptions should be as simple as possible, even unrealistic, but there could still remain a large number of alternative sets. Moreover, there is no guarantee that the simplest set of assumptions is the best. The consequent may be true, the logical derivation sound, but the premise false. The number of possible assumptions can be further reduced by checking empirically the extent to which they reflect some characteristics of the social process of which they are deemed a simplified version. Nagel (1963) argued that an ideal type would meet this requirement, while sets of assumptions that were false simply meant that the model was inapplicable. Checking the validity of assumptions, as for example in seeing whether British collective agreements include the 'last in, first out' clauses for lay-offs found in many American agreements, may require use of different types of research method from those used in testing the model's predictions. But there is no reason why economics should confine itself to a single method of investigation, and to a single type of data, such as official statistics, especially, in view of some of the pitfalls in using such data.

This chapter looks at three areas in which labour economists have sought to deal with the influence of institutions upon labour markets by showing that their action can be fully integrated into the standard framework of micro-economics, and that there is consequently no need to draw on the results of work in related disciplines. The three areas concern analysis of the employment contract, the hierarchy of authority within the enterprise, and the attempts to provide a micro-economic basis for our understanding of union action. In each case, the main themes will be set out, and then evaluated in terms of the extent to which they capture or omit central features of the processes they purport to describe. It will be argued that in each case the problem has been defined too narrowly to capture key features observed in particular by industrial relations specialists and industrial sociologists.

2.2. THE EMPLOYMENT RELATIONS AND IMPLICIT CONTRACT THEORIES

The 'downward rigidity' of money wages in the face of a fall in the demand for labour has perplexed many economists. As mentioned earlier, Keynes (1936) and Hicks (1974) suggested that the reason lay in the importance of workers' ideas of fairness in relative wages. Different groups experience a fall in aggregate demand for labour only as it affects their own prospects, and are reluctant to take a cut in pay because they believe that other groups will not take a corresponding cut, and that pay relativities will be disturbed as a result. Consequently money wages do not fall, and unemployment emerges. The same kind of argument applies at the level of an industry. Hicks' view of such norms of fairness was that they might vary over time, and differ between countries, but that these were probably part of the social structure within which markets worked, and as such are given.

In contrast, the implicit contract theorists set off from the same conceptual problem of why wages appear not to fall to market clearing levels when the demand for labour falls, but propose a radically different solution which has nothing to do with fairness.

A central part of the 'implicit contract' argument is that wages are unresponsive to changes in the demand for labour because employers offer contracts which average out fluctuations in the value of workers' output (in their marginal revenue products) over the business cycle. In effect, one might think of employers as offering such contracts to insure workers against such variations. Hence the wage differs from the workers' marginal revenue product over most of the cycle. In the upswing, when product prices are rising, wages are less than the value of workers' output, and the employers take the difference as an 'insurance premium'. When firms do less well, employers compensate workers by paying out of their insurance fund. Azariadis and Stiglitz (1983) suggest that one might think of firms as consisting of separate production and insurance activities. The firms are assumed to be risk neutral, in that they care only about the total wage bill summed over several periods, and so they are prepared to average out income fluctuations, whereas the workers are risk averse, as they prefer a stable income flow. It is argued that firms are less risk averse than workers because their broader asset holdings, as compared with workers who have only their human capital, enable them to spread their risks more. It is usually assumed that the insurance element is 'actuarially fair' so that expected contributions balance expected payments.

Two problems arise: why workers should prefer stable wages to stable employment, and why we do not observe such contracts in practice whereas they would need to be widespread if they were to cause aggregate wage rigidity.

The first problem is that although risk aversion might explain why workers should wish to have both stable wages and stable employment, it is not immediately clear why they should be prepared to sacrifice stable employment, as spells of unemployment could nevertheless expose them to considerable income variations. The implicit contract theorists advance a number of arguments to explain this.

First, the existence of unemployment benefit may explain acceptance of lay-offs. Firms may not be able to provide insurance against income loss under all circumstances. For example, if product demand falls very greatly, the financial burden on the firm may prove too great. Hence, firms offer only partial insurance against income loss, and include provision for lay-offs. In this case, the burden is then shifted onto an outside agency, often the public unemployment insurance schemes. This introduces an additional element of risk spreading. Lay-offs occur because workers have to stop receiving income from their employer in order to qualify for unemployment benefit. There is in addition debate as to whether benefits lead to higher or lower levels of employment than would otherwise be observed (Azariadis

1981) but this lies outside the present discussion. However, as Sutton (1981) points out, in many countries lay-offs took place long before there was any such unemployment insurance, which limits the applicability of this argument. Sutton further points out that this particular result could also be obtained if workers were risk neutral.

The second argument purporting to explain the acceptance of lay-offs is that the existence of 'last in, first out' clauses in collective agreements or as long-standing management policies would reduce the risk of lay-off to longer service workers, giving them both stable wages and stable employment. If union decision-making processes are dominated by longer service workers, union negotiators will follow the interest of some 'median worker' and discriminate against those with least seniority. The problem then is to explain why short service workers should accept this and not seek to negotiate a separate agreement. One possibility is that they treat the lower expected income, after allowing for the greater risk of lay-off, as an investment, analogous to that in on-the-job training.

The third argument relies on asymmetric information such that employers are better informed about the state of product markets than are workers, and they are also better placed to assess the true performance of the firm, and the true value of the workers' services. If workers have no easy way of assessing the truthfulness of employers' statements about fluctuations in the value of their services, then they might also opt for a fixed wage, but they still have the problem of discovering the average value of their services. In this case, Azariadis and Stiglitz (1983) argue that the optimal contract occurs at a position at which the employer is better off if he tells the truth than if he lies. This will occur where the loss in profits from declaring that conditions are bad and adjusting production levels and the demand for hours of work accordingly offsets any gain from a lower wage settlement. But, they argue, this will often be at lower levels of employment than under conditions of symmetric information, so that there would be fixed wages and involuntary unemployment.

The second problem, why such contracts are implicit, is

not answered directly, although one answer might be that like marginal analysis in employment and pricing decisions, as Machlup (1946) argued, firms do not need to think explicitly in such terms if market pressures and profit maximisation push them in this direction. Most of the thrust of their analysis has been to examine what kind of contract would be optimal: that is, what mix of stable wages, insurance against output fluctuations and probability of lay-off would be chosen by both employers and workers given certain assumptions about their objectives, their attitudes to risk and the conditions under which such contracts are agreed, such as whether employers and workers have equal access to information on the value of output.

The problem for such models is that, in fact, employment contracts and the institutions regulating them appear to behave rather differently.

2.3.   JOB LOSSES IN PRACTICE

The narrowness with which implicit contract theorists have defined the problem of job losses and their relation to income security is revealed by looking at the regulation of employment reductions in practice over recent years. This can be dealt with under four headings. First, lay-offs or redundancies are only a relatively small proportion of the total number of jobs lost for economic reasons. The most common procedures for work force reductions in medium-sized and large firms use redundancies as the last of a whole series of instruments. Secondly, the philosophy behind much of the legislation of the last twenty years on redundancies has been that people should be compensated for job loss, and that such compensation should facilitate economic adjustment. Moreover, these laws and agreements reveal no indication of any implicit bargain over wage stability and job security, whereas a number of related themes are treated quite explicitly in agreements. Thirdly, the process usually involves fairly extensive consultation, in western Europe at least, which is not consistent with the idea of contracts with fixed provisions, and it introduces a large number of

additional interests which help to shape the final outcome.
Finally, in the latest recession, redundancy has been
accompanied by extensive reorganisation of production and
reform of working practices and conditions. These will be
dealt with in turn, the intention being to show that the
implicit contract models are not simply unrealistic, but also
their definition of the problem to be resolved, namely why
do we apparently observe sticky wages and lay-offs in
recessions, is far too narrow.

(a) Redundancies and other means of reducing employment

First, lay-offs or redundancies are but one aspect of job
loss, and, statistically, workers made redundant are only a
fraction of those entering the unemployment register. For
example, in Britain, in the year of fastest increase in unemployment, in 1981, redundancies accounted for only 13 per
cent of entrants onto the register, and in subsequent years
it varied between about 5 per cent and 10 per cent.[1] These
figures will also have included a number of plant closures,
thus reducing further the proportion of people entering
unemployment as a result of what might be thought of as
cyclical lay-offs from the point of view of the individual
enterprise.

This is reflected in legislative and collectively agreed provisions for redundancy. Particularly under the French and
West German legislation, but also in practice in Britain,
there is heavy pressure on employers to use a range of
alternative measures to redundancy, and to keep this very
much as the last resort. Indeed, in France, both agreements
and law require employers to show their workforces that all
other alternatives to redundancies have been used. The
usual steps are first to cut recruitment, and to reduce overtime, then to use redeployment, short-time working, and
finally, if more permanent reductions are still needed, voluntary or compulsory redundancies. These stages are also
set out formally in a number of agreements in the UK, such
as the Ford UK agreement of 1966. There is also a strong
financial incentive for employers to minimise redundancies

owing to the need to provide compensation to those laid off.

(b) Collective agreements and legislation yield no evidence of implicit insurance

Secondly, agreements and legislation on redundancies do not appear to reveal the key presumption said to underlie implicit contracts, implicit insurance. There are two areas in legislation and collective agreements on redundancies in which one might seek evidence of these: the definition of dismissal for economic reasons as distinct from other possible reasons, such as discipline or incapacity, and the reasoning concerning compensation. Legislative provisions are usually at least a partial reflection of employers' and workers' practices because before employment legislation reaches the statute book, there is usually an extensive process of consultation with interested parties so that new rules can mesh in with the existing practices of employers, unions and workers. Consequently, although the legislator's intention is to amend and reform existing practices, most new law should be enough of a compromise between the aspirations of the different parties so that it can be accepted and enforced.

As concerns the definition of redundancy used currently in agreements and in legislation in Britain, France, Germany and Italy, the emphasis is upon changes in the employer's demand for labour as a result of product market changes or of commercial decisions by the firm. The definition in the British Employment Protection Act 1978 illustrates this:

dismissal is attributed wholly or mainly to (a) the fact that his employer has ceased, or intends to cease, to carry on the business for the purposes of which the employee was employed by him . . . or (b) the fact that the requirements of that business for employees to carry out work of a particular kind . . . have ceased or diminished or expected to cease or diminish.

There is no reference to any understanding, formal or informal, between employers and employees concerning the idea that the refusal of wage flexibility might be an element in redundancy.

Equally, the French national agreements of 1969 and 1974 and the subsequent legislation of 1972 and 1975 make extensive provision for the definition and regulation of dismissals for economic reasons (defined as relating to the state of business and having nothing to do with the individual employee), but contain no hint of the idea that these might be consented to as part of a *quid pro quo* for stable wages. The same can be said of the legislation and collective agreements on labour force reductions and restructuring in West Germany reviewed by Delamotte (1971), and of the main agreement (in 1965) dealing with redundancies in Italy. Thus in each of these four countries, there is little evidence in major collective agreements and in legislation on redundancies of any presumption by the parties that there is an implicit contract involving wage insurance and redundancies as an alternative to wage reductions in periods of recession.

One might take the philosophy of compensation for redundancy as some reflection of the mutual understandings between workers and employers. The philosophy of the British legislation is summed up as follows:

The stated purpose of the redundancy payments scheme is two-fold: it is to compensate for loss of security, and to encourage workers to accept redundancy without damaging industrial relations. A redundancy payment is compensation for loss of a right which a long-term employee had in his job . . . redundancy pay is to compensate a worker for loss of a job, irrespective of whether that loss leads to unemployment. It is to compensate him for loss of security, possible loss of earnings and fringe benefits . . . and the anxiety of change of job. (President of the Industrial Tribunals in Wynes v. Southrepps Hall Broiler Farm Ltd 1968)

Again, there is no mention of any presumption by worker and employer that redundancy is the price of a stable wage rate which might be offset against an award given as possible compensation. Nor is any such reference to be found in the French or German legislation. Indeed, not only do formal texts of agreements and legislation on redundancies reveal little sign of the presumption by either employers or workers underlying implicit contract theory, but there is also little evidence of this in the, albeit limited, research on informal workplace rules and 'custom and practice'.

Nevertheless, an implicit contract theorist might reply using Machlup's (1946) argument, mentioned above, over the implicit uses of marginal analysis in wage and employment decisions, which he compared to a driver controlling a car without consciously applying Newton's laws of motion. If the wage insurance contracts can be shown to be those which utility-maximising employers and workers would choose under certain conditions, then if those conditions hold, one might expect such contracts to develop, albeit implicitly.

But there are two objections to this. First, Machlup's example did not relate to a distributional problem between workers and employers, whereas implicit contract theories do. Unlike marginal analysis in Machlup's example, implicit contracts have to be enforced or self-enforcing in some way, hence the importance of contract determination under conditions of asymmetric information when employers are better informed than workers about product market conditions. Thus Machlup's argument is not wholly applicable. In any case, his argument was suspect because even though drivers might be ignorant of mechanical physics, application of such knowledge is central to engineering design in car construction.

The second objection is that many examples of explicit wage and employment guarantees can be found in collective agreements. It is quite common for employers to agree to guaranteed minimum levels of pay in the face of certain types of interruption of production such as mechanical breakdown or a shortage of materials if not caused by an industrial dispute in the firm. It is also quite common to find general statements about the desirability of stable employment and measures to be used to minimise redundancies, and for workers to accept consequent redeployment, and so on. If these items can be stated explicitly, and covered by established grievance procedures, it is hard to understand why the supposed insurance and lay-off elements, together with the means of enforcing actuarially fair insurance, should not also be covered explicitly, especially in view of their potential cost to employers and their potential benefit to workers.

It is generally taken that the expected contributions and payments from the insurance are actuarially fair, but the outcome depends upon the incentives against employers providing false information. It might be supposed that many profit-sharing schemes and output-related bonuses similarly contain inherent incentives against false declarations by employers because the scheme would eventually cease to motivate employees. Nevertheless, it is quite common for there to be a degree of joint supervision by the employer and employee representatives explicitly provided for. Under the French legislation on profit sharing, where it was feared that certain employers would not cooperate, the parliament decided to link such schemes to declared profits in company accounts as this is the most readily available information. There is also a procedure in case of dispute. In view of the extent of institutional supervision of profit sharing and output-related bonus schemes, it is surprising that there should be none for the implicit insurance contracts.

Procedures for negotiating redundancies

Turning now to procedures for handling redundancies, there has been much legislation in recent years in many advanced industrial countries regulating redundancies, such as the revised provisions on redundancies in the Employment Protection Act 1975; the French redundancy law of 1975, which prescribes a legal minimum floor in terms of consultation, notice and minimum financial compensation; and in Germany the provisions for joint decision making on redundancies under the 1972 revised Works Constitution Act. Neither Italy (under inter-industry agreement of 1965) nor West Germany have detailed legislation providing for compensation levels. In both cases, detailed provisions are left to negotiation as the need arises. Despite the existence of a legal minimum level of compensation in Britain, mostly unions have traditionally not entered standing agreements setting out terms for redundancies as they are unwilling to accept them on principle, and prefer to negotiate specific terms and conditions as the need arises. Even in cases such as at Ford UK where there is an agreement setting out procedures and compensation in advance, in the recent cases of redundancies there has nevertheless been a great deal of negotiation (Marsden *et al.* 1985). There has been no sign of acceptance among the workforce and their union negotiators that job losses are the *quid pro quo* for stable wages.

An important feature of obtaining redundancies is the extent and subject matter of negotiations involved even where the law or previous agreements provide an initial framework. Consequently, there appears to be no pre-established set of rules on which workers could calculate expected benefits and probabilities of lay-off at the moment of their engagement, as seems to be implied in a number of implicit contract models. But there is instead collective regulation of the terms and conditions for redundancies. In both France and West Germany, the employer is legally required to establish a 'social plan' with the enterprise level employee representatives, respectively the enterprise committee (in most medium-sized and large establishments) and the works council (in establishments with at least five employees). If such agreement is not reached, in France the issue may eventually go to full collective bargaining with the unions, and in West Germany the mechanism of codetermination is such that if the works council members are not satisfied with the employer's offer, they can be less cooperative on other questions on which the employer is legally obliged to have their agreement. They can also take the matter to the conciliation commission for a decision. Particularly in the French legislation, there is strong pressure on employers in the social plan to show that as much of the manpower adjustment as possible has been achieved through internal redeployment of staff, and in practice there are similar pressures on German employers to use similar methods because of the necessity to agree a 'social plan' detailing manpower adjustment measures with the works council. In Italy also collective bargaining plays a very important part in handling redundancies, the principal negotiations being between the employer and the factory council (a form of shop steward committee established by collective bargaining rather than by the law). In Italy too, the state plays an important part, especially through the lay-off fund (Cassa Integrazione) which assumes up to 90 per cent of the pay of employees who would otherwise have been made redundant. In some respects, Britain may be closer to the United States as unions have been less ready in many instances to accept redeployment which requires alteration of existing skill demarcations, but this may be because of the strong identification of many skilled groups in large parts of British industry with their occupational labour markets.

Practice in the United States is very different from that in western Europe in that there appears to be a measure of *ex ante* acceptance of redundancies in collective agreements by unions and their members, and there is no federal redundancy scheme. In terms of procedures, the case for the implicit contract model is perhaps strongest in the unionised sector of the United States on account of the detailed seniority provisions which regulate lay-offs, giving employers flexibility to adjust their total labour costs during a downturn in their product markets by reducing employment rather than varying wage levels. Nevertheless, in the recent major employment reductions in the US car industry, there was a great deal of negotiation over job losses and related changes.

(d) Redundancies and reorganisation of working arrangements

Finally, in the current recession, redundancies in many cases both in Britain and elsewhere have been accompanied by extensive reorganisation of management and of working practices and the procedures regulating them within the firm. In a study of manpower adjustment in the British car industry, Marsden *et al.* (1985) found that in all of the major producers in the UK (BL, Ford, GM and Talbot) job losses were accompanied by major changes in management organisation, in working practices and in the industrial relations procedures regulating these. The companies' aims were to cut unit costs by improving efficiency as much as by cutting their labour forces, hence the restructuring of management grades, moves to ease job demarcations, and to reduce the amount of negotiation with shop stewards over small changes in work assignments, for example. Similar changes have taken place in the British steel industry, and now in shipbuilding and other parts of engineering. In similar fashion, the case studies in the MIT Future of the Automobile project show that in other European countries and the US, improvements in efficiency in management organisation and work organisation have been as much a feature of the restructuring in the industry as have job losses (Streeck and Hoff 1983). Another example of the degree of internal reorganisation accompanying redundancies, this time for France, is provided by Freyssinet's (1982) study of employment strategies of major industrial groups.

Another important set of observations is that even when faced with a fall in product demand, many British firms do not just retain their existing labour forces, as they might do if honouring an implicit insurance agreement with a lay-off provision, but they frequently continue to recruit to replace those leaving. This emerged from a survey of labour hoarding in British industry by Bowers, Deaton and Turk (1982). Their explanation of this paradoxical behaviour was that union and work group restrictive practices compelled employers to work with fixed teams of workers whose members were reluctant to cover for those leaving. Consequently, the employers would opt for redundancies only when faced with a major decline in demand, and then they would often opt for wholesale plant closures. This again highlights the importance of the relationship between redundancies and workforce reorganisation.

To conclude, a number of points emerge from this discussion. First, the idea that workers enter a contract whose terms concerning wage security and redundancies are fixed at the outset is not borne out in practice. Secondly, redundancies represent a fairly small fraction of job losses, the majority being achieved by other means. Thirdly, Machlup's argument about implicit marginal calculations in firms' employment decisions is not applicable. The terms of implicit contracts are distributional, and the outcomes chosen are of great concern to individual workers and employers. Even though such contracts might be self-enforcing in theory, it is surprising that there should be no reference in agreements and in labour legislation either to implicit understandings such that redundancies are the *quid pro quo* of stable wages, or to procedures for dealing with disputes as there are for other measures which might equally appear self-enforcing in theory.

In view of the many arguments used in pay negotiations, why do we not find that employers cite the insurance element in stable wages as an advantage they offer to their workforces? Also when there are quite explicit agreements concerning guaranteed payments in the event of disruptions to production through no fault of the workforce, and quite explicit agreements on profit sharing and similar benefits, why should wage insurance remain implicit?

Moreover, unions seeking such benefits would surely make such objectives known to their membership as they depend upon their ability to mobilise support in order to conduct effective negotiations. Thus the very nature of unions, and other types of workers' representation, would lead one to expect any insurance element and risk of lay-off to be made explicit if it were indeed the basis of the employment relation.

Finally, the implicit contract analysis takes no account of the degree of supervision and negotiation which precedes employment reductions in practice, and it also takes no account of the important degree of negotiation and reorganisation within the enterprise which often accompanies such changes. Redundancies are often not an isolated reaction to product market pressures on the firm, but one part of a wider bundle of adjustment policies, many of which have to be negotiated. The terms of the contract are not fixed definitively at the moment of a worker's engagement because many of the crucial features, for example relating to redundancy, are negotiated subsequently, although this may be more true of western Europe than of the United States.

2.4.   HIERARCHICAL ORGANISATION OF WORK

A notable feature of the employment contract compared

with other types of economic relationship is that employees enter into a position of subordination or control by their employers. Although this is no longer the sole criterion used by British labour law, it remains one of the three necessary conditions for distinguishing an employment contract. Similarly under French law the idea of personal subordination to an employer is a central criterion, as it is under the law of many countries. This distinguishes the employment relationship from partnership, self-employment, and other types of relationship governing the supply of economic services.

One of the difficult tasks undertaken by some neo-classical economists has been to explain why the employment relationship should involve subordination when different contractual forms predominate in other markets, why such a relationship should emerge out of a world of freely contracting individuals, and why it should be sustained in such an environment. The main thrust of their argument has been that while the cost of coordinating work of many individual workers by means of open-market transactions is greater than that of organising such work within a firm, people will use the latter method. This view of the relative costs of coordinating economic activity provides in addition to a possible explanation of the emergence of the employment relationship, possible explanations of firm size, and of the structure of vertical and horizontal integration.

This section first outlines the central features of this way of analysing the employment relationship and the hierarchical structure of the firm, and then argues that it fails on two counts: it does not sufficiently follow through the impact of inter-group conflict on the internal organisation of firms, and it ignores important external institutional influences on internal organisation. As such it can claim to have highlighted some important aspects of the employment relationship, but not to have provided the basis for a new theory.

The origins of the present debate can be traced back to Coase (1937) who argued that the firm provides an alternative method to the market for organising economic transactions. He wrote:

A factor of production (or the owner thereof) does not have to make a series of contracts with the factors with whom he is cooperating within the firm, as would be necessary, of course, if this cooperation were as a direct result of the working of the price mechanism. For this series of contracts is substituted one. (. . .) The contract is one whereby the factor for a certain remuneration (which may be fixed or fluctuating) agrees to obey the directions of an enterpreneur *within certain limits*. The essence of the contract is that it should only state the limits to the powers of the entrepreneur. (Coase 1937 p. 391)

Coase then asks what determines whether particular transactions will be coordinated through the market price mechanism, and which ones will be coordinated within the firm, and he goes on to describe the firm as superseding the price mechanism. This way of posing the question assumes the logical priority of atomistic markets. His answer is that under certain circumstances the costs of organising transactions through the open market exceed those of internal coordination within the firm. Firms will expand the number of operations they control directly until the cost of so doing becomes equal to that of relying upon open market transactions.

As is evident from the quotation, Coase saw the employment contract as fundamentally different from other contracts, defining the limits of managerial prerogative rather than a specific set of services to be rendered. His view of this distinction has been challenged by subsequent work, notably by Alchian and Demsetz (1972) and to some extent by Williamson (1975).

Alchian and Demsetz argue that:

To speak of managing, directing, or assigning workers to different tasks is a deceptive way of noting that the employer continually is involved in renegotiation of contracts on terms that must be acceptable to both parties. (Alchian and Demsetz 1972 p. 777)

In their view, the employment contract is a sequential spot transaction subject to continuous negotiation. Such transactions take place within the firm because of the problems of measuring individual output in team operations in which an individual's output is not separable from that of the rest of the team. This gives rise to opportunities for individual members to 'shirk'. The problem then is to devise suitable methods of supervising individual effort under such conditions, and Alchian and Demsetz consider a number of alternative structures comparing their costs and effectiveness.

On their assumptions, why should the hierarchical pattern displace more egalitarian forms of organisation? The problem with team production, as they see it, is that:

Clues to each input's productivity can only be secured by observing *behaviour* of individual inputs. When lifting a cargo into the truck, how rapidly does a man move to the next piece to be loaded, how many cigarette breaks does he take, does the item being lifted tilt down towards his side? (Alchian and Demsetz 1972 p. 780)

They argue that mutual supervision by fellow workers still leaves the danger that some may also skimp in this activity because the main incentive would consist of some form of profit sharing, and those who did not take their supervisory duties seriously would suffer a less than proportionate loss of income. To obtain efficient supervision, there needs to be, in most cases, a specialist supervisor, and to maximise the effectiveness of his activities, he should take the residual profit after all the other members have been paid. Thus, Alchian and Demsetz argue that the employment relation differs only in a formal sense from market transactions, and that underlying the institutional form is a process of negotiation and of monitoring of output. For them, it makes little difference whether a group of workers hires a specialist supervisor and pays him according to profits, or whether the supervisor hires the workers.

Alchian and Demsetz's argument about the need for supervision was an intuitive one, but in complex organisations supervision is rarely left to simple observation of behaviour, and where such methods are used, the supervisors themselves are employees. In such organisations there are usually formal channels of communication. Kolm (1969) has argued that the hierarchical structure in these cases too may be optimal depending on the combined cost of establishing such channels, and of transmitting information along them. His argument was that direct communication between individuals concerned could convey a high quality of information, but as the numbers involved increased, a need for more formal channels emerges. But such channels have an initial set-up cost, and have to convey information in a more standardised form. Where the number of messages is fairly high, and their content fairly simple, then a hierarchical structure which minimises the number of channels is the most efficient.

2.5. QUALITY OF INFORMATION AND LACK OF CONSENSUS

The pure informational interpretation of the employment relationship has a number of serious weaknesses, one set of which have been explored by Williamson (1975) before he incorporated this interpretation into part of a wider view of the transactions argument. In many organisations job-related knowledge is not freely available to management, and work groups' control over this is an important source of their bargaining power. Indeed, the revolution in management early in this century was based on the simplification of skilled jobs, and the introduction of work measurement, and this represented a major attack on workers' control of job knowledge, and hence upon their bargaining power. However, management's success in introducing these measures was uneven, and was not always sustained.

It has been suggested that even in semi-skilled work in modern factories, despite work measurement, many jobs are far from standardised because of the need to adapt both jobs and machines to local circumstances within plants, and even within workshops (see Chapter 5 on skill specificity). In Williamson's words, many jobs become highly idiosyncratic. These defy incorporation into complex informational systems, and confound some of the economies of a centralised hierarchical structure. In addition, according to Williamson, they create possibilities for individual groups to withhold information from management, and provide an important basis for small group bargaining. These give rise to important transaction costs within organisations which have to be set against open-market transaction costs, but they also destroy much of the simplicity of Alchian and Demsetz's argument. The reality of these problems is well illustrated in the large number of cases in which workers and their unions greatly restrict the methods of work measurement which management may use, prohibiting for example use of stop watches or filming people at work, or insisting on the presence of a shop steward, as has been common in many parts of British manufacturing industry. The problems, arising from the inseparability of individual output in team production are therefore only one of the informational difficulties within the firm, and probably not the most fundamental.

A second group of objections to the approach adopted by Alchian and Demsetz, which applies also to some extent to Williamson's theory of transaction costs, is that they give little attention to broader institutional and societal influences upon hierarchical organisation. Some recent work in western Europe and in Japan reveals major differences between countries in the nature of hierarchical organisation of production both in terms of the number of grades or levels used, and in terms of the nature of authority. The pervasiveness of these inter-country differences suggests that factors external to the firm are as important as transaction costs in determining organisational structure.

Evidence of systematic differences between countries in the type of hierarchical organisation in firms even within the same industry, using comparable production techniques, and of similar size has been found in a number of cases, the best documented being the comparison between the internal hierarchies of a matched sample of French and West German manufacturing plants by Daubigney and Silvestre (1972) and Maurice, Sellier and Silvestre (1978) which showed that the French firms employed a higher proportion of technical and managerial staff relative to manual employees. That they also paid them a bigger differential over their manual employees than did their West German counterparts suggests that price differences between these categories of labour was not the prime cause of the different employment patterns. A follow-up study by Maurice, Sorge and Warner (1979) and by Sorge and Warner (1978a, and b) showed that firms in Britain employed a greater share of technical and managerial staff than in Germany, but less than in France. Japanese firms have yet different hierarchical structures with, on the whole, a smaller number of grades within the hierarchy, a different relation between skilled workers and their supervisors, and much less division of workers along specialist departmental lines (Dore 1973).

Perhaps more telling, however, are the different processes by which authority is embodied in these structures, and also the number of influences that shape them, and hence which show that they are not simply the result of optimising decisions under the conditions envisaged by Alchian and Demsetz, or by Williamson.

In the French–German comparison it was found that the more extensive hierarchy in the French firms involved a smaller degree of devolution of authority to lower levels of management and to skilled workers. One of the principle reasons for this lay in differences between the two countries in national systems of technical education, and the much stronger technical education of lower levels of management and of skilled workers in Germany enabling firms to decentralise authority more, and to rely less upon centralised methods of work study than their French counterparts. Equally important were differences in the bargaining power of skilled workers in the two countries, those in West Germany having transferable skills on account of the stronger system of technical education, and hence having local skilled labour markets which enable them to quit more easily if dissatisfied. All three factors interact with each other.

In his comparison of Britain with Japan, Dore (1973) emphasised the big differences in group structure and the organisation of authority in comparable firms (in electrical engineering) in the two countries. Best (1984) showed similar contrasts in the steel industry in the two countries. In Britain, tasks were more sharply defined and the distinction between control and execution sharper than in Japan, with a greater degree of devolution of authority in the Japanese firms. Dore suggests that a greater feeling of a common interest between workers and managers in the Japanese firms, combined with a weaker social class divide between them than in Britain, facilitates greater devolution of control in Japanese firms. For example, Japanese firms rely much more on the assembly workers doing the job for quality control and elementary rountine maintenance than on specialist inspectors and specialist maintenance workers.

These examples can only illustrate the important institutional and broader social pressures helping to shape the patterns of authority within the enterprise. But they highlight some of the other factors present neither in Alchian and Demsetz's model, nor in Williamson's transaction cost model. While both of these models provide valuable insights, their strategy for explaining the emergence of hierarchical employment relations out of atomistic contracting arrangements precludes proper account being taken of other institutional and social factors which are also important features of the environments in which firms operate, but yet whose presence would be inconsistent with atomistic contracting.

2.6. TRADE UNION ACTION AND THE LABOUR CONTRACT

In most advanced industrial countries the contents of many workers' employment contracts are not determined by bargaining between many individual workers and employers but through representative institutions of one kind or another. A number of factors have combined to renew interest in the effects of trade union action upon labour markets. Among the most important have been the desire to improve the modelling of trade union action in aggregative studies of labour markets, such as how the presence of unions affects the reaction of the economy to major external shocks such as the oil crises or the advent of a major recession, and how the presence of unions can affect a possible trade-off between inflation and unemployment. The traditional concern of economists was in how unions might push the wages of their members above the level that would prevail under competitive conditions. More recently, the question has shifted to how unions affect the behaviour of wages over time—how they might stop them falling to market clearing levels in the face of a drop in demand. The emphasis has thus been moving away recently from estimating union/non-union wage differentials towards understanding what objectives unions might seek to maximise, and in particular what mix of wage and employment levels they would seek to achieve.

This section examines three moves to trace union influence on the nature of employment contracts, which to some extent run parallel to the developments on implicit contracts. Because work in this area is developing very rapidly any conclusions are inevitably provisional, so the section will concentrate again on some of the broader issues involved in these models. As Oswald (1983) pointed out in a recent review of this work, there is a gulf between the work of economists on these questions and that of industrial relations specialists. One aim of this section will be to look at the nature of this gulf, and examine how far some of the key assumptions underlying these models contribute to it. It will be argued that as theories of trade union action they are very incomplete as they neglect large areas of their activity. This is not necessarily a problem if the aim is to explain the macro-labour market consequences of union behaviour, but it will be argued that here too the models omit elements of union activity and structure which contribute to their influence at this level. The work to be examined includes Dertouzos and Pencavel's attempt to investigate union objective functions econometrically, Oswald's and others' work seeking to base union goals (represented by their objective functions) upon the preferences of their individual members, and Booth's attempt to build an element of union internal structure into this.

In launching the debate on union objectives in the 1940s Dunlop (1944) had suggested that unions could be regarded as behaving like monopoly sellers of labour, although they did not strictly speaking supply labour themselves, and that in consequence they faced a downward-sloping demand curve for labour, setting a trade-off between wage and employment levels as a constraint on their bargaining activities. In addition, he considered a number of alternative objectives for unions: to maximise the economic rent earned by their members, to maximise the wage bill, to maximise the wage bill plus public or private unemployment insurance, and to maximise trade union membership as given by some membership function. These were all maximised subject to the constraint of the labour demand curve. To these Cartter (1959) added the idea of a union wage expansion path which gave rise to downwardly sticky wages when demand decreased, and upwardly flexible wages when demand increased.

The problems picked up in the more recent work are that there was no empirical investigation of sets of objectives that unions pursued in their negotiations, and there was little attempt to show how union objectives might be derived from their members' interests. Consequently economic research in which union objectives entered tended to be based upon guesswork as to what mix of wage and employment levels unions might choose.

The path taken by Dertouzos and Pencavel (1981) was to postulate a general form of objective function on wages and employment of the kind developed by Cartter (1959), which is maximised subject to the trade-off between the two imposed by the elasticity of labour demand, and to test it on data from one union, the American International Typographical Union. They used an objective function of the form:

$$U(w,L) = (w - \gamma)^\theta (L - \delta)^{(1-\theta)}$$

in which w is the wage deflated by the cost of living, L is union employment, $w - \gamma$ and $L - \delta$ represent the amount by which real wages and employment exceed certain reference values, and θ is the relative importance the union attaches to either of these. When γ and δ are equal to zero, θ measures the relative weight the union attaches to wages and employment. Dunlop's maximisation of the wage bill by a closed-shop union is given by $\gamma = \delta = 0$ with $\theta = 0.5$ in the objective function. Alternatively, the rent maximisation hypothesis is captured when $\delta = 0$, γ is equal to the competitive wage, and $\theta = 0.5$. Equally, if γ equalled the wage rate achieved by another union, the function could embrace an element of comparability. Thus, as Dertouzos and Pencavel point out, their model is capable of comparing a number of simple hypotheses about union objectives on their data.

This was tested on data from the International Typographical Union's Cincinnati local for 1949–65. The authors' findings were that the union valued both wages and employment (θ was less than 0.5, but significantly greater than 0), that it valued not merely wages, but their excess over some reference level (γ was greater than 0); but there appeared to be no such reference level for employment as δ was not significantly different from zero. They found an elasticity of substitution of wages for employment of 0.69, consistent with the notion that the union took account of the employment effects of its wage policy. Dertouzos and Pencavel also tested the wage bill maximisation and the rent maximisation hypotheses on this model, but found they performed less well. Results for other locals displayed a range of estimates providing some broader support for their view that both wages and employment should be included in the objective function, and that the rent and wage bill maximisation hypotheses performed less well than the others.

Generalisation from this study is limited by a number of special features of the ITU during this period. The period ended just before major technical change occurred in the industry; the union's structure closely paralleled that of the industry's geographically segmented product markets; labour was fairly homogeneous with all workers having undergone similar training; the union had a democratic structure with a two-party system, and so could be more directly reflective of members' interests; remuneration was negotiated at the local level; it had a closed shop; vacancies were filled from lists of irregularly employed members; there had been stable union–employer relations so that each knew the other's constraints; the union was in a dominant position *vis-à-vis* the companies, so it was not a case of bilateral monopoly. These factors combine to make the ITU a fairly exceptional union. In particular, this is likely to affect the weight attached to employment. Other unions, particularly in western Europe at the moment, are deeply concerned about employment, but this has shown up more in negotiations about a reduction of working time, and this has not influenced wage negotiations to any great extent, probably because of the difficulty of enforcing an agreement which accepted lower wage increases for greater employment, and of convincing members that it was being enforced.

The other direction from which work has been conducted is to derive union objective functions from the utility functions of individual members, and to see how assumptions such as risk aversion by members, or the ratio of wages to unemployment benefit affects union goals. As Oswald (1983) points out, in its simplified form the union's objective function can be written as

$$U = nu(w) + (m-n)u(b)$$

where m is union membership, n the employed members, w the union wage, b the level of unemployment benefits, and $u(w)$ and $u(b)$ the utility members derive from receiving the union wage and unemployment benefit (or an alternative non-union wage) respectively. In this case, the function is 'utilitarian' in the sense that the union is seeking to maximise the sum of its members' utilities. In an alternative form, the union seeks to maximise the expected net benefit of its members:

$$U = n/mu\ (w) + (m-n)\ /mu(b).$$

In this formulation, members are faced with a probability of n/m of a job at the union rate, and of $(m-n)\ /m$ of unemployment receiving only unemployment benefit. If m is fixed the two formulations are equivalent, but not if m is variable and influenced by the union.

Oswald's (1982) micro-economic model of union objectives (it does not deal with bargaining) seeks to derive a union's objective function from individual members' preferences. He treats the union as a coalition of workers with similar skills, and as a monopoly sufficiently large to be able to influence the wage either by controlling entry to the occupation, or by imposing a wage rate, and stipulating that workers should not work for less.

He further assumes that individuals choose the hours they work, and that firms determine employment. In analysing the decision to form a union, Oswald sets up the workers' expected net benefit function from having a union, which is a positive function of the union mark-up and the marginal utility of unemployed workers, and a decreasing function of both the elasticity of labour demand, and the workers' aversion to risk (the risk of loss of income through becoming unemployed after the union is formed). He suggests that the probability of unionisation is an increasing function of individual workers' expected net benefit.

He further assumes a competitive industry with *identical workers* (i.e. skill and seniority do not affect the probability of unemployment) and is able to show that the probability of unionisation in such an industry is a decreasing function of:

(a) the degree of workers' relative risk aversion,
(b) the price elasticity of product demand,
(c) the elasticity of labour supply in hours,
(d) the elasticity of substitution between labour and capital,
(e) the relative cost of labour in the final product (provided the elasticity of substitution of capital for labour is greater than the price elasticity of product demand).

Items b,d, and e are three of the familiar four Marshall rules as refined by Hicks (the fourth being the elasticity of supply of cooperant factors of production).

He assumes that unions have utilitarian preferences, namely that they seek to maximise the sum of their members' utilities, which is equivalent to maximising the expected utility of their representative member if membership is constant. He shows that if a union has such preferences, and its members are risk averse, then there exists an increasing, quasi-concave objective function defined on wages and employment. Thus in Oswald's model, employment matters in contrast to the rent maximisation models—and he has been able to show that this can be derived from certain assumptions rather than postulating it in an *ad hoc* fashion. This enables Oswald to derive a number of predictions about union behaviour including: the union sets a wage level which maximises the expected utility of its employed and unemployed members, the latter receiving unemployment benefit, or possibly a lower wage in a non-union firm; and a change in the size of a union's membership does not alter the union's optimum wage. The marginal benefit to the union is the marginal increase in the wage times the number of members benefiting, and the marginal cost is the number of members losing their job as a result of the higher wage times the difference between the employed and the unemployed member's utility. The size of the membership does not affect this outcome. In this respect it is a model explaining the optimum wage level chosen by a union given its current membership level, and in the absence of bargaining.

There are other models within this broad approach, as Oswald (1983) points out. His own is classified as a 'monopoly model' in which the union sets the wage and the employer then decides on the level of employment. But while the outcome in this case lies on the tangency between the labour demand curve and the union's objective function, it is not *pareto optimal*. Another approach is what he called the 'efficient bargain model' in which the outcome is *pareto optimal*, but lies to the right of labour demand curve. In this the union seeks to set both the wage and the employment level, but the result is not stable because the employer can move to a higher profit level by moving back onto the demand curve. Moreover, the applicability of the second type of model is more restrictive than the first as few unions have such ability to set both wage and employment levels.

Whereas Oswald's model seeks to derive a union's objective function from the preferences of all of its members who are assumed to be homogeneous, a different approach, adopted by Booth (1984), is to recognise that members long established in certain jobs may have a lower probability of being laid off as a result of a wage increase than less senior workers. The two main results are first, as expected, in the median voter model, the union's wage policy changes only if changes in labour demand affect the median member, which generates a degree of wage stickiness, and secondly, that making membership dependent upon trade union policy rather than treating it as fixed generates greater changes in wages in response to changes in demand.

2.7.　WAGE DETERMINATION AND JOB REGULATION

Returning to the gulf between these economic models and those of industrial relations specialists that Oswald referred to, perhaps the most important factor in these attempts to define union goals or objective functions is that, although still in a state of flux, they concentrate on a rather narrow area of union activity. Indeed, this is recognised by Oswald and particularly by Booth who recognises that different unions have different internal structures. Indeed, Oswald (1982) points out that his model of unions did 'not imply that other factors—sociological and political influences for example—are unimportant, merely that economic forces have some effect upon why certain sectors are unionised whilst others are not' (p. 579), but he does not give any indication as to how these effects might be integrated into his model. The limitations on the empirical applicability of these models as they stand is also recognised implicitly by Dertouzos and Pencavel in their listing of the special characteristics of the ITU.

Although their work captures important features of collective bargaining, it is as well to try and trace out some of the elements which still are missing. Two broad problems arise: that unions also engage in job regulation, to be explained shortly; and in many cases there are several levels of bargaining, all of which can help shape the levels of pay finally emerging, a factor which has been one of the biggest problems in making incomes policies effective.

Much of the economic debate and research about union

	Wage determination	Job regulation
Individual level	A	B
Collective level	C	D

Figure 2.1

activities has focused upon their wage-determining activities, on the union mark-up and on the trade-off between wage levels and stability and employment. But an equally important area, which has impinged upon the economic debate about productivity and economic performance (e.g. Pratten 1976 and Freeman and Medoff 1979), has been the role of unions, or of worker representatives, in regulating the way in which the employers can use the labour they have hired. Job regulation might be defined as the fixing and application of the web of work rules which govern the deployment of labour and its reward. Some of these rules are widely seen as restrictive practices, such as restrictive manning rules, or craft demarcation rules, while others are seen as establishing procedures through which grievances can be handled, and others help to establish those limits within which management may direct labour as referred to by Coase earlier on in this chapter.

The relationship between the individual and collective levels, and job regulation and wage determination, is illustrated in Figure 2.1.

Much of the work within economics treats the choice facing individual workers on setting up a union as between individual or collective wage determination, squares *A* and

C. Mostly, the amount of negotiation under *A* will be very small because for most jobs firms will make an offer and the prospective workers can either take it or leave it. It ignores the job regulation side.

This focus has also been present in industrial relations thinking, as is evidenced by the section Flanders (1968) quoted from the Webbs, but careful reading will also highlight one important change in moving from the individual to the collective level:

In unorganised trades the individual workman, applying for a job, accepts or refuses the terms offered by the employer without communication with his fellow-workmen, and without any other consideration than the exigencies of his own position. For the sale of his labour he makes a strictly individual bargain. But if a group of workmen concert together, and send representatives to conduct bargaining on behalf of the whole body, the position is at once changed. Instead of the employer making a series of separate contracts with isolated individuals, he meets with a collective will, and settles, in a single agreement, the principles upon which, for the time being, all workmen of a particular group, or class or grade will be engaged. (S. Webb and B. Webb 1902 p. 178)

The move to the collective level does not just substitute a collective contract for a set of individual contracts. Instead, as Flanders (1968) pointed out, the collective agreement regulates the terms which should go into individual employment contracts. This distinction stands out more clearly if one remembers that in Britain, although collective agreements are gentleman's agreements and so not enforcible at law, individual employment contracts are legal documents and their terms can be enforced. The function of the collective agreement is a regulatory one establishing a set of rules governing relationships between employer and employees, and between employer and unions, what Flanders called 'joint regulation'.

Stressing the importance of the regulatory aspects of collective bargaining does not necessarily detract from the economic models discussed so far, but much depends on how the one function within collective bargaining influences the other. In fact, the two interact in a number of important ways, and these may help to explain part of the gulf Oswald referred to. First, although it is useful to distinguish job regulation from wage determination conceptually, in practice there is no hard and fast division especially under conditions of shop floor bargaining. The insistence upon a restrictive definition of the limits within which management may deploy labour is often a way of signalling to management that additional flexibility will be available if the price offered is right. If management is successful in insisting on a less restrictive definition of such limits, it will not have to pay for the flexibility. The actual amount of bargaining at this level can vary greatly. In the 1970s, in Britain and in Italy it was very great in certain key manufacturing sectors as both countries experienced a major growth in shop stewards. It may be weaker in French manufacturing, as Eyraud (1983) shows work group bargaining to be much weaker in French than in British engineering industries. Nevertheless, it suggests that to some extent at least, the boundary between these two functions within collective bargaining is itself the outcome of a form of bargaining.

Secondly, under various forms of productivity bargaining, in the quest for increased efficiency, employers are continually seeking agreement on changes in existing working practices and work rules in return for conceding a pay increase. This introduces a dynamic element into the wage employment trade-off, but it also increases strains on intra-organisational bargaining within unions as they then have to win acceptance for such changes from their members. The union, even at company level, is often not simply a coalition of members, but a coalition of different work groups. If the union is to make concessions reducing time allowances for workers to clean up at the end of shift, all workers in the plant may benefit from the increased sales advantage that the company derives. But the sacrifice affects only shift workers, and the management might be unwilling to give a special compensatory payment to the shift workers that could upset the company's pay structure.

The third problem, which is not unrelated to the first two, is that in very many cases the wage rate is not set wholly in one central bargain. In many private sector firms, there is also company and plant level bargaining which can add considerably to the initially agreed wage rates at the industry level. This is also true even of countries such as West Germany and Sweden which have relatively powerful central negotiations, at the industry-regional level in Germany, and until recently at the national level in Sweden. In Germany, the works councils have considerable powers of negotiation, if not strictly of bargaining, over wages within the framework established in industry-regional agreements. In Sweden, the extent of wage drift during the 1960s and 1970s was ample testimony of the amount of wage negotiation at company and plant level despite the attempts at the national level to negotiate wage agreements that were consistent with certain macro-economic policy objectives. Again unions do not consist only of individual members, nor of individual members and leaders, but of a coalition of organised groups. Holding together such a coalition has a strong economic component in achieving agreements which satisfy members' wage and job security aspirations, but (i) these wage aspirations include a strong normative element, and (ii) holding together such a coalition is as much a political as an economic process.

The power of many of these groups within unions arises from the employers' need to proceed with a certain level of consent from the workforce. Thus the practice of negotiating over changes in working practices reinforces the power of different groups within unions strengthening their position *vis-à-vis* the central negotiators. Sometimes unions can consciously devolve power onto representatives of these groups, as did the TGWU and the AUEW in the late 1960s as they recognised that their organisational power had shifted down to this level.

Fourthly, the wider economic importance of these structural aspects of collective bargaining cannot be neglected, for example in incomes policies. The problems of running incomes policies in Britain, even with the active support of union leaders, when rank and file members are opposed, and pressing against wage controls were well illustrated in the late 1970s. In Sweden too, the wage drift which arose when a local bargaining went beyond the limits fixed in the agreements between the central manual workers' union LO, and the central employers confederation SAF, was a constant threat to the 'Swedish Model' of economic regulation. The wildcat strike movements in West Germany, especially those of 1969 provide another illustration of rank and file pressures on higher level wage bargaining, and their threat to the control of inflation (Schumann *et al.* 1971).

2.8. CONCLUSION

This chapter has looked at some recent attempts by economists to analyse certain institutional characteristics of the labour market treating them as the consequence of the preferences and actions of individual workers and firms operating under specific market conditions. Both for implicit contracts and for Alchian and Demsetz's theory to explain the element of subordination in the employment relation and hierarchical organisation of the firm, the emphasis has been upon building a model that explains how such institutional forms might emerge in an economic system consisting of individual workers each in competition with the others and of competitive firms. This involved taking both perfect competition and the choices of individual utility maximisers as the starting point of the explanation. While the theoretical models of union objectives and their ideal contracts did not assume perfect competition, the authors nevertheless sought to build up their models from the preferences of individual members. The position of Dertouzos and Pencavel is somewhat ambiguous. While their intellectual sympathies might be with the individualistic research programme, and their work is quoted to support the validity of the construction of union objective functions, they did not derive their union's objective function from individual preferences, and their empirical findings stand independently of any micro-economic foundations. Indeed, their use of quantitative research methods could well be adopted by institutionalists to supplement other research methods.

Although these represent important developments towards a better understanding of institutional influences upon labour markets, there remains a wide gulf between them and the findings of those with a more institutionalist approach. The causes of the gulf discussed in this chapter might be summarised as follows. There were four major problems with the 'implict contract' theories of the employment relation: even at the height of the employment 'shake out' in Britain between 1980 and 1982, redundancies were not the most important method of reducing the size of a firm's labour force; there is no evidence in negotiations nor in redundancy law that the parties are aware of an implicit understanding that wage security implies a degree of job insecurity, despite the existence of procedures to supervise explicit agreements on guaranteed pay levels and output-related bonus schemes, for example; the procedures for dealing with employment reductions in practice are mostly not automatic, and involve a good deal of negotiation and consultation at least in most western European countries; and finally redundancies are also frequently accompanied by fairly extensive internal reorganisation of working arrangements and practices, as is illustrated by the recent employment adjustments in the car industry.

For the hierarchy theories the main problems were that they assumed that information about effort and the content of skills could be obtained by simple observation by a supervisor, which effectively ignored the use of such information in conflict between workers and management, and their interpretation of the management hierarchy really hinges on ignoring such conflicts and the more authoritarian type of hierarchy that might be introduced in order to control these. Alchian and Demsetz also underestimated the extent to which hierarchical relations vary between countries. There is no single model of a managerial hierarchy, and management hierarchies differ in the number and size of grades, the amount of delegation, the distribution of technical competence, their basis of consent, and so on, and the reasons for these lie outside Alchian and Demsetz's model. The assessment of individual workers' output is an important function, but it is only one of many which influence hierarchical structure within firms.

The trade union models did not deal with 'joint regulation', which is a major part of a union's activity, and which, it was argued, could not be rigidly separated from wage determination activities. Joint regulation also accounts for the need for a number of different organisational levels of trade union action, and these can become supplementary foci of wage bargaining. One implication of this is that trade unions are not coalitions of individual members, or median members plus leaders, but they are coalitions of groups. The problems for union leaders of managing such coalitions has major economic consequences visible in the problems of 'wage drift' surrounding centralised industry and national wage bargaining and prominent during periods of incomes policy.

One of the reasons for the gulf that Oswald referred to between research by economists and that by industrial relations specialists in this area is that the economic models discussed in this chapter are mostly not seeking to explain the form of employment contracts as observed empirically, but stylised forms of these; this is particularly true of the implicit contract and the hierarchy theories, and there is a danger of the same kind in the theories of trade union objectives.[2]

It was argued that it was hard to justify these stylised representations of contracts and of hierarchical organisation. Such an objection differs from criticising the realism of a theory's assumptions. The criticism bears on the representation of the phenomenon to be explained. Friedman's argument that lack of realism of assumptions mattered little compared with the final empirical test of the predictions derived from these does not, therefore, apply in this case. Nor, it was argued, did Machlup's argument in defence of marginal analysis of firms' wage and employment decisions. Employment contracts set the terms of the distribution of income between employers and employees. Workers would have to be extremely confident of their employer's intention and interest to stick to the terms of the contract for them to leave such key benefits as wage insurance and employment security implicit. Machlup had applied his example of a driver not needing to know the laws of mechanical physics and yet still successfully handling a car to analysis of implicit decision rules involving no negotiation.

Keynes' and Hicks' view that wage stickiness was the result of comparability norms has been criticised by several authors on the grounds that it had no clear micro-economic basis and that it was '*ad hoc*'. The *ad hoc* argument needs to be used with some care. Economists are right to be suspicious of researchers who invoke a particular event which did not form part of their initial hypotheses in order to explain why their predictions failed. Another *ad hoc* strategy is to refine the initial assumptions in order to make the predictions fit the final set of observations. Of this too economists are rightly suspicious. But what of apparently deviant observations such as the persistent failure of wages to fall in the face of a fall in demand as predicted by micro-economic theory? Here the charge of *ad hoc* depends upon the subsequent attitude to the basic theory. If a person maintains that standard micro-economic theory provides an adequate model of the labour market, but that 'factor X' intervenes to stop wages falling to market clearing levels, then the *ad hoc* invocation of some 'factor X' gives rise to inconsistency. Consistency can be restored by showing that 'factor X' stems from standard micro-economic assumptions combined for example with workers' imperfect information or attitudes to uncertainty. Most of the authors reviewed in this chapter have followed this path. But this has accentuated the gulf between these disciplines, especially as research in these disciplines would broadly support Keynes' and Hicks' view on pay comparability.

There are, however, limits to the usefulness of the *ad hoc* rule. When Hicks (1974) for example was seeking to explain wage stickiness by means of norms of pay comparability, he was not looking for a 'one-off' explanation of a failure of wages to respond to a fall in demand as predicted by standard supply and demand theory. From his analysis of relevant examples, he was clearly seeking the causes of this stickiness. And his examples could be supported by a number of studies of the action of comparability in pay bargaining be it at the national, industry, plant or shop floor level. Assuming it had been shown that variations in the extent of wage flexibility did indeed correspond to the strength with which workers defended pay comparability, should this explanation be treated as *ad hoc* (especially as there is no direct evidence of implicit contracts)? It is hard to see any justification for so doing. The task then for theory would seem to be either to explain the development of comparability in terms of standard micro-economic assumptions (perhaps through the role of comparability in conditions of imperfect information for example), or to look for ways to bridge the conceptual gulf between labour market economics and industrial relations and industrial sociology. The former approach would most likely reproduce explanations open to the same kind of objections as those raised so far. The latter might well start with a project to see how comparability affects wage settlements, and how employers try to break the link sometimes, but mostly fail.

NOTES

1. *Department of Employment Gazette*: redundancies confirmed as due to occur to the MSC. They exclude redundancies involving less than ten workers. Moreover, workers with their current employer for less than two years do not qualify for protection. Thus the figures understate the actual numbers of redundancies, but it is unlikely to be more than double the figures quoted.
2. Although there is currently an attempt to examine the contents of major collective agreements at the LSE's Centre for Labour Economics (e.g. Oswald and Turnbull 1984).

3 Individualism and Group Norms in Labour Markets

3.1. INTRODUCTION

This chapter looks at the attempts by a group of labour economists to apply the 'measuring rod of money' as conceived by Marshall and Pigou to the action of collective norms and attitudes in labour markets. In order to achieve this, they seek to formulate the problem in individualistic terms which can be integrated into the calculus of the theory of individual choice. The argument of this chapter is that although this group goes a long way towards recognising the non-economic basis of many workers' and employers' attitudes observed in labour markets, in the end their attempts to deal with these in a purely individualistic framework fails. The latter part of the chapter takes a small number of major empirical studies of workers' attitudes in the labour market in order to give more substance to the idea that many such attitudes are collective schemes of interpretation used by workers and employers to understand and act upon their environment, and mostly cannot be assimilated to individual tastes.

One of the most interesting features of the models of Becker, Lévy-Garboua and of Wood to be examined in this chapter is that they seek to analyse the impact of discrimination and social norms on the labour market by treating them as non-monetary motivation and non-profit-maximising behaviour. In contrast, many of the theories of labour market discrimination either look outside the labour market to the family and the education system, or else treat discrimination as a form of cost-minimising behaviour. For example, Stiglitz (1973) reviewed a number of theories in which a person's race or sex is treated by employers as an indicator of his or her likely productive characteristics. The theories reviewed in this chapter, while maintaining the conceptual core of economic analysis, seek to integrate the action of social norms, treating them as social norms and not attributing an economic function to them.

Becker offers a general method for dealing with a whole class of non-monetary motivations in the labour market:

> This theory can be applied to 'discrimination' and 'nepotism' in all their diverse forms, whether the discrimination be against Negroes, Jews, women, or persons with 'unpleasant' personalities, or the nepotism be in favour of blood relatives, countrymen, or classmates, since they have in common the use of non-monetary considerations in deciding whether to hire, work with, or buy from an individual or group. (Becker 1971 p. 11)

It was developed for analysing the impact of racial discrimination on the labour market, but has also been applied to discrimination by sex, and by social class. A related theory has been developed by Wood for the impact of wage comparability norms. In essence, Becker's broader target is the impact of collective norms and group relations on the labour market, and he seeks to show that the individualistic conceptual apparatus of neo-classical micro-economics can be applied successfully to these.

In more detail, taking Becker as an illustration, the strategy of this chapter is to show that stability of the labour market equilibria with discrimination depends upon the fact that discriminatory behaviour is generated by group norms. In the case of discrimination by employers, Becker has great difficulty in explaining the persistence of discrimination in a competitive economy because one would expect non-discriminating employers to drive discriminating ones out of business in the long run. The pressure of competition could be reduced if there were community pressures to make a sufficient proportion of employers in a particular area discriminate equally, but Becker's individualistic premises rule out such an eventuality. Similarly, in the case of discrimination by workers against other workers, it is argued that the job segregation between black and white workers which Becker's theory predicts will only persist if there are sufficient group pressures to maintain it, which is inconsistent with Becker's premises for the same reason.

For Becker, discrimination is a strong case of a social

norm active in labour markets. Notwithstanding the importance of discrimination as a social problem, the main issue
at stake in this discussion is the nature of the influence
of social norms on labour markets. It is, therefore, more
appropriate to examine the more general work of industrial
sociologists on workers' attitudes than to confine the discussion rigidly to the nature of discrimination.

The latter part of the chapter is devoted to an outline of
the way in which group pressures can act in order to enforce
group norms in the labour market, and thus provide some
explanation of how stable patterns of group behaviour may
persist in a competitive economic environment. In addition
to material self-interest, which it is argued is not a sufficient
condition for such stability, there are four main types of
pressure: direct sanctions by other group members; moral
sanctions such as exclusion, and those arising from internalisation of group norms, such as feelings of shame and
guilt on the transgression of group norms; a sense of group
identity; and the tendency for members of such groups to
hold certain common ways of interpreting their environment
and the action of other groups.

The basic strategy of Becker's method

The method used by Becker for analysis of the impact of
social norms has been widely used by other economists, for
example for discrimination on grounds of sex (Chiplin and
Sloane 1974) or of social class (Lévy-Garboua 1979). The
basic idea on which their approach rests has a long history
within economics, and can be traced back to Pigou's idea
of the 'measuring rod of money' (Pigou 1921, Pt. 1, Ch. 1,
S6), and to Marshall who expressed it thus:

An opening is made for the methods and the tests of science as the force
of a person's motives—not the motives themselves—can be approximately
measured by the sum of money, which he will just give up in order to
secure a desired satisfaction . . . the economist does not claim to measure
any affection of the mind in itself, or directly; but only indirectly through
its effect. (Marshall 1920 Bk. 1. Ch. 2, S1)

In Becker's theory, discrimination arises because workers
have a 'taste' for either working or not working alongside

people of a different race, or sex, as do employers for employing or not employing certain categories of people. In order to satisfy such tastes workers are prepared to forego higher earnings, and employers higher profits, so that under competitive conditions, the strength of the taste can be measured by the amount of income they are prepared to forego in order to satisfy them.

Discrimination can be seen as a critical case of the application of individualistic analysis to group phenomena because it implies (i) an attitude by one individual towards members of another group, (ii) the individual him or herself is also a member of a discriminating group, (iii) which thus implies one is dealing with inter-group relations, and (iv) it is frequently also associated with expectations within the discriminating group that individual members should conform, so that one may also legitimately see discrimination as a social norm as well as an attitude. Thus if Becker's method is successful, it opens the way for a full-scale analysis of the impact of social norms upon labour markets. The other two studies in this vein to be dealt with are Lévy-Garboua's adaptation of Becker's method to the analysis of the impact of social class upon earnings, and Wood's (1978) analysis of the impact of workers' tastes for particular pay relativities upon wage determination.

This chapter does not reject the principle of net advantages but only its application to certain types of attitude, notably that in such matters as job choice, and employment decisions discrimination can be treated on a par with the effect of physical working conditions.

3.2.   AN OUTLINE OF BECKER'S ANALYSIS

Becker presents his theory as one of quite general application to the influence of all forms of non-monetary motivation on the labour market. He begins by proposing that an employer with a taste for discrimination against a particular group, for example by group W against group B, behaves as if the net cost of employing individuals from that group were $w(1 + d_i)$, where w is the equilibrium wage rate in the absence of discrimination and d_i is the ith employer's discrimination coefficient (DC). Similarly, a worker who discriminates against working with someone from another group behaves as if the net wage were $w(1 - d_j)$ where w is the wage rate offered, and d_j the worker's discrimination coefficient. In both cases, the financial cost of the taste is given by the wage rate times the discrimination coefficient wd_i and wd_j. However, what is observed statistically is what Becker calls the market discrimination coefficient (MDC) which varies in proportion to the individual discrimination coefficients, but which also depends very much on the degree of monopoly and monopsony on the labour market, and on the degree of substitutability between W and B labour. It is thus not an average of the individual discrimination coefficients. Becker defines it as $(w_w - w_b)/w_b$.

The tastes for discrimination translate into income differences between W and N workers through the working of labour, capital and product markets. Becker sets up a simple model consisting of W workers and capitalists, and of B workers and capitalists, in which W possesses relatively more capital than B, W and B workers are perfect substitutes, and W has both more capital and more labour. Under these conditions, trade without discrimination between W and B would result in W supplying capital to B and B supplying labour to W, and this would lead to the equalisation of factor prices. But if W discriminates against B, reducing trade in W capital and B labour, then the losers will tend to be W capitalists and B labour, reducing B workers' incomes relative to those of W workers. Why do B workers not retaliate and refuse to trade at all, resulting in two completely separate economies? Becker argues that the gains from even a small amount of trade are positive, so that B workers will continue to trade with W.

In the case of discrimination by employers, the link between the individual discrimination coefficients and the MDC can be illustrated for a competitive industry as follows. If B labour represents a quarter of the overall labour force, and W labour the other three-quarters, and B and W workers are perfect substitutes in production, then the MDC will be at the lower quartile of the distribution of individual DCs. This is because employers with a DC below the MDC hire only *B* labour, while those with DC above the MDC will hire only *W* labour. Thus the MDC is influenced both by the average level and by the dispersion of DCs of individual employers. In the long run, those with the lowest DCs, having the lowest unit costs, will tend to expand faster, and this will reduce the dispersion of DCs among existing firms, and exert a downward pressure on the MDC. Thus one of Becker's predictions is that discrimination will be greater the less the degree of competition.

In the case of discrimination by employees, an employer has to pay a discriminating worker more for working with a member of the group discriminated against. Consequently cost-minimising employers will avoid mixing *W* and *B* labour which, if they are perfect substitutes in production, will produce labour market segregation between firms employing *W* and those employing *B* labour. At this point, the trading analogy enters to determine the size of the MDC. However, if discrimination is by labour only, then factor price equalisation could come about by adjustments in the capital market producing market segregation without wage discrimination. If a third group of labour is introduced, which is a complement employed in fixed proportions to each of *W* and *B* labour, then the MDC will be determined from the individual DCs of this third factor in the same way as it was for discrimination by employers.

3.3. SOCIAL DISCRIMINATION AND THE RELATION BETWEEN EDUCATION AND EARNINGS

One of the most important studies of social discrimination inspired by Becker's theory has been Lévy-Garboua's (1972 and 1979) analysis of the relationship between education, earnings and social origin in France. Unlike Becker's study, Lévy-Garboua's was primarily empirical, consisting of an econometric analysis of the results of the 1964 French national survey of labour force training and qualifications carried out by INSEE.

Lévy-Garboua shares with the human capital theorists the idea that individuals invest in education in order to obtain some future monetary return, but his theory of education and earnings is that education does not create human capital which is directly productive, and that, instead, educational diplomas serve to indicate the level of innate ability or the productive potential of individual workers. He thus adopts a more general empirical formulation for his earnings function in order to test whether investment in education is directly productive as the human capital theorists such as Becker (1975) or Mincer (1974) argue, or whether it acts as a detector or filter of individual workers' innate abilities, such that the diplomas obtained certify these for prospective employers, as suggested by Arrow (1973) or Spence (1973).

Lévy-Garboua defines the individual's productive capacities as anything bringing about a difference of pay under conditions of perfect competition. If educational diplomas merely certify that individuals have a certain minimum endowment of such capacities, then the marginal product, and thus the earnings of workers who have just reached a particular diploma, will reflect both their investment in obtaining that diploma and their remaining unfiltered capacities. The basic form of his earnings function is:

$$E_{ij} = F^*_{ij} + F_{ij}$$

where

$$F_{ij} = \int_0^j r_t \, C_{it} \mathrm{d}t \ .$$

In this, E_{ij} represents the earnings of the ith individual of age j years. This can be decomposed into F^*_{ij}, representing the return on unfiltered capacities, and F_{ij}, the return on education. C_{ij} is the marginal cost of the ith individual's training net of depreciation. His estimating equation is of the form

$$\mathrm{Log} \ E_j = r_s S12N + r_p P + aj - bj^2 + c$$

where $S12N$ is the net duration of schooling, and P the time equivalent of post-school training (both on and off the job), and r_s and r_p the private rates of return on these.

Lévy-Garboua then brings the theory of discrimination to bear on the interpretation of differences between the age earnings profiles thus estimated for people with similar levels of education but different social origins.

Four main observations arise from his study, the first two of which relate to Lévy-Garboua's own theory of education and earnings, and the latter two relate to discrimination as applied in this context. The first observation is that non-filtered capacities are substitutable for filtered ones; the second is that screening implies the existence of a 'parchment' or diploma effect such that investment in education which does not lead to the next highest diploma produces no return; the third is that the behaviour of different social groups in occupational choice produces social segregation in employment; and the final one is that 'cultural nepotism' by employers means that unfiltered capacities are rewarded according to social origin, at least in the early part of a person's career.

The substitutability of filtered and non-filtered capacities is supported by the observation that the earnings profiles of sons of manual and of clerical workers cross at two ages, as the latter overtake sons of manual workers at about the age of twenty-four and are overtaken by them in their late thirties. Lévy-Garboua's explanation for this is that for equal ability, sons of clerical workers invest more in education than do sons of manual workers, and consequently have a higher level of filtered or certified capacities early in their working lives which is attractive to employers. However, as employers become aware of the unfiltered capacities of manual workers' sons the longer they employ them, manual workers' sons' earnings catch up with those of sons of clerical workers.

The second, the 'parchment effect', is related to the first, and describes the situation in which additional years of education working for a diploma which was not completed receive no income. This is a central part of Lévy-Garboua's version of the screening theory. In his regressions, this effect is picked up by dummy variables in his main estimating equation for each of the main diplomas.

The third influence is that of social segregation. Lévy-Garboua explains this by the tendency for people of a particular social background to follow particular streams within the French educational system, leading to particular types of occupation. For example, sons of blue collar workers tend to follow the technical stream, while sons of white collar workers tend to follow the general stream. This might be analysed in terms of discrimination between workers leading to labour market segregation of the kind described by Becker, as a disinclination to work with people from a different social background would affect occupational choice.

The difference between the earnings profiles of sons of blue collar and of white collar fathers then arises from the smaller liquidity of the technical diplomas taken by blue collar workers as opposed to the general diplomas of the same level taken by white collar workers. The former, because of their greater specificity to particular types of job, are more frequently out of line with labour demand, thus reducing individual workers' bargaining power, and added to this, the greater tendency of blue collar sons to follow their father's occupation generates a crowding effect in their labour markets.

The fourth influence described by Lévy-Garboua arises from discriminating behaviour on the part of employers who favour job applicants of certain types of social background. 'Cultural nepotism' by employers leads to differences in earnings between workers with the same level of higher education but of different social origin. The profiles show that sons from the higher socio-professional groups start at a higher level of earnings, although those from lower groups catch up later in their careers. As both groups of sons are likely to have the same distribution of unfiltered innate capacities, this means that employers reward these unfiltered capacities more generously for sons of higher social groups. If all of these unfiltered capacities were productive, then the earnings difference would persist over the workers' lifetime. But this is not the case as the earnings differential disappears in later life. According to Lévy-Garboua, this means that employers initially misjudge job applicants from higher socio-professional groups, although they realise their error later after working with them.

In Becker's terms, cultural nepotism would be equivalent to treating the net output of the offspring of lower socio-professional groups as reduced by a discrimination coefficient. In fact, as Lévy-Garboua points out, his own definition of 'cultural discrimination' is somewhat broader than Becker's as it relates to the effect of social origin upon the remuneration of unfiltered capacities, and includes both the non-pecuniary motivation Becker refers to and elements of possible misinformation.

3.4. THE PERSISTENCE OF NORMS OF DISCRIMINATION IN A COMPETITIVE ECONOMY

A point on which Becker's theory of discrimination has been much criticised, but which applies equally to Lévy-Garboua's theory, has been that of accounting for the persistence of such discrimination within a broadly competitive economy. Both Becker and Lévy-Garboua were keen to develop a theory which did not depend upon imperfect competition because, although there may be many imperfections in American and French labour markets, in both economies there is a considerable degree of entry and product market competition. The problem can be looked at from the point of view of both employers and employees.

(a) Discrimination by employers
As stated earlier, the essence of Becker's approach to discrimination is that employers should forego some income in order to satisfy their taste so that, compared with non-discriminating employers, those discriminating will earn a smaller monetary return on capital employed. Thus one would expect discriminating employers to grow more slowly, to go out of business or to be bought out more often than other employers, so that in the long run discrimination by employers would be eliminated from the market. This was

indeed Arrow's (1972) argument against Becker. This would cause the distribution of discrimination coefficients among existing employers to decline as those with the highest coefficients had the greatest chance of going out of business. So over time, the median coefficient would fall, and with it, the W/N pay differential, even though the distribution of discrimination coefficients in the wider society remained unchanged.

Becker may have been aware of such difficulties when he recognised that discrimination might be more prevalent the less the degree of market competition. Nevertheless, Becker's and Lévy-Garboua's theories were meant to be more general and to be applicable to a competitive or near-competitive market environment.

If their theories are to work for competitive conditions, then there has to be some force easing the pressure on discriminating employers. The obvious one is the ratio of discriminating to non-discriminating employers in a particular market. Thus the theory could continue to work if there were a sufficiently large proportion of discriminating employers, and if there were enough discriminators among new entrants to maintain discrimination as the dominant pattern. In theory, under conditions of constant returns to scale, a single non-discriminating employer would suffice to drive all discriminating employers out of business, and indeed, one could cite the case of desegregation among American baseball teams in the 1950s, when one man, Bill Veeck, started hiring black players.[1] However, the nature of competition in many industries differs from that in professional sport because success does not depend upon position in a championship table, and in practice, even under near-constant returns to scale, expansion can be a costly and uncertain business and may involve considerable organisational problems for firms, and this could slow the speed at which less discriminating firms drive out the more discriminating ones.

Discrimination is also likely to be more persistent the smaller the dispersion of discrimination coefficients. A large dispersion would lead to large disparities of income between those discriminating to different degrees and this would have a similar effect to the existence of a higher proportion of non-discriminators.

In addition, if firms with high discrimination coefficients have a higher chance of going out of business, the maintenance, in Becker's model, of a given distribution of coefficients among firms would require that there be a correspondingly higher proportion of employers with high coefficients among new entrants. If the latter had the same distribution as the wider society, then the median coefficient among employers would still decline, as those with lower coefficients have higher survival chances. To maintain the pattern among employers new entrants would have to include a higher proportion of high discrimination coefficients than the wider population, and there is no obvious reason why this should be so.

The distribution of discrimination coefficients among employers might be maintained by the influence of social groups to which discriminating employers belong such that the groups constrain individual employers to conform to a particular pattern of discrimination. At least these might considerably slow down the elimination of discriminating by competition, and prevent highly discriminating firms from copying the practices of their less highly discriminating competitors. However, to maintain their individualistic assumptions, Becker and Lévy-Garboua would have to provide a model of group pressure which was constructed from individualistic premises, but the difficulty of achieving this has been shown by Arrow, and by Olson. Arrow's (1963) 'voting paradox' argument shows that transitive individual preference orderings cannot necessarily be aggregated into a collective transitive ordering unless certain prior restrictions are imposed which rule out incompatible preferences. Olson (1971) takes a different tack, and shows that groups based on individualistic premises have certain unstable tendencies in the way that cartels are always inherently unstable because of the gains that individual members can hope to make by violating the cartel's restrictions on output or on price.

Thus Becker and Lévy-Garboua are left with the problem that although group membership might help maintain the distribution of discriminatory preferences among employers to ensure persistence of discrimination in a competitive economy, the individualistic premises from which they set out provide little hope for constructing a theory of group preferences out of individual preferences. Thus they are left in the position that they could account for the persistence of discrimination by employers in a competitive economy if they can show that membership of discriminating social groups maintains the distribution of tastes for discrimination among established employers and among new entrants. But this solution is closed to them because it would be inconsistent with their premises that such group norms are in fact to be treated as tastes in individual preference functions, without requiring any reference to social groups, except as a shorthand for individuals with shared tastes or objectives.

One possible alternative is that the groups might be assumed to have a group utility function in the way that Oswald (1982) (see Chapter 2) treats unions as having a utility function. The justification in this case is that the arguments in the union's utility function are fairly limited, and the fact that people are free to either join or not provides a possible way out of the Arrow paradox. It could be argued that if membership of the group is elective then the individual utility functions may be aggregated for these issues up to the group level, as those who feel that their own preference orderings are violated can opt out (if there is no closed shop). However, membership of social groups is usually based on ascriptive criteria such as race, sex or social origin and so is not elective. Thus the analysis does not seem appropriate.

There is an additional reason why it is not appropriate, namely that elective membership usually presumes that the individual derives some net gain. But this would contradict the basic assumption of Becker's analysis of discrimination: that discriminating individuals are prepared to forego income in order to indulge their tastes. Thus one is left with groups of people whose utility functions for some reason contain a number of similar arguments, and which can discriminate as groups, but whose scope and cohesion are taken as given. Thus Becker and Lévy-Garboua are not just taking tastes as given, but they are also taking as given the social groups to which these tastes relate.

Group action need not be explained in purely individualistic terms. Indeed, the strength of individual attachment to group membership is well illustrated by the fact that one of the most effective sanctions groups apply against dissident members is to exclude them, as for example when workers send uncooperative work-mates 'to Coventry' by refusing to speak to them. Discrimination frequently bears the hallmarks of social norms because of the threat of sanctions by other members of the group, at least as important as individual preference. One has only to reflect on the treatment of individual members of a discriminating group who do not themselves wish to discriminate: for example, members of catholic or protestant families in some parts of Northern Ireland who wish to marry someone from the other church. Another example might be the community pressures among the South Wales miners during the strike in 1984–5 which maintained a very high degree of unity during the year-long strike and which enabled them to avoid almost entirely the mass picket lines used in the North of England. Similarly, in communities in which 'piston' or nepotism is practised in order to obtain preferential treatment for group members applying for a job or for promotion, the practice depends partly on intra-group solidarity, and the expectation of the informal exchange which, if not granted, may result in penalties. The person in the position of power is expected by members of his or her group to give favourable treatment almost as a moral obligation.

(b) Discrimination among workers

Discrimination among workers according to Becker's theory should lead to job segregation because employers would have to pay over the odds to persuade a worker to accept a job with members of the group against which he or she discriminates. But it is open to question why this job segregation should be any more persistent in a competitive economy than discrimination among employers unless group pressures are introduced into the picture. This can be shown as follows.

In Becker's model, white and black workers are assumed (i) to be perfect substitutes in production. As a result a non-discriminating employer is indifferent between workers from either group. If we assume that (ii) only workers discriminate and further assume with Becker that (iii) tastes for discrimination are randomly distributed among the white workers and that (iv) they are of varying intensity, what happens if we have a number of job seekers of either group? This can be looked at under the assumption of negligible hiring and job search costs, and then the assumption that they are positive.

Under negligible hiring and search costs, if all W workers discriminate to the same extent, then the recruitment of a B worker by the employer will result in mass resignations. Alternatively, if some W workers discriminate and others do not, only discriminators will leave. In the absence of hiring costs, employers will be indifferent between hiring W and B workers. Under these conditions, W workers will have higher average turnover rates than B workers. They will also have a higher unemployment rate because whereas B workers may apply for jobs in all firms, many unemployed W workers will apply only to all $-W$ firms. These will have lower turnover rates and thus lower vacancy rates than mixed firms, other things being equal. But most empirical studies of discrimination show that, other things being equal, unemployment rates are usually higher among groups which are discriminated against. In addition, the type of job segregation observed would not be stable. In the absence of hiring costs, employers with all $-W$ labour forces would be likely sooner or later to take on a B worker, provoking resignations among some or all of the W workers.

The introduction of hiring and search costs considerably alters the picture because discriminating W workers can now inflict a cost upon their employers by resigning if a B worker is recruited. But likewise, resigning also imposes a cost on such W workers. In the absence of collective action, workers might still have higher resignation and unemployment rates because if individual discrimination coefficients are randomly distributed, then employers will not know how many if any of their W employees at any one time would resign if a B worker were taken on. Those in a hurry to recruit might well risk taking on a B worker rather than wait for a W applicant and play safe. This would lead to lower average annual incomes for W workers because of the spells of unemployment. This again seems to be at odds with the empirical research.

Collective action, be it in the form of union action, or informal group pressures from existing employees of the firm, however, could be a source of pressure on an employer not to take on B workers. In this way, W workers could threaten to impose collective sanctions on the employer including possible resignation *en masse* if a B worker is recruited. However, if it is based upon randomly distributed tastes for discrimination, again the result is unstable. Under such conditions, if the employer were about to engage a B worker, W workers with low discrimination coefficients would accept working with such a worker if the distaste is outweighed by potential search costs. But to apply collective sanctions, they would have to be prepared to support workers with higher discrimination coefficients, and it is the latter who gain from collective action, while the former gain nothing. This is quite different from the economic theories of trade union membership under which all members are likely to gain some increase in welfare. Thus on purely individualistic grounds, it is hard to account for collective pressures for discrimination, unless of course the dispersion of discrimination coefficients among W workers is very small. But one reason for Becker's assumption of randomly distributed coefficients was that the theory should not depend upon any systematic factors governing their distribution, such as social group pressures.

Thus as with discrimination by employers, we see that stable patterns of discrimination among workers are hard to explain in the purely individualistic terms set out by Becker and Lévy-Garboua, and calls for some recourse to the action of social groups.

3.5. WORKERS' PAY NORMS AND PAY RELATIVITIES

Becker's treatment of discrimination provided one illustration of the way pay differentials might arise because of non-market influences. A somewhat different approach, but one also seeking to remain within the mainstream of economic theory, was undertaken in an intriguing study, in which Adrian Wood (1978) sought to construct a theory of the impact of people's ideas of fair pay relativities upon the process of wage determination fixing the parameters within which it takes place. But, again the difficulty with his model lies in the assumption of individualistic premises which preclude the kind of group pressures which might make wage comparability norms more effective.

In common with Becker, Wood's main point of departure is to assume that employees' utility functions contain, in addition to the usual arguments of pay and working conditions, arguments relating to fair pay relativities. Employers are assumed to have standard objective functions, except that they have to maximise these functions subject to possible costs inflicted on them by employees whose pay norms may have been violated. An additional similarity is that Wood assumes that workers might forego the opportunity to maximise their earnings if this raised their relative earnings above what they felt was a fair differential *vis-à-vis* some other group.

Fundamental to Wood's analysis is the distinction between 'normative' and 'anomic' pressures on employers and workers. Normative pressures derive from workers' ideas of fair pay relativities, while anomic pressures relate to the market forces. The main behavioural assumption concerning pay relativities is that people resist being paid less than what they feel is fair, $\bar{w}$, and although not averse to being paid more, they will not fight for it. A wide range of pressure tactics can be used by employees to force the employer to pay in accordance with their norm, including strike action, reduced cooperation, a reduction of effort, and labour turnover. All of these inflict costs upon the employer such that failure to satisfy a group's idea of a fair

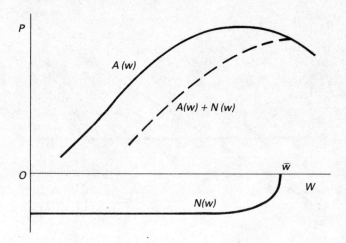

Figure 3.1: The anomic and normative pressure functions facing an employer.

relativity causes loss of profits. The other constraint on the employer arises from 'anomic' or normal economic pressures. Failure to pay enough to recruit and retain labour of the desired quality also reduces profits through the costs of under-manning, wastage, while paying too much leads to a cost disadvantage.

Thus Wood can represent the employer as facing an anomically optimal wage function, $A(w)$, and a normative pressure function, $N(w)$, which both express profits, P, as a function of the anomically optimal wage and of the pressures imposed for the normative wage relativity. Thus the employer selects w so as to maximise

$$P(w) = A(w) + N(w).$$

This is represented in Figure 3.1.

The analysis can be illustrated for two bargaining groups in an enterprise which are concerned only with their pay relative to each other, and its absolute level. Suppose that group X's desired relativity is $\bar{w}_x$, and group Y's, $\bar{w}_y$. In

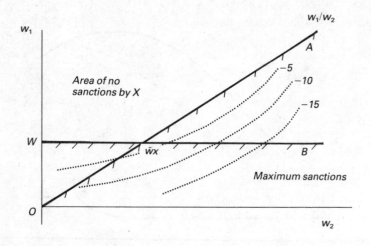

Figure 3.2: The area of acceptable and unacceptable pay for group X.

Figure 3.2 the ray from the origin through the point $\bar{w}_x$ represents the same relativity between the two groups. The horizontal line through $\bar{w}_x$ represents the absolute level of pay w_1 (or an external relativity with another group outside the firm). Group X will resist any combination of pay levels for the two groups to the right of OA as this would imply a smaller relativity compared with group Y, and it will also resist any absolute pair of pay levels below the line WB, but it will be happy with any combination in the area above $W\bar{w}_xA$. The further the pay relativity and level drop below this line, the stronger will be the resistance by group X, and the stronger the sanctions they will impose on the employer. This could be represented by a series of isoquants representing the cost to the employer of different levels of sanctions from members of group X.

A similar analysis can be done for another group Y, which when superimposed on Figure 3.2 shows the size of the area of agreement between X and Y over possible relativities. For both groups $\bar{w}_x$ and $\bar{w}_y$ might coincide so that there would be a relativity which would incur no sanctions against the employer. But it is easy to envisage cases in which there will be such disagreement on pay norms that there is no combination of wage rates for the two groups which will enable the employer to avoid sanctions from one group or the other. The problem of cost minimisation facing the employer becomes more complex still when we remember that he has also to take account of the anomic wage function.

The analysis so far has been conducted for two groups within a firm, but it can be extended to any number of relativities. Thus in $A(w)$ and $N(w)$, w can be thought of as a vector of $k-1$ relativities with one absolute rate (or one external comparator):

$$w_2/w_1, \ w_3/w_1, \ \ldots \ w_{k-1}/w_1$$

Of course, as the analysis becomes more complex, the occurrence of irreconcilable pay norms becomes increasingly likely, which then raises the question of which norms should prevail (those of the strongest groups?), and whether groups might not benefit from forming coalitions and compromising on their pay norms.

The second stage of Wood's analysis deals with external relativities, which introduces the problem of the sequence of pay settlements and of inflation resulting from incompatible norms. This can be illustrated with three groups A, B and C. Figure 3.3 includes on its axes relativities between A and the two other groups—the third relativity being determined by the other two. A's region of complete satisfaction is given by the vertical line through α, to the right of which lies its preferred relativity with group C, and the horizontal line through α, above which lies its preferred relativity with group B, and so on for the other groups' preferred relativities. If the three groups reach their pay settlements in the order $ABCABC$, then when A settles, the relativity between B and C is given as it can determine only the rate for its own members. Consequently, its range of possible settlements is given by a ray from the origin though γ, and it will want to settle at least at the rate at which the ray enters A's region of complete satisfaction, which we call a. Next, when

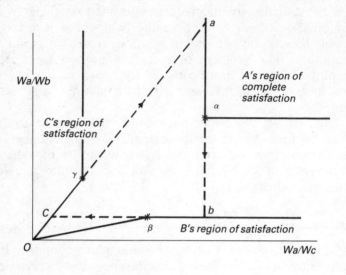

Figure 3.3: Pay settlements with three groups.

B settles, the rates for *A* and *C* are fixed, so its range of possible settlements are given by the vertical line through *a*, and it will aim at least for the point at which this line enters *B*'s area of complete satisfaction, at *b*. It is likewise for *C*. Thus there develops a dynamic for pay settlements from tension between the pay norms of the three groups, none of which can be simultaneously satisfied.

The difficulty with Wood's theory lies less in the dynamics of wage behaviour than in the mechanics by which wage comparability norms are made effective. Early in his book, he opted for treating such norms as arguments in workers' utility functions, and thus opted for the same individualistic premises as Becker and Lévy-Garboua.

By remaining silent on the nature of the pay norms, and by opting for premises familiar to most economists, he greatly eased his task of exposition, but as with Becker and Lévy-Garboua, there then emerges the problem of how stable norms arise and persist in a competitive economic system given individualistic behavioural assumptions. The biggest problem is why workers within the same bargaining unit should all have incorporated the same wage norms in their utility functions. This may be easier to explain for groups with a clear occupational identity and long-standing union organisation, such as certain groups of craft workers. For these, the bargaining unit and the occupational group are closely linked even though the same union may conclude separate agreements with many separate employers. Craft unions in Britain defend long apprenticeships on the ground that young workers need to learn not only the technical side of their skill, but also the culture and traditions of their trade. But it is less clear for groups whose identity depends mainly upon the firm to which they happen to have been recruited. To introduce new arguments into a worker's utility function each time he or she changes job and bargaining group seems unsatisfactory as utility functions are only observable by their consequences.

In Wood's case there is the additional problem as to why the distribution of individual workers' pay comparability norms should coincide with bargaining units. In fact, studies of wage comparability in shop steward bargaining, such as those of Willman (1980) or of Batstone *et al.* (1977), indicate complex political processes at work in mobilising, defining, and defending such norms.

This is especially true of French industrial relations where the bargaining unit frequently depends upon the unions' ability to mobilise workers in defence of a particular wage norm, or working practice. In one sense this resolves Wood's problem of why the norm and the bargaining unit might coincide, but as Eyraud (1983) has shown the norm is defined partly with an eye to the problems of mobilising support. He argues that French unions often define wage demands in general terms and defend them with general arguments in order to mobilise as much support within the firm as possible. But it also introduces a degree of instability into Wood's model as the lack of well-established bargaining units is one of the factors behind the instability of relations between French unions and employers.

These work group pressures behind norms are not inconsistent with Wood's analysis of wage dynamics if we treat the norms in his model as 'revealed' in the sense Samuelson uses for consumer demand analysis. But it seems much more questionable to relate them directly to individual workers' utility functions.

3.6. THE NATURE OF GROUP PRESSURES

The argument so far has been that some form of constraint over individual action by the group has been necessary in order to get the results Becker and Lévy-Garboua seek from their models, which is in fact inconsistent with the basic individualistic premises upon which they are built. It remains to be seen, however, what is the nature of such group constraints in the labour market, and what sustains them.

For the present argument, group pressures can be divided into four kinds. The first concerns the direct pressures upon deviant members who fail to conform to group norms involving material sanctions, and the second, moral pressures such as exclusion or shame. The third concerns elements of group consciousness, and the fourth shared perceptions and orientations by group members which can lead them to interpret their situation and the action of other groups in a similar ways. It is not difficult to see how direct pressures can work, but they do presuppose the existence of fairly cohesive groups. While this cohesion can be, and often is, partly based upon individual self-interest, it is also based upon a shared acceptance of certain group norms, a sense of belonging to a group, and on common ways of interpreting one's surroundings. Apart from the material sanctions, these pressures are mostly omitted from individualistic theories of group behaviour. Yet they provide the cohesiveness which makes group action more stable and more effective, including in a competitive environment. Moreover, they are hardest to integrate into an individualist choice theoretic framework, especially since, as noted earlier, Arrow's voting paradox, and Olson's work should suggest that there is no simple way of aggregating from the individual to the group level without introducing some restrictions on individual choice, or unless group membership is voluntary.

Material and moral sanctions

There are many illustrations of direct group pressures. The literature on small group behaviour in workplace regulation provides many illustrations of norms developed by work groups and the sanctions they use to enforce these *vis-à-vis* management, but more important for the present argument, *vis-à-vis* group members who might be tempted to violate them. In the cases of overtime and piecework 'banking' under payment-by-results systems (under which workers develop a degree of control over the pace of work by storing up overtime of piecework chits issued by their supervisors, using them to even out fluctuations in pay) and of other methods of controlling the pace of work by group go-slows or 'gold-bricking', close cooperation and collusion between group members is essential. In both of these cases, practices such as sending fellow workers 'to Coventry' (refusing to speak to them), or hiding their tools, are common sanctions indicating group hostility to individuals violating the group norms. Such exclusion both makes work more difficult, and also makes life very unpleasant for the individual thus excluded. Thus the element of self-interest for most workers is bolstered by the threat of sanctions, and notably of exclusion.

Other examples of group pressures of a moral kind on individual workers can be found in the 1984 British miners' strike. Large numbers of pickets shouting 'scab' are intimidating of themselves, but for individual miners crossing them, there is the additional opprobrium that their fellow workers from the same communities are accusing them of disloyalty (the meaning of 'scab'), and will probably not accept them back into the community after the end of the strike. The language is not one of rational calculation of

self-interest but one of morals—of loyalty and obligations
to one's fellow workers. In contrast, in the Nottinghamshire
area, the miners had voted against strike action, and a
majority continued to work despite mass pickets from neigh-
bouring Yorkshire. They did so claiming that the strike call
was not legitimate, and had been called in violation of union
procedures for calling a national strike.

Moral sanctions derive additional force according to the
degree to which individual members have internalised group
norms, so that transgression brings, in addition to disapproval, feelings of guilt and shame. Social science research
on this in relation to work group norms is scarce, perhaps
because of the intrinsic difficulty of exploring people's feeling of guilt, but literature can provide some insight. A well-
known example, in Robert Tressell's (1955 Ch.2, p. 36)
novel about building workers, is that of the craftsman who
is browbeaten by his foreman into accepting less than the
union rate for his work, about which he feels both guilty
and ashamed.

Group consciousness

The third pressure is the idea that one is part of a group
with which one shares certain similar ways of seeing things,
and with which one feels a moral bond. Consciousness of
being a member of a social group can be decomposed into
three main constituents: a principle of identity which defines
the group in terms of its principal activities, a principle of
opposition which defines it in relation to other groups which
impinge upon these activities, and finally a principle of
totality which defines the overall context for group members
in which these relations take place, and which provides the
interpretative scheme through which they understand these
relations (Touraine 1966). The third principle is the key to
group consciousness, being both the element which provides
cognitive unity to the group, and at the same time offering
a basis for empirical investigation.

Some evidence for this can be found in the three major
post-war European studies of workers' attitudes to their
work and to society, by Popitz *et al*. in West Germany, by
Touraine in France, and by Goldthorpe *et al*. in the UK.

The findings of these studies can to a large extent be taken as cumulative in that the French study was greatly influenced by the earlier German one, and the British one was influenced by the other two as is evidenced by numerous cross-references.

Although about fifteen years elapsed between the German and the British studies, during which prosperity greatly increased, each one showed that there was, among its sample of manual workers, a strong degree of consciousness of belonging to a distinct community of manual work. This was strongest in the German study which was located in the steel industry of the mid-1950s, but was still clearly visible in the sample of high-wage engineering (mostly cars) workers in Britain in the late 1960s despite the acquisition of many of the material benefits of middle class existence.

The idea of belonging to the community of manual labour (*die Arbeiterschaft*) was a major theme running through Popitz' interviews with German steel workers. This comprised two elements: an awareness of belonging to a particular collectivity (*Kollektivbewusstsein*), and of being engaged in a particular type of activity and living by their skill (*Leistungsbewusstsein*). The latter consisted of an awareness of a collective skill belonging to the whole of labour force, and although stronger among skilled workers, was not confined to this category. It is important to remember that many of the skills in the steel industry were developed by long experience on the job. The *Leistungsbewusstsein* distanced the manual workers both horizontally from other groups of employees, notably white collar workers, and vertically from the works management.

The two fundamental constituents of worker consciousness (Arbeiterbewusstsein), namely the worker's recognition of the technical skill of his work, and his awareness of a shared social condition, are thus determined by his social distance, and his differentiation from the 'others'. (Popitz *et al*. 1957 p. 242).

The belief that society is divided into two parts ran through all the types of image of society identified in their research, and it was closely intertwined with the belief in a community of manual labour (*Arbeiterschaft*). This, Popitz and his colleagues argued, could be contrasted with the hierarchical view of society held by white collar workers (not included in the sample).

In view of the different class structure of French society, and the different patterns of authority in the enterprise, one would expect there to be differences in the form and content of manual workers' consciousness. This was indeed found by Touraine, although he too noted certain fundamental similarities between his own sample and the German one.

A high proportion of manual workers in all three types of consciousness identified in Touraine's study were against capitalism, believed that technical change was of benefit only to their employers, were hostile to office workers, wanting manual occupations for their children, and saw collective struggle, rather than individual action, as the most likely path to improved conditions. The ideological tone was somewhat different from that revealed in the German study, which could have been the result of the more strongly socialist and communist outlook of the main French trade unions. They thus had a high degree of group identity in terms of the groups in opposition to which they defined themselves, in terms of their own life chances, and of what it was desirable to aspire to in life. Their opposition to capitalism (not necessarily in Marxist terms) indicates a degree of unity in terms of their interpretation of the society.

The idea that high material standards of living among manual workers will cause them to develop middle class attitudes and values (the *embourgeoisement* thesis) was tested, and rejected by the British study. It also showed that adherence to more traditional working class ties remained strong:

The social horizons of the members of our Luton sample certainly proved to be wider than those taken as characteristic of the traditional worker, and in other respects apart from material standards of living. However, it is also evident from the results of our enquiry, first, that the aspirations of our respondents were still in important ways shaped and defined by the social realities of their position as manual wage workers—that is to say, by their distinctive class situation; secondly, that their more 'middle class' aspirations were often not held with any great belief in the possibility that they would be realised or were not associated with attitudes and behaviour conducive to their realisation; and thirdly, that only very rarely were aspirations specifically focussed on status enhancement in the sense of there being a desire to emulate, and to gain the acceptance of, persons regarded as belonging to a superior status group. (Goldthorpe *et al.* 1968 p. 122)

The results of the 'Affluent Worker' study are particularly illuminating because they are based on a group among which one would expect the grip of consciousness of belonging to a manual working class to be weakest, but yet in terms of the research team's indicators of social aspirations and political allegiances, there had as late as the late 1960s been little substantial erosion of this awareness.

Group perceptions among manual workers
The fourth pressure reinforcing self-interest in generating group cohesion is shared group perceptions. These studies were not designed to test the existence of group consciousness as such among sub-groups within the manual working class, but they do provide another element for the present argument—namely evidence for the existence of group perceptions in the form of orientations to work, other groups and to society.

The form in which the findings of the Popitz study were presented do not allow one to assess how far the different perceptions of work and society it detected related to membership of different groups within their sample. But Touraine's and Goldthorpe *et al.*'s findings permit at least a partial view of this.

Touraine sought to relate the orientations detected in his survey to the stage of socio-technical development of work organisation. His central idea is that technical change provokes changes in work patterns and in the nature of skilled work and of supervision, and that this shapes their perception of the underlying nature of authority relations in the firm, and of the relation of their own technical competence to production (e.g. whether their skills are general or whether they are closely tied to their employer's immediate needs). Their relationship with their employer affects their views of the possibilities of collective action, and of their relationship to the ultimate goals of production, and thus their view of society. Touraine formalised this view arguing that one could identify three stages in this socio-technical evolution which coexisted in many firms. Phase *A* relates to the craft or artisan form of socio-technical organisation, phase *C* to the automated form of production, and phase *B* to an intermediate form of production associated with assembly line production. In his view, these were group perceptions and not individual ones as they arose out of the reaction of the social organisation of work to technical change, and developed more through collective than individual experience of their conditions and the forms of conflict to which they gave rise.

Within this framework three principles of identity, opposition, and totality have different contents and different relations to each other in each of these phases. In phase *A*, the principle of identity focuses on the worker's skill or craft which embodies a different relation of skill to work to that found in the phase *C*, in which Touraine argues individual skill is absent because of the degree of automation. While opposition in phase *A* tends to be against individual bosses who might exploit market weakness of workers at a particular time, in phase *C*, the principle of totality dominates that of opposition as the key concern is the functioning, and control, of an abstract productive system, such as in the contemporary gas, electricity or oil-refining industries. In between these two comes the phase *B*, that of semi-automated processes in which craft skills still maintain a role, as in maintenance work, but one which differs from that in the craft system and is more dependent on the technical system of production.

In contrast, manual workers, subjected to the pressures of the organisation, see their work situation first as part of a system of economic exploitation, dominated by deskilling and by the 'intolerable work rhythms'. They can no longer rely on the autonomy given by their skill, and they define themselves by reference to their role in an organisation. Here self-consciousness takes on its modern form, whereas consciousness of opposition is, as in the previous phase, directed above all against the employer's profits, which are seen as being the purpose behind the patterns of work adopted. This can be described as consciousness of belonging to an economic class. (Touraine 1965 p. 287)

In contrast, the type of images or consciousness associated with the phase *C*, Touraine argues, should not be a class consciousness of the traditional kind, but one more general and more abstract, and directed at the organising principles of society.

Workers' demands are no longer expressed in defence of their social and professional role within the enterprise, nor even as a demand for planning for the whole of society. They require not only greater participation, and deeper integration, but pose a desire for control as an alternative to the dominant rational models of society and their bad consequences . . . (Touraine 1965 p. 293).

Thus Touraine's argument is that workers have certain key attitudes which form into a coherent picture of society and their position within it. These attitudes bear particularly upon the meaning they attach to their work, their relations in work, and to the type of industrial and political action in which they might engage.

Touraine's empirical results broadly justify this view and can be illustrated. First, there emerges a broad picture of workers in phase *A* based on craft patterns of work organisation who define their activity in terms of their skill, and organise their economic and social defence around this. This colours their view of work, and of fair remuneration, their view of class, their view of the characteristics required for personal success, and their view of trade union action— as much a struggle against the bosses as a pressure tactic. In contrast, workers in phase *C*, the technical system of production, have no craft basis around which to organise their economic and social defence, but identify themselves more with their industry than with their occupation, and see their work more in terms of production. They also see social conditions as a major determinant of success, and see the economic and social system in more abstract and less personalised terms—thus their emphasis upon the role of union action in reducing inequalities between classes, and in improving working conditions, and their view of strikes as a pressure tactic rather than a weapon against the bosses.

An important question is whether these views fall into distinct types, or whether they simply form part of a continuum. If the influence of technical change on workers' orientations acts through its impact on the socio-technical organisation of work and upon the groups into which workers are organised then one might expect a degree of discontinuity. If, on the other hand, the influence of technical change is fairly direct upon workers' orientations, then the degree of continuity between the different phases identified by Touraine might be greater, especially as Touraine hypothesised that the phase *B* of assembly line working was transitional between craft and automated production.

According to his findings, the different forms of workers consciousness do not form a continuum. Phase *B* includes elements of the work organisation and technology of both phases, and the contradictions resulting engender their own form of worker consciousness. This is particularly notable for the views about economic class, supervision, and obstacles to marriage, as workers in this phase believed more strongly than those in either of the other two phases that, for example, there were only two social classes, that supervision was oppressive, and that there were social obstacles to marriage.

Thus Touraine argues that the social and technical organisation of work, through its impact upon people's skills and the nature of the mental and physical activities they undertake, and the type of work group to which they belong, shapes their way of seeing and understanding their relation with their employers. These schema fall into discrete logical types, which imparts a degree of stability and enables them to serve as a basis for group action, for example, in industrial disputes.

The Affluent Worker study, although specifically focused upon manual workers, also brought together a good deal of earlier research on orientations. It distinguishes three broad orientations which were not intended as an exhaustive list. The first is the so-called 'instrumental' orientation, which is characterised by the primary meaning of work being as a means to ends external to the work situation such that workers seek to maximise economic returns. Consistent with this, their involvement in the firm employing them is primarily a calculative one based on the economic return from continued employment in that firm. As work is not valued as an activity in itself, the amount of personal involvement is low—it is not a source of self-realisation—and workers will have a sharp division between their work and their non-work lives.

The second orientation is described as 'bureaucratic', in which the primary meaning of work is as service to an organisation in return for a career or rising income and status, and long-term job security. In this, economic rewards are not tied to particular amounts of work done. Consequently, involvement in the firm contains a definite moral element rather than deriving from a purely market relationship. Because work involves progression in earnings and in jobs, the worker's conception of him or herself will be related to career, and to future position and status in the organisation, which will also be a source of social identity. As a result, there should be no sharp dichotomy between work and non-work life.

The third orientation is 'solidaristic', in which work has an economic meaning, as it does in all three orientations, but is experienced additionally as a group activity. The group could be a firm or an enterprise, but it could also be a work group. Such workers might forego some economic benefits in order to maintain group solidarity or group norms. Involvement in work will also be of a moral kind, but the attitude to management could be cooperative if the moral attachment is to the enterprise, or it could be highly conflictual if the focus of the moral bond were the work group. Consistently with this, personal involvement in work will be strong, and in addition to its instrumental element, work will be found emotionally rewarding. Because work and its relationships are a source of satisfaction, the division between work and non-work life will be diffuse, and work colleagues may often also be friends outside the work environment.

The authors argue that particularly the bureaucratic and

the solidaristic orientations depend on the type of group to which the workers holding them belong. For workers with the instrumental orientation, the allegiance to groups other than that already noted to the manual working class is less obvious, if only because a large number of those involved had uprooted themselves in order to get jobs in these higher paid industries. But two observations on the correlates of instrumentalism were striking. First, it was considerably higher among semi-skilled production workers than among craftsmen, which echoes some of Touraine's observations. Secondly, and more important, it was highly correlated with downward social mobility. Thus one could argue that although instrumentalism was not directly linked to work-related groups, it was in fact related to workers' perceptions of themselves in relation to other groups in the wider society (Goldthorpe *et al.* 1968 Ch. 7).

Thus the emphasis of these studies has been that these orientations are characteristics of groups of workers shared by their individual members rather than simply the perceptions of different and otherwise unrelated individuals. Even in the case of the instrumental orientation the influence of a strong reference group was at work.

There has been a good deal of other evidence of both workers' images of society and of orientations to work, again treating these as group characteristics rather than individual ones. While it would be wrong to say that there was a consensus on their nature and extent, much of the controversy had centred more on their causes, their diversity, and patterns of change than on whether the concepts have any value. Two of the main controversies around the Affluent Worker study, for example, were on how new a phenomenon 'instrumental' orientations to work were in fact, whether they were not also present in more 'traditional' working class communities, such as in shipbuilding (see Cousins and Brown, 1975), and whether 'instrumentalism' was the new pattern in worker orientations to work towards which the British working class was moving. The other main controversy was the extent to which such orientations were determined by factors outside the workplace as compared with immediate work experience. Thus, while several of the studies brought together by Bulmer (1975) contested detailed points about the content of the images of society attributed to workers by earlier studies, they broadly produced evidence in support of the existence of such images.

The main note of dissent was from Blackburn and Mann (1975 and subsequently 1979). Their study of unskilled and semi-skilled workers in the Peterborough labour market produced evidence of weak orientations to particular types of work, especially to work out of doors with the autonomy of supervision that implied (Blackburn and Mann, 1979), but of only weakly defined images of society (Blackburn and Mann, 1975). However, a central part of their argument was that for the type of workers in their sample, the amount of variation in jobs was very limited so that the lack of choice accounted for the weakness of specific orientations.

Thus an additional source of strength for group action lies in the perceptions of work and of other groups shared by members of a particular group. These are mostly shaped by shared experiences in and away from work, and although the precise content of such group orientations is hotly contested among industrial sociologists, there is more consensus on their group-related nature, and on the way they act as interpretative schemes. The problem facing Becker and Lévy-Garboua, and to a lesser extent Wood, lies in their attempt to base group norms as in discrimination and wage norms upon individualistic premises. They need these other collective elements in order to obtain stable patterns of group behaviour.

3.7.   CONCLUSIONS

This chapter has sought to examine the way in which some economists have dealt with the influence of non-monetary motivation on labour market behaviour by using Marshall's idea that the strength of such motivation can be measured by the amount of other goods a person would just be willing to forego in order to satisfy such desires. The strength of this approach is that it enables economists to maintain the basic structure of individual utility maximising, apparently without making assumptions about the underlying processes behind these motivations. As Marshall wrote, the economist does not seek 'to measure any affection of the mind in itself', but only through its effect on market choices.

There is, however, a difference between Marshall's use of this principle as it might be applied in his 'principle of net advantages' in job choice, and the questions to which it has been applied by the three authors discussed in this chapter. Although social status is undoubtedly attached to certain types of working conditions, such as those concerned with the removal of waste, as they affect the great majority of workers it is usually a question of a physical or psychological nuisance which is connected with the inherent characteristics of the job. But Becker and Lévy-Garboua apply the same principle to one's relations with workers from other social groups. Thus one is dealing no longer with inherent characteristics of the job concerned, but with relations between social groups, and their effect upon labour market behaviour. Becker's intention is fairly explicit, namely to show that from the point of view of labour market behaviour social relations with workers or employers from other groups can be treated on a par with a taste or distaste for certain working conditions. Discrimination is for him a strong case out of a whole class of social relations acting upon the labour market.

The basic problem of this approach which arises for all three authors lies in the consistency between their treatment of these group norms, be they for discrimination or for wage comparability, as arguments in individual workers' or employers' utility functions, and the stability of such patterns of behaviour in a competitive economic system. The problem arises with the derivation of stable patterns of group behaviour from the assumption that the norms appear only as tastes in individual utility functions. Arrow argued that in the case of discrimination by employers, on these assumptions, one would expect non-discriminating employers in the long run to drive the discriminators out of business. Thus for the persistence over time of patterns of discrimination one needs some kind of group pressure to restrict the freedom of employers who otherwise would not discriminate, and possibly some guarantee that there would be a high proportion of discriminating employers among new entrants replacing those going out of business. Likewise, on the side of discrimination by workers against fellow workers, it was argued that without group action to enforce discriminatory behaviour one could easily arrive at lower annual incomes and higher rates of unemployment among those workers who discriminate than among those who are discriminated against. Thus both Becker and Lévy-Garboua (who applied Becker's framework to discrimination by social class) need some kind of group pressure in order to maintain the patterns of discrimination in a competitive environment.

Wood's theory of the action of norms of wage comparability is more ambivalent than that of Becker, but it too sets off from individualistic premises suggesting that such norms may be in individual workers' utility functions. However, as already shown for Becker's theory, some mechanism for generating group cohesiveness is needed given the instability of groups in which cohesion is based solely on self-interest. There is the additional problem in Wood's theory that the groups are in fact bargaining groups, which requires the rather arbitrary assumption that arguments of individual workers' utility functions change when they change bargaining group, an assumption many economists, including Becker, would reject as these are unobservable. But one could treat his model as being based upon 'revealed' wage comparability norms for different groups in the way Samuelson used revealed preferences as the basis of his analysis of demand, although the relationship between pay norms and bargaining groups in his model remains unresolved.

The latter part of the chapter was devoted to outlining some of the principal pressures groups exercise over individual members over and above the element of self-interest. It was suggested that there are four main pressures arising from direct sanctions over individual members: moral pressures of exclusion and those arising from internalisation of group norms, a sense of belonging to a wider group, and

the extent to which group members share ways of interpreting their environment and their relations with other
groups. These do not preclude association for mutual gain,
but it is suggested that these pressures provide the additional
cohesiveness so that such groups can continue to function
in a competitive economic system.

The individualist approach to the influence of social
norms on the labour market, discussed in this chapter, has
been to treat them as tastes in individual workers' and
employers' utility functions. The approach is an interesting
one because it seeks to treat these norms as instances of
non-monetary motivation in the labour market, as distinct
from more conventional treatments of discrimination, which
regard it as a disguised form of cost minimisation by
employers. As such, the theories of Becker, Lévy-Garboua,
and of Wood represent a major attempt within economics
to broaden its analytical scope to deal with problems also
raised within sociology and in industrial relations. Nevertheless, it has been argued that these models have important
weaknesses in the way they represent social norms. The
biggest problem arises because they collapse collective
phenomena into individual phenomena, the only link
between the individuals being that they are treated as sharing certain preferences in certain activities. Indeed, Becker
was keen to show that such group phenomena could in
fact be dealt with quite adequately without introducing any
reference to the characteristics of groups which could not
be reduced to statements about their individual members
and their preferences and actions, hence his interest in
tackling discrimination as a critical case of a social norm.

The view of social norms implied by this approach is that
one can say all that is important about social norms in the
labour market by treating them as tastes in a utility function,
and that there is no need to invoke groups except as collections of individuals with some interests and preferences
in common, such as discriminating employers or workers.
This representation of norms is very restrictive in that it
rules out a number of aspects of norms highlighted in this
chapter. There it was argued that they involved the use of
material and moral sanctions, consciousness of belonging to

a group, and certain shared ways of perceiving other groups' actions. Moral sanctions such as displays of disapproval and exclusion require some acceptance by the person being punished that the norm is legitimate. A taste for being approved of would capture some of this but not the element of legitimacy. The consciousness of belonging to a group and shared perceptions by group members offer no obvious means of integration into an individualistic choice theory as both are related to the meaning members attach to their social relations. While it might be possible to translate some of this meaning into expectations about the likely costs to be incurred by undertaking certain courses of action (e.g. perception of an employer's willingness to endure a strike, or of the sincerity of an employer's proposals in negotiations) much that might be relevant to the form of conflict and the participants' ability to mobilise support would be omitted.

Nevertheless, could one not treat social norms as stable, and then introduce them into individual utility functions? Becker himself argues that tastes should be treated as stable for methodological reasons. However, if their stability depends upon group pressures, while the nature of these groups is not explained in terms of the individualistic calculus (as in the voting paradox discussed earlier), this strategy amounts to abandoning Becker's aim of explaining group action and norms in purely individualistic terms. The other major problem is that using a broader concept of group action as a premise for individualistic analysis of choice is in effect combining two very different types of explanation, and it is not clear under what conditions the different sets of assumptions on which they rest would be mutually consistent.

NOTE

1. I am grateful to Shirley Dex for this observation.

4 The Long and Short Periods, and the Relationship Between Competitive and Customary Forces

4.1. INTRODUCTION

This chapter examines another common strategy used in labour economics and in industrial relations for dealing with the joint action of market and institutional and social forces upon wage structure and labour market adjustment, looking in particular at the treatment of customary norms in pay determination. The strategy seeks to articulate the action of market and these other social forces in such a way that the latter may be powerful in the economic short-run, but in the economic long-run, because of the pressures of competition and substitution, market forces are held to predominate. This chapter sketches out the nature of the strategy in some detail, and then deals with its consequences. It will be argued that despite the attractiveness of this way of articulating the time component of economic and social processes, it gives a very truncated view of, for example, labour market custom when compared to the evidence from empirical studies of work rules and 'custom and practice'.

There are many social forces operating on labour markets and on wage structures, as Wootton (1955) has argued, but perhaps the most controversial has been that of custom. Because of its importance in a number of debates, this is the principal 'social force' discussed in this chapter. The problem, as in the other chapters, is that the concepts, such as custom—used by labour economists, sociologists and industrial relations specialists—are built up from different sets of empirical observations. It follows that one cannot ignore or reject one of these discipline-based concepts without also denying the relevance of some of the empirical observations on which each is based. It will also be argued that custom should not be treated always as a rigidity which is eroded in the long-run, and that it can, particularly in the workplace, be an active force generating new patterns of pay relativities.

Marshall's (1920) distinction between the economic short and long periods provided a ready framework for this strategy for reconciling, at the conceptual level, the action of economic and social influences on labour markets. These periods were defined in terms of the time of economic processes and not of actual time.

Of course the periods required to adapt the several factors of production to the demand may be very different; the number of skilled compositors, for instance, cannot be increased nearly as fast as the supply of type and printing-presses. And this cause alone would prevent any rigid division being made between long and short periods. But in fact a theoretically perfect long period must give enough time to enable not only the factors of production to be adjusted to the demand, but also the factors of production of those factors of production to be adjusted and so on . . . . (Marshall 1920 Bk. 5, Ch. 5 S8)

Indeed, Marshall's view of the influence of custom upon relative prices is perhaps best encapsulated in his remarks preceding his discussion of the peculiarities of labour as a commodity:

the direct effects of custom in causing a thing to be sold for a price sometimes a little higher and sometimes a little lower than it would otherwise fetch, are not really of very great importance, because any such divergence does not, as a rule, tend to perpetuate and increase itself; but on the contrary, if it becomes considerable, it tends to call into action forces that counteract it. Sometimes these forces break down the custom altogether; but more often they evade it by gradual and imperceptible changes in the character of the thing sold, so that the purchaser really gets a new thing under the old name. These direct effects then are obvious, but they are not cumulative. (Marshall 1929 Bk.VI, ChIV, S1)

The other case Marshall discusses is that of cumulative influences of custom, but these are seen essentially as factors inhibiting economic progress.

Marshall's device has been used in two main forms which are equivalent despite certain differences in form. The first is the explicit ordering of the time of market and customary processes into the long- and short-run framework, and the second is the treatment of customary and organisational forces as acting within a certain range of tolerance left by market forces. The equivalence of the two can be seen from the fact that the constraint on social pressures pushing the wages of a particular group outside the range of tolerance is the acceleration of substitution either by consumers for the final product, or by employers looking for alternative methods of production (whether by employers immediately concerned, or by other employers not directly concerned but whose business prospects are improved as a result).

The argument of this chapter will be that this strategy for taking account of both market and social and institutional pressures on labour market behaviour has much to recommend it, notably that it goes some way towards recognising that such non-market processes may well not be reducible to individualistic rational calculation, and may not be market processes under another guise. But it has certain quite serious limitations because of the need to conceive of such processes as subordinate to the long-run working of labour market forces, especially those of competition and substitution. It will be argued that the price of this accommodation is that certain institutional and customary processes are treated either as phenomena in the process of disappearing under the influence of market pressures, or as phenomena generated from within the enterprise and thus of a more ephemeral nature than the broader forces of the market. It will be argued that on the evidence we have, custom in differentials and customary rules for determining pay do not fit easily into this framework. This provides prima facie grounds for doubting whether the wages of groups displaced from their long-run equilibrium level will automatically be brought back into line, and indeed whether it is sensible to define long-run equilibrium so as to exclude customary and institutional influences.

This chapter examines the way in which Hicks has used the device of the Marshallian short- and long-runs, and in which other labour economists, such as Lester and Reynolds and Taft, but also more recently Brown and Sisson, and Mackay *et al.* have used the idea of a margin within which non-market forces can determine labour market behaviour.

Against these it will be argued that it is mistaken to confuse patterns of relative wages which may have been sanctioned by 'custom', and the process of custom itself which is a method of social regulation.

4.2. HICKS' VIEW OF CUSTOMARY WAGE DIFFERENTIALS

Among economists, more than most Hicks has sought to reconcile the importance of claims of justice and fairness which appear to motivate wage bargainers and the workers they represent with the impersonal forces of market competition. His analysis was developed partly as a response to Wootton's (1955) argument that the structure of wages in Britain did not correspond to the economist's view, and that it was instead subject to the opposing sentiments for defending customary differentials and for reducing inequalities. Hicks' counterargument is that differentials which have acquired the force of custom, or which have come to be accepted by workers as 'fair', are mostly ones which were previously caused by market pressures of supply and demand, but which have become ossified with the passage of time, and so ceased to correspond to current market conditions.

Hicks' argument can be applied to differentials which have lost their former justification because of technical or product market changes, but the example he gives is even more general, and so perhaps more interesting. His argument is well summarised in his own diagrammatic presentation showing the relative wage of a particular occupation and numbers of workers suitably endowed to enter that occupation (Figure 4.1). At time t_0, the existing labour supply is $ON1$. In the very short-run this cannot be increased, and the supply curve becomes vertical at $ON1$. As more time is allowed, more people can train, and training facilities can be expanded, so the slope of the curve is reduced, but employers usually cannot afford to wait, so, Hicks argues, they would be likely to opt for a new wage rate below $N1Q1$ but above $N3Q3$ so that vacancies can be

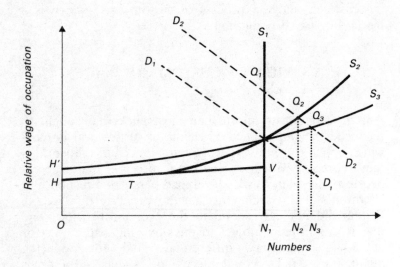

Figure 4.1: Emergence of a customary wage differential.

filled sufficiently quickly to meet the increased product demand. As a result, a wage differential emerges which is above the level that would be suggested by long-run equilibrium conditions, and it is easy to see that once people have entered the occupation they will be anxious to maintain their differential. But being above the long-run level, it will be subject to market pressures to bring it back into line eventually.

The short-run supply curve lies below the long-run curve up to $N1$, reflecting rates of pay just sufficient to retain workers in the occupation, but not to replace losses through natural wastage.

In a later work, Hicks (1974) suggests that one of the reasons for the importance of custom in wage differentials lies in the continuity of the employment relation, as distinct from many, but not all, economic transactions. This continuity provides the basis on which established custom and practice can grow:

Now it is necessary, purely on grounds of efficiency, in regular employment that both parties, employer and employed, should be able to look forward to some durability in their relationship. Yet if the worker is to be free to move . . . there can be no such reliability unless there is contentment, or to least some degree of contentment. So it is necessary for efficiency that the wage-contract should be felt, by both parties but especially the worker, to be fair . . .

A system of wages which will satisfy all the demands of fairness that may be made upon it is quite unattainable. No system of wages, when it is called into question, will ever be found to be fair . . . That has always been true; how is it then that we have got on, in the past, as well as we have? Only because the wage system has not much been called into question. That can happen; but it is necessary, for it to happen, that the system of wages should be well established, so that it has the sanction of custom. It then becomes what is expected; and (admittedly at a low level of fairness) what is expected is fair . . . Employers were reluctant to raise wages, simply because of labour scarcity; for to offer higher wages to particular grades of labour that had become scarce would upset established differentials. They were reluctant to cut wages, simply because of unemployment; for if they did so they would alienate those whom they continued to employ. The 'stickiness' is not a matter of 'money illusion'; it is a matter of continuity. It would of course be reinforced by the standard rates of trade unionism; but there would be a tendency in the same direction even apart from trade union pressure. (Hicks 1974 pp. 64–6)

Thus Hicks' view of custom, particularly as it affects wage structure, is that custom and fairness grow up around patterns of differentials that have already been established by normal market pressures. They may well serve a useful economic function of stabilising workers' and employers' expectations concerning relative wages, or they may inhibit certain medium- and longer-term adjustments, but their action is essentially retardative, and they do not generate new structures of their own. Moreover, in this view, wage norms based on concepts of fairness or of custom are also likely to weaken over time, giving way to new structures generated by changes in the labour market. Thus if there is a process of selection determining which differentials are to survive, it is most likely to be their continued approximation to the patterns of relative pay given by long-run equilibrium. His main addition to Marshall's and Clay's view was to introduce the additional source of flexibility in the economic system arising from the capacity of the system as a whole to accommodate normative pay structures which differed from those of standard long-run equilibrium, thus his reference to the shift from the Gold Standard to the 'Labour Standard', the interpretation of which change will be discussed further in Chapter 6.

A similar view can be detected in Mackay and his associates' (1971) summary of the findings of their labour market study:

The adjustment process in the market may then be slow, and strewn with errors of judgement, but in the end the plants do react to labour market pressures in a manner which is by and large consistent with our a priori expectations, and the same is true of the actions of employees. (Mackay *et al.* 1971 p. 397)

In addition, Mackay *et al.* explicitly endorsed Slichter's (1950) view that managers had a 'range' of discretion in fixing relative wages (p. 391).

4.3.   RANGE THEORIES OF THE ACTION OF LABOUR MARKET PRESSURES

A similar device for relating the action of labour market and institutional pressures on wages and labour market behaviour has been to suggest that within a certain range non-market forces can exert quite a strong influence upon relative wages. This type of approach has been widely used to help explain the big dispersions of inter-plant earnings within occupations, as well as other apparent deviations of observed wage structures from standard competitive theory. The problem, as Lester, one of the strongest exponents of the 'range theory' of wage differentials, described it was to explain: 'the continued existence of sizeable differences in local wage scales not offset by other job attractions or by differences in the quality or effectiveness of labour . . .'. (Lester 1952 p. 488). Lester presented the idea of a 'range of indeterminacy' in a strongly intuitive fashion, using it to describe the wide disparities of wages within occupations in firms in the same locality, and to explain the differences in the structure of occupational differentials in different localities. The competitive model of the labour market, as Lester and others saw it in the late 1940s, predicted that competition would produce uniform rates of wages for all those in a particular occupation in a particular local labour market.

The survey data on which Lester and others, notably Reynolds, based their view did not permit them to test directly either qualification of pure competitive theory, namely equality of 'efficiency wages' or equality of 'net advantages', but interviews with a small number of firms in Lester's case provided his justification for observing that non-pay advantages tended to be higher in higher paid plants, and after allowing for greater investment by the firms in training and experience, higher wage firms did not recruit a noticeably higher quality of labour.

Lester argued that the forces active on the labour market could be classified under three headings: anti-competitive; impeditive; and competitive. The predictions of standard competitive theory would only be realised if the competitive forces were strong enough to override the other two sets of forces. In the case of local and occupational differentials examples of anti-competitive factors he cited were: employers' practices of restricting hiring to certain entry grades at the bottom of job ladders, heavy reliance upon internal upgrading, the tendency for many jobs to have no equivalent in other local firms, and the corresponding reliance upon on-the-job training—factors subsequently picked up by Doeringer and Piore (1971) in their account of internal labour markets. Examples of impeditive factors were that people grow accustomed to certain patterns of differentials (thus the differences between occupational wage structures in different localities), information about jobs and pay is often hard to obtain, many workers are reluctant to change jobs once they have settled, and a great part of such mobility as takes place is random. As a result of these factors, Lester argues that the effect of competition is largely confined, on the supply side, to those seeking their first job, to the unemployed who do not intend to return to their old job, and to short-service workers, and on the demand side, to those companies which are seeking new employees. As a result Lester argues that: 'Competitive forces do operate with respect to the hiring and pay of production workers, but they may not be strong enough to predominate, to overcome the anti-competitive and impeditive factors' (Lester 1952 p. 491). Lester identifies four types of competition affecting labour markets: between companies for new labour; for community reputation with respect to employment; in product markets; and trade union rivalry.

it seems likely that a wage position established by a firm anywhere within a community's wage range would be an equilibrium position even from a long-run view point. Assuming underemployment or even relatively full employment such as the economy has enjoyed during the past decade, there appears to be little in the way of competitive pressures to force a firm to alter its relative wage position. Of course, certain conceivable changes, such as a need to expand its employment rapidly or the location of a new higher-wage plant nearby could serve to make a firm's established wage position untenable. (Lester 1950)

He goes on to argue that in the absence of some such exogenous change, there is little reason why the pattern of interfirm variation in wages in a particular locality cannot persist, and that there exists a significant range of indeterminacy. This range he identifies with the observed dispersion of interplant pay levels.

In a similar vein, Reynolds (1951) argues that there is a 'range or band of feasible wage levels at which a firm may operate', and that once established at a particular level, its position is stable in that 'it can continue to recruit as many workers as it needs', and although Reynolds points out that the lower wage firms almost certainly get less able workers, he suggests that this does not fully compensate for the differences in pay levels, and that there is still a fair dispersion in wage levels per efficiency unit.

However, the actual range of indeterminacy for any one firm is not necessarily the same as the whole dispersion of pay levels in its locality, and if a high paying firm were to try to drop to the bottom of the league, it would most likely suffer from problems of morale among its existing employees, and have difficulties in recruitment. Thus although labour market forces might leave a fairly large range of feasible pay levels for firms in a particular locality, it may be much more difficult for individual firms to change their position once it has become established.

On the question of skill differentials, in the same chapter, Reynolds sought to explain why they should be so much greater in the United States than in France or Sweden. His answer is of some interest because of its similarity to some of the customary forces noted by Hicks. He suggested that the reason why

employers have continued, decade after decade, to pay skilled wage rates well above the level necessary to induce upward mobility . . . (which) seems to indicate an established belief among employers that skilled workers *ought* to be paid much more than the unskilled. This belief does not seem to be based mainly on competititve reasoning but on a variety of other considerations: acceptance of the fact that skilled workers (many of whom are at least second- and third-generation Americans) have customarily had a markedly higher standard of living than the unskilled (many of whom are of recent immigrant stock), and a belief that this difference of living standards should be perpetuated; a feeling that wages should be related to specific productivity, under technological conditions in which the gap between the specific productivity of skilled and unskilled workers cannot be closed by substitution of one for the other; a feeling that skill and training are meritricious in themselves and should be rewarded . . . ; a recognition that the skilled workers are natural leaders of the labour force and are also potential foremen and supervisors, and a consequent desire to strengthen their loyalty to the company . . . . (Reynolds 1951 p. 239)

The margin of indeterminacy, he suggests, is not so much constrained by actual substitution of workers of one category for those of another in individual firms, as by the gradual substitution arising from differential growth rates of firms owing to competition and substitution in product markets—the Hicksean and Marshallian long-run *par excellence*.

Writing with Taft five years later, he argued that the range of indeterminacy was circumscribed by market pressures:

Further, there is a built-in safeguard against excess zeal on the part of trade unions or governments, for when wage differentials are reduced below the minimum tolerable level, organisational decisions appear to lose their effectiveness. The market takes over once more and pulls up higher wage rates sufficiently to restore differentials to an adequate level (Reynolds and Taft 1956 p. 374)

Thus for Lester, and even more so for Reynolds and Taft, the main source of pressures limiting the margin of indeterminacy surrounding feasible wage levels in labour markets is provided by the same factors that Hicks and Marshall treat as forces of the economic long-run.

From this discussion, it is clear that Hicks' and Marshall's approach to the interaction of competitive and organisational factors and social norms on labour markets has been frequently used by other economists and labour relations specialists.

4.4. CUSTOM AND LABOUR MARKET REGULATION

In their treatment of social custom and wage differentials both Hicks and the exponents of the 'range' theory of differentials allowed custom and other organisational and social factors a good deal of influence in the Marshallian short-run, while suggesting that in the longer run such rigidities in relative prices, and labour allocation would be constrained and possibly broken down by market forces. The origins of customary differentials were explained by Hicks in terms of levels of relative wages that had been established by market forces in the past, and to which people had become accustomed. Reynolds also spoke of custom in this way. He spoke of people growing accustomed to certain differentials, and of this custom having a strong moral force 'skilled workers *ought* to be paid more than unskilled workers', but the origin of the differential itself lay in the past pattern of relative supply of and demand for skilled and unskilled labour. In the passage quoted, the impression is very much that the force of custom is the belief that this differential should be perpetuated. Lester also referred to the tendency of people to become accustomed to certain differentials as one of the 'impeditive' factors to labour market competition. The idea underlying these views is that such forces as social custom preserve rather than create new differentials or patterns of behaviour, while market forces provide much of the impetus for change. Thus market pressures are treated as both historically and logically prior to those customary and organisational factors which contribute to the margin of indeterminacy.

This raises a number of important questions, the central one being whether such forces as custom in labour markets are merely passively registering past market equilibria, or whether custom, and related forces have an important dynamic of their own. To be answered, this question needs to be broken down into a number of subsidiary questions. First, to what extent is it true historically that custom merely sanctified market determined relative wages (section 4.5)? The second and third questions relate to the role of custom in workplace bargaining, and in regulating whole labour markets respectively (sections 4.6 and 4.7).

It will be suggested that there has been a tendency to conflate two things: a particular structure of wage differentials which has received the sanction of custom, and the process of customary regulation itself. The first may well be something which is continually undergoing change and being broken down by market pressures in the same way as the structure of prices of other goods, but the second is a process of social regulation active both within and beyond the bounds of the enterprise. Moreover, it will be suggested that customary regulation does not sanction all practices and differentials which develop, but is highly selective, and is often as important as market pressures in determining which practices and differentials will become established.

Evidence on the working of custom in the labour market is somewhat fragmentary, so the argument of this section will of necessity be rather tentative.

4.5. CUSTOM AND DIFFERENTIALS IN HISTORICAL PERSPECTIVE

Much of the historical evidence relating the role of custom

in labour markets suggests that it was more a system of regulation and that, to a degree, it preceded collective bargaining. Indeed, one writer, Rowe (1928), argued that one of the key methods of collective bargaining as described by the Webbs, namely the estblishment of a 'common rule', was the direct descendent of customary wage levels.

Much writing both on labour economics and on industrial relations starts from the assumption that collective bargaining was preceded by a system of competitive labour markets in which workers competed for work, and bargained over terms and conditions as individuals. This is well encapsulated in Flanders' (1968) critique of the Webbs' view of the development of collective bargaining. He accused them of making the fundamental mistake of believing that collective bargaining was the collective equivalent of individual bargaining instead of a system of industrial government, but he shared with the Webbs the idea that individual bargaining had been the historical precursor of collective bargaining.

However, before the growth of collective bargaining in the nineteenth century there is evidence that custom played an extremely important part in wage regulation in many activities. Customary regulation was a precursor of collective bargaining, and it was itself a method of collective regulation, albeit more diffuse and of a less contractual nature. E. P. Thompson described briefly the role of such custom among agricultural labourers and particularly among skilled artisans:

The wages of the skilled craftsmen at the beginning of the nineteeth century were often determined less by 'supply and demand' in the labour market than by the notion of social prestige or 'custom'. Customary wage-regulation may cover many things, from the status accorded by tradition to the rural craftsman to intricate institutional regulation in urban centres . . . Custom, rather than costing (which was rarely understood), governed prices in many village industries, especially where local materials—timber or stone—were used. The blacksmith might work for so much a pound for rough work, a little more for fine. George Sturt, in his classic study of 'The Wheelwright's Shop', has described how customary prices still prevailed in Farnham when he took over the family firm in 1884. 'My great difficulty was to find out the customary price . . . I doubt if there was a tradesman in the district—I am sure there was no wheelwright—who really knew what his output cost, or what his profits were, or if he was making money or losing it on a particular job'. . . . Customary traditions of craftsmanship normally went together with vestigial notions of a 'fair' price and a 'just' wage. Social and moral criteria— subsistence, self-respect, pride in certain standards of workmanship, customary rewards for different grades of skills—these are all as prominent in early trade disputes as strictly 'economic' arguments'. (E.P. Thompson 1968 pp. 260–1)

Customary methods of regulation were already under attack before the end of the eighteenth century in agriculture, and many industrial employers during the nineteenth century century sought successfully to break down such methods of regulation, as was shown by Hobsbawm's (1964) study of custom, wages, and workloads. Hobsbawm argues that gradually workers learned the rules of the new game, of working employers' payment systems to their own benefit, and developing collective bargaining, but there nevertheless remains a strong link between earlier forms of customary regulation of wages, and certain methods of collective bargaining, particularly among the more skilled groups.

Rowe (1928) argued that throughout the latter part of the nineteenth century customary wage differentials played an extremely important part, and by and large accounted for the considerable degree to which wage rates in different industries moved together (see Chapter 6 in this book). The main exceptions, coal mining and the railways, were the industries in which Hobsbawn argued that the workers had gone furthest in learning to manipulate the new set of economic rules by pressing for as large increases as the market would bear. However, the stability of differentials in other sectors suggests that the strength of customary differentials remained widespread, as Rowe argued. Indeed, Rowe went on to suggest that

the influence of custom may be said to have constituted the real basis of the trade union standard rate. The standard rate was not an original concept of trade unionism: it was essentially the means whereby principles which custom stamped as right and proper, were solidified into a system, which it was the function of trade unionism to maintain as rigidly as possible. At the end of the nineteenth century, as throughout its course, the medieval conception of the just wage still lingered in the minds of the wage earners in the guise of a reverence and a trust in custom as affording a criterion which was desirable in itself, and which also afforded practical guidance in steering amidst the reefs and shoals of their negotiations with the capitalist. (Rowe 1928 p. 156)

Rowe suggests that custom accounted for the apparent symmetry of the wage structure in the late nineteenth century, but also that custom was declining in importance up to the First World War. The rest of his chapter was devoted to the factors underlying the breakdown of the 'common test of comparison' up to and after the First World War under a variety of influences, including technical change, the expansion of socialism in trade union circles, and inflation and flat-rate pay increases. Nevertheless, the stability of the inter-industry pay structure in both the short- and long-run during the inter-war years and the partial re-establishment of skill differentials during the 1920s and 1930s suggest that, despite the changes brought about during and after the First World War, norms of fairness continued to exercise great influence upon wage structure.

Indeed, Rowe overtstates the decline of normative pressures on pay structure as Hicks (1974) observed when he remarked that the ability of the wage structure to withstand the economic pressures set in motion by the war and subsequent recession was greatly helped by the abandonment of the Gold Standard. This made the bond between real and money wages flexible. Rowe may also have overstated the degree of consensus in the late nineteenth century, although it had also been observed by other post-war writers, such as Clay (1929).

One strand running through the writing of a number of authors, including Flanders, is the idea that before collective bargaining negotiations were mostly conducted on an individual basis. This is true in the sense that individual workers would present themselves to individual employers (much as they do under collective bargaining), but in those trades in which customary rates predominated, both employers and workers were price takers, and it would be wrong to suppose that in the absence of unions, workers (and other employers) were bereft of means of enforcing the customary wage norms. In the rural and small town communities referred to by E. P. Thompson the skilled artisans were also members of the community, as were their employers, which exposed them to a wide variety of informal pressures. The breakdown of such customs would have been greatest in the casual trades, and in those industries in which technical change was breaking down traditional job structures, but slower in others, such as construction, and in small firms, which then accounted for a major share of employment.

An important counterpart to the idea of fair and customary differentials is that of fairness in the amount and quality of work supplied. Hobsbawm again provides limited evidence that the two went together especially during the first part of the nineteenth century. Where people worked in groups, or worked frequently in close contact, the social pressure to conform to established norms of effort was not dissimilar from those documented in more recent studies of work group constraints on output.

This evidence is fragmentary, but the idea that custom was just obeyed because it had become imprinted on people's minds seems unsatisfactory. It is important to look to the social mechanisms of enforcement, and the processes of adaptation of custom.

One final question is whether the action of custom was simply a method of labour market regulation, or whether it also implied the existence of stable sets of pay relativities. Rowe and Clay appear to indicate the effect of custom on stable differentials, although Hobsbawm's evidence is less clear in this respect. However, Phelps Brown and Hopkins' (1955) work on skill differentials in the building industry over seven centuries revealed very long period stability, including in the nineteenth century. Phelps Brown (1977) also found stable occupational differentials through the nineteenth century for a number of other occupations, with the notable exception of coal miners. Parodi (1962) demonstrated a similar stability and subsequent change of wage structure in France after 1862. It therefore seems likely that custom maintained a stable structure of wages despite major fluctuations in the demand for different categories of labour through the nineteenth, and into the early twentieth century.

Is such long period stability of differentials consistent with Hicks' model? Probably not because if the economy is adjusting to changes in demand, such very long period stability of differentials suggests that employers and consumers would have been adjusting their investment and consumption decisions to take account of the cost of stable wage relativities. This action would lead to qualitative and quantitative adjustments which would ease some of the product market pressures for change in relativities.

The next section looks more closely at the working of custom in modern industrial relations, and how it relates partly to pay relativities, and partly to rules for determining pay. In both of these there is an element of almost random change often generated by unintended consequences of management decisions which is filtered by shop stewards. This process can also generate new differentials and changes in them, although there are also pressures on companies to contain labour costs, and some from the labour market through possible problems of recruitment and turnover which may constrain them. But this requires a more active model of custom, which is discussed in the next section.

4.6.   CUSTOM AS A FORM OF REGULATION

The view of customary differentials, and restrictive working practices discussed so far is one which sees them as 'rigidities' which impede the free action of market adjustment, even though at times it may be conceded that they have some economic justification. Even the evidence quoted so far on wage differentials in the nineteenth century and earlier focuses mostly on the stability over long periods of time of such differentials. The process by which particular sets of relative prices and certain working practices become 'customary' is unexplained, being at best a preference for things as they are.

But custom changes. In this section it will be argued that custom as it affects relative wages and working practices is a great deal more than a process by which existing patterns become 'ossified' as they receive the sanction of custom.

On the contrary, customary rules in labour markets are flexible, although not always in the direction and at the speed employers might wish, and there are social processes at work selecting which practices and which pay rules will receive the sanction of custom. Moreover, although stability of certain pay norms can arise out of attachment to a particular differential, it often stems from attachment to particular rules and procedures for determining pay levels of individual groups. By focusing on these, it will be possible to see that the Hicks-Marshall view of such customary practices and relativities as reflecting what was economically optimal in the past is mistaken. Their view has been shaped by comparative statics (as for example in Figure 4.1). The problem is that customary regulation does not just come into action once economic conditions have shifted, as in their analysis, but they help shape the long-run equilibrium itself as it affects the relative wages on which firms base their long-run decisions.

Evidence in favour of treating custom as a form of social regulation of labour market conditions can be gleaned from a number of studies of workplace bargaining. This section will begin with a discussion of evidence for Britain and France relating to customary rules in the workplace and then move to other levels of bargaining. Besides stressing the flexibility and selectivity of customary regulation, it will also look at some of the reasons why it functions differently in other countries, and in particular, how differences in union workplace organisation in the two countries affects the working of precedent. It will then be argued that precedent derives its force from the web of rules, formal and informal, governing worker-employer relations. Three central studies in this respect are those of W. A. Brown (1973), Flanders (1964), and Morel (1977 and 1979). It then turns to the use of custom and precedent in higher levels of bargaining.

(a) Customary rules effective within the plant in Britain and France

Brown's (1973) study of piecework bargaining in ten engineering firms in England brings out several key facets of the working of 'custom and practice' rules. The rules he studies were mostly confined to particular workplaces, sometimes even particular work groups, and although mostly acknowledged by both workers and management were unwritten, and in many cases had superseded the written procedure and payment agreements governing relations in the workplace. They were also 'non-negotiated', in that they did not arise out of a formal process of collective bargaining, but they were known about by both management and shop stewards, and mostly accepted as legitimate. In many respects, this body of 'custom and practice' served as the day-to-day work rules governing such things as the application of payment systems, job variations, and the scope of managerial discretion as concerns jobs. Brown described them as non-negotiated transaction rules.

To a limited extent only do these rules conform to Hicks' view of custom as a form of sanctification of existing differentials and practices. Although some shop stewards do 'try things on' and try to pass off certain advantageous practices as custom, most of those interviewed by Brown did not appear to behave in this way, and saw themselves as the guardians of workplace custom rather than as its initiators. Most new custom and practice arose from management actions or decisions, or sometimes from their absence of action. Once a precedent had been set, it then became incorporated into the body of workplace custom. So far, this is quite consistent with Hicks' interpretation. But Brown also found evidence that shop stewards were *selective* in which practices or management decisions they would press as precedents. Equally, management would sometimes stress that certain actions were not to be interpreted as precedents, and sometimes they were successful and sometimes not.

One of the chief methods by which custom and practice rules grow is by one group of workers obtaining a favourable decision from management which then sets a precedent which other groups might follow. Examples Brown gave of this concerned the use of stop watches in work study. But among the shop stewards studied, two things were notable. One was their general respect for custom and practice rules and for precedent, even when it was not favourable to the workers concerned, as is shown by the following example:

It had been normal to pay men in the production shop the time-rate earnings of the toolroom when they were asked to do occasional one-off jobs (because of the excess work load in the toolroon). The rate for the toolroom had fallen behind the average earnings of the man's section and, in any case, his own normal piecework earnings were well above that rate per hour. Did he have to do the job, and did he still have to have that rate? The convenor pointed to the coding on the job card and said that there was little choice—the man was 'on thin ice' in contesting the matter and should not 'push it too far'. The shop steward then took the matter to the Works Manager who confirmed that the payment was 'accepted practice' but said that in future, such a job would go to one of the lower earners so that no-one would be penalised. This verbal (and hurried) statement by the Works Manager was taken by the steward as an authoritative ruling which can be seen to introduce a new rule of inflexibility in work allocation. (Brown 1973 p. 100)

This occurred in a factory in which the workers regularly used sanctions against management, but they were nevertheless prepared to accept the power of a custom and practice rule, even though disadvantageous.

Thus, even though there are occasions on which shop stewards 'try things on' to see if management will accept bogus precedents, Brown's study shows that on the whole, they act as the guardians of custom and practice. Second, although custom and practice rules grow out of management errors and past decisions, shop stewards are selective in the way they incorporate them into new custom and practice. A common way in which piecework systems gradually deviate from their original design is by management making concessions over timing of jobs because some parts of the job, or the materials used, change and some adjustment is needed to readjust earnings levels. Once such concessions have been made, they tend to become part of custom and practice. One example given by Brown involved the 'misrecording' of waiting time in one factory.

The misrecording of waiting time in the factory increased over the late 1960s, especially among the four gangs of fitters who made up one quarter of the direct labour force. These gangs tended to compete in earnings among themselves and they tended to keep gang earnings close together. The average earnings of all four gangs had been above those of other piecework groups in the factory for at least fifteen years. Over the 1960s they maintained their average earnings between 5 and 10 per cent above the average for the whole factory. In 1970, however, the misrecording of waiting time by the fitters got out of hand. In a sort of 'normative breakdown' the competing gangs drove each other to mis-record more and more. The spiralling of earnings that resulted drove fitters' average earnings for 1970 to 25 per cent above the factory average. This flagrant exploiting of the system forced a hitherto tolerant man-agement to intervene. It froze their earnings unilaterally and, when the fitters came out on strike for several weeks, the rest of the factory refused to join them. The political integration among the workforce had been inadequate to prevent this cumulative competition among the fitters and it was clear that the workforce resented the breach with management that it had brought about. (Brown 1973 p. 80).

In this case, the other stewards and work groups clearly felt that the fitters were getting too far out of line, so this particular path of potential growth of custom and practice was restricted. In another factory Brown studied a similar type of differential had emerged from slack piecework values, again creating a 25 per cent earnings differential between groups of semi-skilled workers:

Over the next five years the differential remained between 22 and 26 per cent despite the fact that all the jobs were reobserved or changed many times over the period. Although there was no difference in the nature of the semi-skilled jobs at which the men worked, and although they worked under the same roof, both management and senior stewards said that comparisons 'just aren't made'. If they were made, it was said, they were ruled out as inapplicable. Even though the aberrant differential had arisen through a management error the shop stewards' committee accepted it and actively prevented comparison. (Brown 1973 p. 80)

Here Brown argued that the stewards' committee was aware of the potentially high cost to management of removing the differential, and so were content not to 'push things too far' by pressing for it in order to maintain their bargaining relationship with management. In this instance also, the stewards did not seek to press the growth of custom to its fullest extent, but were highly selective as regards which practices should become part of workplace custom. The study also illustrates how, under piecework bargaining, pressures from custom and practice can alter pay structure, albeit in a rather haphazard fashion. Indeed, such pressures have been widely observed by managers as a cause of disruption of plant wage structures agreed at other levels of negotiation. For example, a common problem in industry has been for the earnings of assembly workers on piecework or payment by results to increase faster than those of craftsmen and supervisors paid on time rates, and to reduce, and occasionally even invert the normal differential. The organisational pressures maintaining normative order in pay among groups of assembly workers might give less protection to differentials of craftsmen and supervisors who are usually organised into separate bargaining groups.

In French firms, there is no real equivalent to the British shop stewards, yet Morel (1977, 1979 and 1981) provides many instances in which customary rules give rise to significant deviations from the letter of written collective agreements and from company rules. His examples cover working time, bonus payments, and deviations from the principle of linking wage rates to jobs rather than to individual workers. In Morel's study too, the deciding factor in the survival of such custom is the bargaining relation between the work force and their employer. Moreover, he describes the influence of custom in similar terms to those used by Brown:

The employees invariably see, in each individual and each collective personnel decision, precedents to which management has a duty to refer in future decisions. Hence, a precedent is formed each time that a rule is not applied, and each time a special solution is devised for a particular problem, and this becomes the supreme reference. Formal rules are therefore permanently being eroded by precedents which contradict them, and which stem from the discretionary powers of management, and so new tacit and unwritten rules emerge based on precedent. (Morel 1981 p. 123)

(b) Customary rules and work groups in Britain and France

Brown's study focused on relations within individual plants, and his analysis of the factors affecting the evolution of custom and practice rules is correspondingly focused on the plant level. The main constraint on shop steward activity at

this level, for Brown, is the need for the stewards to maintain the alliances between different work groups within the
factory, without which the system of custom and practice
rules could not be maintained. This meant that different
groups' views of fairness in relative pay and conditions were
important—thus the lack of support for the fitters in the
example. This was tempered by the stewards' desire also to
maintain a good bargaining relation with management which
can speed up the bargaining process, and reduce the need
for the use of costly sanctions by either side. Finally, Brown
suggests that the reduction of uncertainty is a factor determining the evolution of custom and practice rules, so that
stewards will use their power in order to make the functioning of the rules more predictable, and will use the rules
to make management's action more predictable. In this, his
analysis approaches those of Crozier (1963) of informal
work rules in French industry, and of Morel (1981) of the
'indulgent pattern' of work relations.

Nevertheless, in France, work group organisation is relatively weak, as Eyraud's (1983) comparison of plant level
bargaining in engineering Britain and France shows, and
consequently, work group custom is more fragile than in
British plants. According to his study, in France informal
rules rely heavily upon informal understandings between
workers and their supervisors, and are often not recognised
by higher levels of management, which is in strong contrast
to the position in British engineering. As a result, according
to Morel, unions adopt an alternating strategy of decentralisation and recentralisation in which individual groups'
custom is allowed to develop, and then the union seeks to
extend the advantage to all groups in the plant. The weakness of individual occupational groups means that the
unions, at plant level, have to keep a close eye on developing workgroup custom in order to maintain unity, and to
concentrate action on those precedents which can be most
fruitfully generalised. This strategy contains essentially the
same elements as that used by British shop stewards, but
places less reliance upon informal rules because of the greater difficulty of getting management to accept them.

(c) Some historical evidence on workplace bargaining

One potential objection to the use made of Brown's and Morel's studies is that they may relate to an exceptional period, the 1970s, when union power was at its height. Indirect evidence for earlier periods in this century in Britain can be found in Cole's (1923) study of workshop organisation before and during the First World War in the British engineering industry, and in Goodrich's (1920) study of shop floor control in the same period. Piecework was greatly expanded during the war, but even before the war, its use was common in the industry. The 1901 engineering agreement secured a more advantageous recognition of piecework for the employers, and also retained and reinforced the principle of 'mutuality'—that piecework prices should be fixed 'by mutual agreement between the Employer and the Workman or Workmen who perform the work'. Cole traced the development of this:

When a particular job recurred often in a particular shop, a standard price for it was naturally evolved. Moreover, it was inevitable that the prices accepted by one man should react upon the prices which other men in the same shop could obtain from the foreman. Consequently, it became, in most well-organised shops, a regular practice for informal consultations to take place before any questionable price was accepted . . . . In some works, these in formal consultations served as a basis for more formal organisation . . . In the Crewe railway workshops, for example, there arose 'Piece-work Committees', which kept 'books of prices' for the various trades, and, *by the gradual accumulation of precedents*, worked out something like a standard price list for the whole establishment, the list of course being modified, as the need arose, for each fresh job or new method of doing an old job. (Cole 1923 p. 15) (Author's emphasis)

Although Cole does not go into much detail in describing the logic of the bargaining process over piecework, many of the management and union problems thrown up by piecework during the 1914–18 war were very similar to those described by Brown in the same industry fifty years later. Moreover, the key actors in the negotiations in both periods were the shop stewards, whose numbers and powers had increased greatly by 1919. Some additional confirmation of

the similarity of the processes of regulation between the
two periods is given later in Cole's book when describing
the development of payment by results in engineering during the war:

In practice, as we have seen, the methods of fixing and adjusting piecework prices and other forms of remuneration under payment by results
varied widely from case to case. In some instances the employer fixed
prices at will ... and the workers lodged a general complaint if they
considered (their aggregate weekly earnings) to be inadequate. In other
cases, 'mutuality', modified by a measure of informal joint action among
the workers of the same trade or shop, was actually in operation; in yet
others, more or less complete and recognised forms of collective workshop bargaining had been developed. 'Scientific Management', or any
attempt to fix prices on the basis of an accurate study of times and
motions, was only in operation in a very few establishments, and was
generally disliked by employers as much as by workers (Cole 1923 p. 58)

Goodrich (1920) also provides some evidence of informal
regulation, but also shows that piecework was regulated
differently in different industries (see especially Chapter
12). In the cotton industry, for example, piece price lists
were fixed by formal collective agreements covering every
process in the trade, which contrasted strongly with the
working of the 'mutuality' principle that prevailed in the
engineering industry. Goodrich's main focus was on
encroachments on managerial prerogative that had become
embodied in formal agreements, but he nevertheless recognised that the 'mutuality' rule had the potential to lead to
various forms of informal bargaining:

(under mutuality) ... there are always the rudiments of a collective
bargain. One man's acceptance of a bad bargain is obviously the other
men's loss, and the men doubtless talk over their rates. From this informal
understanding there are various stages to full collective bargaining. Certain unions make regulations that their men shall not accept rates below
those set by a majority of members working in the shops. (Goodrich
1920 p. 168)

Out of this process, Goodrich argues, the establishment of
shop stewards and their committees, and of standardised
price lists within the establishment is a natural, although
often difficult, progression.

Thus although it has not been possible to demonstrate that the same kind of process of custom and practice rules described by Brown was at work in the engineering industry in the early part of this century, it is clear that there was not only, especially at the time of the First World War, a fairly widely developed system of informal workplace bargaining, but also an acute awareness of the inter-dependence of the individual bargains struck by individual workers or work groups.

(d) The influence of customary rules beyond the workplace

The discussion so far has related mostly to rules of precedent within the workplace, but there are a number of mechanisms by which it spills over from one group of workers to another. Two important influences on its spread are industrial and union organisation. Union organisation outside the plant can also play an important part in consolidating workplace custom, so that the two levels of bargaining are to some extent interdependent.

Industrial organisation influences the spread of customary rules as it determines which categories of worker will come into contact with each other. Notable cases in Britain in which such contact has been important include the links between coal miners and workers at coal-fired power stations. Why should the rules relating to two groups of workers with different employers but handling the same material, and coming into frequent contact differ? This has been one of the long-standing comparability links in pay negotiations. Similar links apply between workers in the coal and steel industries, and between those in gas and in water distribution who may supply services to the same households from the same underground channels. Such examples could be multiplied many times over. In such a way, customary rules generated among one group of workers can be spread to other groups, creating a complex web of comparability. It is such rules and wage differentials which generate fixity in industrial pay structures rather than attachment to the abstract categories of official statistics.

As concerns the influence of union organisation, craft

rules provide another example of rules which spread beyond the limits of individual workplaces, and in this case across occupational labour markets. Craft demarcation rules relate to the sets of tasks that constitute the 'job territory' of workers in different skilled occupations, particularly among maintenance trades. Although some of these tasks will have been built into formalised job descriptions, in most firms work study has been applied less by management to craft jobs (partly because of the greater control *vis-à-vis* management such workers operate over their work as compared with semi-skilled production workers), and where they have, the formal job descriptions mostly reflect the pre-existing job territories. Indeed, a recent study of the British car industry (Marsden *et al.* 1985) indicates that despite new technology, and a major reassertion of managerial control over the work process, and the ending of a number of informal custom and practice rules, changes affecting craft jobs have been relatively small, the one exception being perhaps Austin Rover in the maintenance of some of the its new robotic equipment.

These craft demarcations have been changed by negotiation at company and plant level rather than industry level, although the provisions for apprenticeships and access to craft work are negotiated at industry level. This is strong indication of the importance of job and work group level control over craft job territories. In contrast to the plant level rules discussed in the previous section, the nature and the content of these craft rules apply to workers in these particular occupational labour markets in whichever firm they are engaged. When negotiations take place at the industry level, as happened recently in the British shipbuilding industry in 1984–85, the agreement had to be ratified in individual yards before coming into force.

Of course, there is some variation between companies in the strictness with which craft demarcations are enforced, notably they are usually more tightly defined in larger establishments, and there are numerous accommodations made on a piecemeal basis in individual plants under local custom and practice, but they remain a form of customary rule effective across a whole occupational labour market. It would, therefore, be mistaken to believe that these customary rules were limited in their development as in their operation to individual establishments. The nature of demarcation rules shows that the emphasis placed by Hicks on the *duration* of the employment relation as a source of custom can at best be only a partial explanation of the phenomenon.

The key to maintaining such rules lies in the occupational pattern of British trade union organisation. Even within the general unions, craft workers tend to be organised in their own special sections. This helps to sustain the links between craft workers in different firms and thus to maintain the rules of their craft. It also provides a base from which they can influence the training of future craftsmen, and ensure that craft culture is passed on with the necessary technical skills.

The rules governing craft organisation are not the only ones to benefit from the protection of union organisation outside the plant. The same is true of those described by Brown, which are also protected by more formal bargaining arrangements at higher levels. These can provide a basic framework of protection for shop floor activities, for although a tight labour market might help to extend the range of issues governed by custom and practice rules, the more formal agreements can provide more permanent protection, particularly to the shop steward organisation, should the market slacken. Recent examples of such support can be found in recognition agreements in which employers recognise, but also delimit, the powers of union representatives in the workplace. The classic example of such an agreement was the 1922 procedure agreement in the British engineering industry which held sway for the following fifty years, under which the employers recognised that a certain range of issues could be dealt with by shop stewards (see Marsh 1965). Although the amended agreement was finally abandoned in 1971, subsequent agreements replacing it at the company level have maintained this role, as indeed have recognition agreements negotiated in new areas of union representation (some examples are reviewed in Marsden 1978). Thus although the powers of shop stewards may wax and wane partly in response to changes in labour market conditions, their strength, and that of custom and practice is to some extent stabilised by formal collective agreements reached at the company or industry level with the relevant unions.

In France, the strength of workers' attachment to rights acquired at the establishment level provides another example of the interaction between custom and negotiation, as is illustrated by the failure of the much publicised national level negotiations to introduce greater flexibility of working arrangements in 1984–85.

The extension of rules from one enterprise to another is also an active process which depends upon action by individual groups of workers. New comparability rules do not always follow the pressures of supply and demand for different categories. The forces maintaining wage and other worker norms respond to the same processes as those described at the workplace by Brown and by Morel, notably the need to maintain solidarity between different groups of workers, and to maintain a good bargaining relationship with their employers.

(e) Custom and collective rules in other countries
There are several puzzling aspects of the analysis of customary rules and the labour market presented so far. One is the degree of similarity of approach of Brown, Crozier (1963), and of Gouldner (1954) in their analyses of the influence of work group pressures on the development of workplace rules although their research was based respectively on Britain, France and the United States. Yet the studies of Brown and Morel indicate important differences in the way custom operates in plants in the two countries.

Despite the existence of highly developed systems of workplace representation in both France and Germany, it appears that custom and practice rules play a more limited role than in Britain. In West Germany, few examples of customary rules in the workplace have been uncovered by sociological research. The examples of seniority rules for upgrading in the steel industry documented by Bosch and

Lichte (1981) also appeared to have something of a twilight existence, and were only effective within the plant and within the work group concerned. In the West German case, works councils and employers have been unwilling to recognise sources of work rules that originate from outside the system of workplace codetermination, and this has been a major factor in preventing German shop stewards from evolving in the direction of either their British or Italian counterparts.

For United States manufacturing industry, Doeringer and Piore (1971) argued that workplace custom has played an extremely important part in the development of the rules regulating internal labour markets (see Chapter 5 below), and in particular in the development of seniority rules. To some extent these differ in form from those found in Britain because a greater proportion are embodied in the legally enforceable collective agreements. This was true of the 'bidding rule' setting out a number of seniority based rules for bidding for internal job vacancies analysed in Gouldner's (1955) study. Nevertheless, Doeringer and Piore (1971) also stress that much workplace custom in the United States is of an informal kind, and that it can be flexible, and they drew a parallel, in this respect, between their own observations of workplace custom in American manufacturing firms and those of Bloch (1939) on custom in medievel society.

The greater strength of customary regulation in Britain, as compared with France, Germany, and the United States, may be the result of the decentralisation of bargaining power to their shop stewards by a number of key unions at the same time as many firms decentralised certain decisions to the plant level. Many factors may explain this movement. First, much skilled work, especially in the maintenance area, is defined in terms not of a particular technical capacity, but of a set of tasks whose execution is the exclusive right of the members of a particular craft. This does not rule out high levels of technical competence, but it rests on a different logical principle. Consequently, the day-to-day adaptation of jobs to employers' requirements has to be negotiated at a fairly low level (as compared for example with

West Germany, see Marsden 1980). In this respect, there is
some convergence between the British and North American
experience. The second reason lies in the different legal
tradition governing collective agreements in Britain where
they have the status of 'gentleman's agreements' which are
not legally enforcible, and this creates a very favourable
climate for the development of customary regulation.

4.7. WHY PRECEDENT HAS SUCH FORCE

The strength of precedent as an argument in work group
level, and also higher level negotiations, would seem to
arise from two related sources, both of which are related
to the limitations of general principles underlying written
job descriptions and work rules. Both Brown and Morel
treat custom and practice as a set of 'transaction rules'.
Brown (1973 p. 84) defines these as 'a pattern of behaviour
governed by a reciprocity relationship between two parties
which both parties regard as legitimate', which points to a
potential convergence between his own work and that of
writers such as Alchian and Demsetz (1972) and Williamson
(1975) discussed in Chapter 2. But absent from these models
are the procedures by which workers regulate their own
jobs jointly with management (but not necessarily without
conflict). If management is given full authority to specify the
final details of the employment transaction at the moment
of execution, what guarantee do the workers have that
management will not abuse this in order to redefine the
scope of the job and thus alter the terms of the whole
exchange? Heavy use of rules based on precedent, as is the
case with custom and practice, can restrict management's
power to do so very effectively.

Custom and practice can constitute a fairly coherent system of regulation. Many jobs involving the application of
some manual dexterity are hard to codify. This is accentuated where work groups are unwilling to let management
observe the work too closely (v. the difficulties work study
engineers often have in gaining acceptance for the use of
stop watches). Hence, the way a job is done tends to become

the definition of the scope and content of that job. New recruits are initiated to current practices as they are taught the job by experienced workers. From them they learn the scope of their jobs, and the limits within which the foreman is customarily entitled to use his discretion in directing workers to particular tasks. Indeed, as Mottez argues, drawing on North American and French experience, even job measurement and work study are essentially processes of negotiation:

The work study engineer does not act simply as a technician, but as a negotiator. He is caught between management, which sees him as a technician, and the workers who seek, in their own interest, to deceive him. The work norm is the result of a compromise. Once it is fixed, the workers take care not to exceed it to such an extent that their good faith in the negotiation would be brought in question. (Mottez 1966 pp. 139–40)

In the broader context, as for example in regulation of an occupational labour market, customary rules can no more define job contents than can formal description by management, but the rules can focus on key indicators such as the type of tools or materials used. Thus in the case of craft work, job contents often are not defined in terms of tasks, but in terms of the materials handled and the tools used (e.g. having a joiner present if a piece of electrical maintenance involves dismantling even a small amount of woodwork, or the rule that only craftsmen should carry certain tools on the shop floor, and that technicians, even if themselves former craftsmen, should not be allowed to carry tools in the plant). Under such circumstances, it is clear that precedent can play an important part in the definition of job contents.

Precedent also plays an important part in the elaboration of written rules, and can eventually supersede them, as Morel's (1979) study shows. Written rules provide only a fraction of the work rules effective in a plant or company at any one time. For example, management's daily decisions (or failure to act) affect the application of even the most explicit written rules (be their origin in collective bargaining or management rules), and any repeated decision can become part of the way in which a general rule is applied. Precedent draws its strength from the fact that the enterprise is an environment governed by a large number of formal and informal rules. To claim that a precedent exists for the payment of a particular bonus is to claim that it forms part of the implicit rules of the workplace.

In order for custom to regulate work life, it must be flexible enough to adapt to changing circumstances. Brown's analysis shows that it is far from static. Usually, customary rules confine the scope of unilateral management decisions, and define the limits beyond which management must negotiate. Thus the customary rules serve not only to define job contents and the terms of the wage-work transaction, but also to regulate the normal limits of managerial authority, and to define conditions under which change can be introduced.

Moreover, bargaining is at the heart of customary regulation and questions of control and of economic reward are closely intermeshed. For example, if technical change, or a change in the nature of the raw materials used brings about a small change in the content of a particular job, the foreman may insist that a new task is part of a worker's normal job, and thus does not require additional payment. On the other side, the worker, or his steward, may insist that it is indeed a new or exceptional element in the job and thus requires additional payment. This illustrates the grey line separating managerial authority from negotiation, as it also illustrates its economic focus.

Another aspect of the internal logic of customary regulation appears if we consider the social situations in which it does not apply. For example, offering a present to a friend does not constitute a precedent requiring a second gift from the donor. On the contrary, it normally creates the expectation of a reciprocal action by the receiver. The practice of doing someone a favour provides another example. It is common in situations in which precedent is normally important, for example in the authority relation. Doing something as a favour creates flexibility because it enables those involved temporarily to step out of such relations and to do something which does not create a precedent for the future. The social significance of this practice arises from the widespread importance of precedent and other types of rule which demand certain actions on a regular basis.

To conclude, custom is a mode of social regulation which has its own logic. Although it can be used in opposition to managerial authority, it is not necessarily a source of inertia. Seen in this light, it fits very uncomfortably into the constraints of the economic short term.

4.8. CONCLUSIONS

This chapter has examined some attempts within economics and industrial relations to articulate the time of economic and social processes active in the labour market. All social processes exist in time and social and economic theories also embody their own conceptual times. Attempts to study the interaction of these, therefore, require some articulation of the times of the different processes they seek to represent. This chapter has dealt particularly with examples of the interaction of market and social forces on labour markets, looking in particular at the question of custom and wage differentials and the forces of competition.

Marshall's distinction between the economic short- and long-run has played a central role, providing what is, at first sight, an extremely practical way of reconciling the joint action of social custom and of market forces upon relative wages. This was explicitly taken as the basis of Hicks' reply to Wootton's argument that economists paid too little attention to the influences of social convention and of hierarchy upon wage structure, but is also implicit in the analyses of many of those who postulate that such customary forces operate within a 'range of indeterminacy' left by the action of market forces.

On the whole, custom is seen as a force of inertia in labour markets. For Hicks, it represents mostly an ossification of differentials which had originally been dictated by reactions to supply and demand. For Lester, and Reynolds, and other writers using the 'range' strategy, the origin of customary differentials is less clear although the impression is nevertheless that market forces have been predominant in creating wage differentials, and that custom again is an impeditive influence in labour markets.

The chapter then turned to some of the manifestations of custom in labour markets, and it was argued that the treatment of custom as acting within the economic short run, or within the range of indeterminacy gave rise to a somewhat truncated concept of its action, and that it was wrong to conflate sets of relative wages that had somehow obtained the sanctification of custom with custom as a regulatory process. The chapter examined custom in three of its main manifestations in labour markets: as customary wage levels which according to Rowe were the forebears of the union standard rate, at least in Britain; as the process of custom and practice bargaining in the determination of piecework earnings within the establishment; and as rules defining job contents across occupational labour markets.

Examination of these manifestations of custom showed that it involved a great deal more than mere sanctification of established differentials, and that it responded to a wide variety of pressures. Brown's study showed it responding to pressures of group action within the workplace, and comparison with other countries showed the influence on custom of the broader systems of rule-making within industrial relations, and also possibly of the nature of the legal system through the acceptability or otherwise of the 'gentleman's agreement'. Thus the dynamics of custom are not really satisfactorily dealt with by assuming that they can be contained within the economic short-run.

The second part of the chapter looked more closely at the working of custom and of customary differentials. Two main conclusions emerged. First, it was argued that custom could influence particular wage relativities not just in the short term, but also in the long and very long term. Phelps Brown and Hopkins' example of the stability of skill differentials in the building industry over seven centuries may have been exceptional, but there were plenty of other examples of stable occupational differentials over prolonged periods despite labour market fluctuations. In the face of such long term stability, it seems likely that economic decisions would be based upon the assumption that such relativities were fixed, and that the burden of adjustment would fall on quality and quantity rather than on price, obviating the tendency that would otherwise exist to bring the relativity more into line with the long-run competitive equilibrium level.

The second conclusion was that custom is an active and not a passive process in labour markets. Although there may be occasions when once economically optimal relativities become customary, there are also many instances in which the forces of custom and practice can generate new relativities, or transform existing ones. To see this, one has to distinguish between two focuses of custom: that on a particular relativity; and that on a set of work rules governing pay. Brown's study illustrated both. The first would usually defend existing differentials, while the second can evolve picking up odd management concessions affecting pay, making certain practices customary (e.g. the misrecording of time slips) and so on. This second focus of custom and practice can indeed alter relativities, and is one of the forces within companies by which piecework earnings can sometimes increase faster than those of supervisors and craftsmen for example paid on time rates. Brown's study also illustrates some of the group dynamics which regulate custom and practice drift, such as the need for shop stewards to maintain the stability of an alliance between different workgroups, and to maintain a stable bargaining relationship.

Do these conclusions contradict the earlier argument about long-term stability? Clearly they call for some qualification, but one should remember the constraint on the evolution of customary rules arising from the need for worker solidarity in the face of their employers. Competition is not the only force preventing individual groups from pushing their pay levels beyond certain limits. The flexibility of customary rules observed by both Brown and Morel, and also by Doeringer and Piore, is therefore compatible with the relative stability of wage structures.

Thus, despite its appeal, Hicks' model based on the Marshallian long and short periods, cannot be regarded as a general explanation of the reciprocal influence of custom and market forces on wage differentials. The same applies to the models based on a 'range of indeterminacy' left by market forces, although both may be valid in particular cases.

The articulation of the economic short and long terms depends on the tendency of wage differences which diverge from their long-run equilibrium level to return slowly to this position. The studies of Morel, and especially of Brown, indicate that this process will be much more unpredictable than Hicks believed, and there is the additional possibility that qualitative and quantitative adjustments will further weaken the economic pressures of product markets upon wage structures. These are given further support by the arguments developed in Chapter 8 below.

5 Labour Market Structure and Institutional Pressures

5.1. INTRODUCTION

One of the central questions behind the debates about labour market adjustment revolves around the nature of processes dividing the labour market into a large number of sub-markets, and the way in which these may affect the rules regulating the supply of and demand for labour. Mainstream neo-classical theory usually starts from the presumption of an otherwise homogeneous market divided up only by the technical limitations on the substitutability of different skills and abilities, and possibly by the constraints imposed by the need to certify the quality of skills. While competition between workers on different sub-markets may be very limited, each sub-market itself remains a zone of competition, in which normal market relationships as conceived by economic theory apply. On the other hand, there is also a long tradition within economics of stressing the institutional and social origins of these divisions, and stressing also the effect these processes may have upon the rules governing the supply and demand relationships within these sub-markets. One very important work in this area which has reopened much of the old debate has been that of Doeringer and Piore (1971) who sought to apply the insights of human capital analysis to the study of labour market structure, and in particular to the working of internal labour markets within firms, and thus to synthesise these two strands of labour market analysis[1].

Their work, and the subsequent debate, raises a number of important theoretical questions concerning the relation between market and institutional processes, and the extent to which one can really talk of a labour market which is divided into a large number of sub-markets which continue to function as markets, or whether they are regulated by different processes.

141

One way of summarising the point at issue would be to suggest that the labour market might be seen as a social space on which actors' behaviour is governed by certain rules. In neo-classical theory these are the rules of optimisation by workers and by firms and of competition. Many neo-classical writers accept that this space is divided into sub-areas, but would maintain that within each of these the same principal rules of exchange apply, while some overall unity to the labour market is provided by the opportunities for substitution by other factors, and pressures of competition on other markets. Thus the labour market is structured into sub-markets by the restrictions on the substitutability between different kinds of labour.

Historically, one important strand of thought articulating the influence of social groups and labour markets was that of non-competing groups as represented by Mill, and Cairnes. For the latter, the labour market was divided into segments within which the forces of competition applied, but between which there was no competition. For Cairnes, these segments corresponded to different social groups, as family wealth determined largely the individual's opportunities for investment in the training necessary to enter any particular non-competing group (these groups being professionals, artisans, labourers, etc.). He envisaged that increased access to education would reduce the inequalities between these groups, and diminish their influence, but he perhaps underestimated the ability of more educated groups to derive more benefit from state support of education than less educated ones.

Writers of a more institutionalist bent have argued that institutional rules, such as demarcation and apprenticeship rules arising out of collective bargaining, and company recruitment practices can also play a major role in defining the limits of sub-markets. In some respects their line of argument can be summarised as saying that the labour market is fragmented by such institutional rules and group pressures. It is 'balkanised', to use Kerr's (1954) expression. The question remains as to whether these sub-markets can be regarded as obeying the same underlying set of rules of exchange, thus justifying the analogy of a 'balkanised labour market', or whether the processes which break up the market also transform the principal rules of exchange within each sub-market. At first sight, one of the attractions of the 'balkanisation' approach is that it offers a neat way of articulating the influence of market economic forces and of institutional, and other social processes. But it remains to be seen how far it resolves the main problems.

This chapter examines these attempts to account for the social and institutional structuring of labour markets, and their implicit assumptions about the nature of labour markets and of these processes. 'Internal labour markets' play a large part in the contemporary theories of labour market structure, and it is important to ask whether they should be thought of as markets, and how misleading is the implicit analogy with 'external' labour markets. This chapter argues that the analogy is misleading because, first, there are important differences between the rules and processes regulating internal and external labour markets, and secondly, the rules and processes which divide off internal from external labour markets can have a profound effect upon the workings of such markets.

The chapter begins with Kerr's argument about the nature of labour market balkanisation, pointing out that although he set the tone for much of the ensuing debate, he did not regard their development as necessarily desirable, and in many respects saw balkanised labour markets as akin to monopolies in need of regulation in the interest of those workers excluded from such markets, as well as the wider public interest. In contrast, the arguments of Doeringer and Piore, of Williamson, and other writers hinge on the mutual benefit to workers, employers and even to consumers of such arrangements under certain conditions.

Doeringer and Piore (1971) tie the uniqueness of many jobs to a corresponding uniqueness of a plant's technology as it is progressively adapted to a firm's requirements, and their theory bases internal labour markets on the minimisation of the cost of investment in the skills for such jobs. Williamson (1975), on the other hand, also takes such uniqueness as his starting point, but then argues that the employees' monopoly of job knowledge in these conditions leads employers to give workers an interest in the long-term profitability of the company, hence the development of internal labour markets and stable employment.

It will be argued that these theories have a number of weaknesses. First, specificity in production technology and non-transferability of skills is not a wholly independent variable, and can itself arise out of employers' policies to promote a stable workforce, and secondly, it is not independent of changes in the firm's structure. Thirdly, the rules governing internal labour markets do not necessarily correspond to cost minimisation considerations, but may be the result of industrial conflict. Fourthly, international comparisons suggest that the same skills can be organised in internal labour markets or in occupational labour markets, which both diminishes the strength of the technology argument, and introduces another factor: the influence of national labour market institutions, such as apprenticeship provisions which establish a basis for occupational labour markets where otherwise employers might reply upon internal labour markets. This last point is also an important qualification on the argument that plant size and product market structure are determining factors.

The view argued for in this chapter will reflect the line begun in Chapter 1 that it is necessary to see internal and, for skilled workers at least, external labour markets as institutional phenomena bound by sets of rules which may be the outcome of negotiation or of unilateral decision, legislation, or of other less explicit processes, such as in particular social custom. This, however, does not preclude them from having an allocative role, nor does it exclude the possibility of certain labour markets approximating to the competitive model.

5.2. KERR AND THE BALKANISATION OF LABOUR MARKETS

Kerr distinguished between three broad types of labour market: unorganised or competitive labour markets, craft labour markets, and enterprise labour markets. For the two latter types of market, entry is determined by administrative rule, be it union apprenticeship or the employer's hiring decision. He contrasted this with the earlier theories of non-competing groups of Mill and Cairnes. In these cases access to the labour markets of each non-competing group was largely determined before entry into the labour market. Kerr's typology relates more closely to divisions limiting the mobility opportunities of those already on the labour market.

Some of the central insights of Kerr's view have been lost in the subsequent debates about internal labour markets and segmentation, which have focused almost entirely on the factors dividing unorganised from internal labour markets. Kerr's emphasis lay upon the types of administrative rule and of quasi-property rights vested in labour markets. The craft market, which consisted of all the jobs in a particular locality which could be done by workers belonging to the relevant craft, was one in which there were of communal property rights over such jobs vested in the union. Access to the market was given by union membership, although employers remained free to select whomsoever they wished from this market. In contrast, in the enterprise market, Kerr saw a form of individual property right over each job vested in individual workers, although access to this particular market was given by the employer. Kerr does not seek to explain the development of these different kinds of administrative market, although he does retain the term 'market' for both types. However, he stresses the importance of the administrative rules determining the boundaries of these markets, as distinct from the technical properties of the skills exercised. Kerr treated both craft and enterprise markets as 'internal labour markets'. In this view, such internalisation of labour markets was not necessarily the result of the greater efficiency of organizing transactions within an administrative unit instead of on the open market, and he seems to have viewed them as more of a restriction of competition, and of opportunities for suitably qualified workers denied access to these markets.

The sources of this enclosure movement are not far to seek. Employing units are larger, and bureaucratic rules take the place of individual judgements . . . Workers have organised into unions which seek to establish sovereignty over a 'job territory'. Within this job territory work the citizens who belong to this private government; outside are the non-citizens without rights. The demands of all citizens must be met before the petitions of aliens are considered. The institutionalisation of labour markets is one aspect of the general trend from the atomistic to the pluralistic, and from the largely open to the partially closed society. (Kerr 1954 p. 96)

Although Kerr is not recommending the abolition of such institutionalised labour markets so much as their greater regulation in the public interest, his emphasis is clearly upon their sub-optimality as compared with the theoretical optimum of competitive labour markets. In this respect his argument differs from that of Doeringer and Piore, and of Williamson, and also from that of the segmentation writers who have stressed the question of control of the labour process in large firms. In Ryan's words (1981), such rules are not 'surrogates' for markets, nor can they really be said to be making markets work more efficiently, in the neo-classical sense, as some would argue in the case of Doeringer and Piore's model.

5.3.   THE IDEA OF A 'MARKET' IN DOERINGER AND PIORE'S THEORY

Doeringer and Piore took over their definition of an internal labour market as an administrative unit within which the pricing and allocation of labour are governed by a set of administrative rules and procedures from Dunlop (1966) and from Kerr (1954), but sought to synthesise the writings of the institutionalist labour economists with the newer developments in human capital theory. This section argues that technological and skill specificity play a central part in Doeringer and Piore's theory, and that these enable them to argue that internal labour markets are a logical devel-opment in a competitive labour market given certain con-ditions, and hence to justify use of the term 'market', as internal labour markets are a form of surrogate market.

They took as their starting point Becker's (1975) analysis of the distribution of costs and benefits of the investment in 'specific' or non-transferable training within the enterprise, that is, training which does not enhance the individual worker's productivity in other firms, because it does not give rise to skills which can be used in them, and thus for which there is no market outside the worker's present firm. This is contrasted with 'general' skills which are useful to a large number of other employers, and for which there is a well-developed external market. Most skills fall somewhere in-between these two extremes. The point of Becker's distinction is that individual employers have little incentive to invest in general skills unless other employers do likewise because of the potential loss of their investment through labour turnover, and so they are likely to want trainees to bear the brunt of the cost. This might be done by paying a special rate to trainees which is below the value of their output. This problem is much reduced for specific skills. Although employers are still likely to need some policies to reduce labour turnover to prevent their investment in specific skills from melting away, at least the financial incentive to individual workers to leave is smaller, as is the incentive to other employers to poach them away. Doeringer and Piore argue that it is the policies which employers and workers develop in order to manage investment in such specific training which gives rise to internal labour markets.

The main steps in their argument may be schematised by the following causal chain linking technological specificity to internal labour market structure:

Technological specificity
|
Job specificity
|
Advantages of on-the-job learning
|
Skill specificity
|
Type of mobility
|
Internal labour market

Of the various forms of specificity, only skill specificity is defined formally—using Becker's definition. Doeringer and Piore locate the origin of internal labour markets in the nature of the production process. Capital equipment is often custom built, and even where it is bought 'off the peg', it is common for it to be adapted to local conditions, so that the range of tasks which workers perform, even working on similar equipment, can vary greatly from one plant to another. In some of his subsequent writings, Piore (especially 1972 and 1973) develops the role of technology as a source of labour market structure further. This variability between establishments in the range of tasks to be carried out gives rise to 'job specificity'. The jobs into which these tasks are grouped will also vary markedly from one establishment to another. This, they argue, has a crucial impact upon the relative costs of different types of training.

Formally organised off-the-job training, be it for general skills, or for specialist skills within the enterprise, involves high set-up costs, and thus requires a sufficient volume of training. In contrast, the set-up costs of informal on-the-job training in which much of the learning is done 'sitting by Nelly' with some instruction from supervisors are very low. But they are likely to increase steeply the greater the number of trainees to each experienced worker, the main costs arising from the time such workers are diverted from their normal jobs. In most cases of job specificity, the numbers to be trained are likely to be fairly small so that informal on-the-job training would be quite economical.

On-the-job training can also reduce foregone production because the trainee is doing the job, albeit less efficiently than experienced workers. Further economies may be realised if the training period can be spread over a whole succession of jobs, with the jobs arranged so that as people progress through them, each job provides some of the experience required for the next. Doeringer and Piore argue that many of the 'job ladders' to be found in American manufacturing industry embody this kind of process, and they have referred to such temporal linkages between jobs as 'mobility chains'.

For Doeringer and Piore, clusters of these internal mobility chains constitute enterprise internal labour markets, and give them their structure. In the formation of such internal labour markets, besides the emphasis upon optimisation decisions by management and by workers (who have an interest in the return on their specific training), Doeringer and Piore attribute an important role to workplace custom, in the form of informal and formal rules regulating the patterns of progression between jobs. Despite the provision of a good number of examples, such rules tend to be treated in a similar fashion to that described in Chapter 4, namely as passive outgrowth of past economic relationships, and as a conservative force inhibiting change.

Custom at the workplace is an unwritten set of rules based largely upon past practice and precedent . . . work rules appear to be an outgrowth of employment stability within internal labour markets. Such stability . . . is of value to both the employer and the workforce, and one of the factors producing internal labour markets is the desire to effectuate stability. (Doeringer and Piore 1971 p. 23)

They go on to argue that such stability facilitates the formation of cohesive groups which cement these norms.

Dependence on 'past practice' means that any procedure, if repeated, becomes customary . . . This characterisation of custom makes it an essentially passive phenomenon which tends to grow up around whatever exists. It implies that a workplace begins essentially as a *tabula rasa* without work rules. Management, at least in non-union enterprises, is free to establish whatever set of work rules are most conducive to economic efficiency. Once these rules are established, custom begins to form around them through a process of application. (Doeringer and Piore 1971 p. 25)

They point out that customs may be brought by workers into new establishments from their previous work environments, but in such cases also, the emphasis is upon custom reflecting practices that were optimal some time in the past.

Because one effect of custom is to inhibit change, it causes the allocative structure to reflect efficiency considerations, employee interests, and the balance of negotiating power prevailing at some time in the past . . . (Doeringer and Piore 1971 p. 61)

Thus through their argument one can see that technological specificity is the prime driving force behind their theory of the development and structure of internal labour markets.

As mentioned, Doeringer and Piore argue that the mechanisms working within internal labour markets are governed by administrative rules rather than open market competition. The adjustment mechanisms within internal labour markets differ from those of competitive labour market theory because firms have to use a number of other management devices, notably job evaluation, engineered production standards, job design, career progressions, administered wage and salary structures and so on. In addition, workplace custom often reinforces these, a notable example that they quote being seniority rules.

The development of enterprise internal labour markets (as indeed of employment protection legislation of the kind discussed in Chapter 2) can greatly reduce the competitive labour market pressures on employers and on workers, owing to the higher cost of dismissal for employers, and of quitting for workers. Even if one rejects the specific skill theory, the use of the personnel practices associated with enterprise internal labour markets is a barrier to labour mobility as accumulated rights in the employee's present firm will be lost, and the main alternative sources of employment may themselves be in other internal labour markets. Hence, the effectiveness of the threat of quitting is greatly reduced. In similar fashion, the presence of a large queue of labour at the firm's employment office exerts a smaller pressure because of the large organisational changes that would be necessary if full use of it were to be made.

In sum, the forces which in neo-classical theory yield a determinate wage establish, in the internal market, only a series of constraints. The equality between the marginal product of labour and the wage of a job postulated by competitive economic theory is reduced to an equality between the discounted present value of expected cost and productivity streams calculated over the distribution of *expected* employment tenure for various *groups* within the enterprise. (Doeringer and Piore 1971 p. 77)

So how exact is the analogy between internal labour

markets in their theory and standard neo-classical labour markets?

The case for treating internal labour markets as markets would seem to rest on two main propositions. The first is that their development and structure are seen as 'a logical development in a competitive market' (Doeringer and Piore p. 39) where certain conditions prevail, notably skill specificity and custom. The second is that despite the administrative nature of many of the rules governing internal labour markets, the external market can still exercise a good deal of pressure at ports of entry at which people may assess their earnings prospects over the whole of their period in the firm, and losses from wastage. In addition to competition for entry, there may still be considerable competition between workers for jobs within an internal labour market. Moreover, following the neo-classical tradition, Doeringer and Piore treat custom as ossifying existing structures rather than generating any of its own.

Moreover, they retain a good deal of the neo-classical apparatus of optimisation. Firms build internal labour markets in order to minimise costs of investment in enterprise–specific human capital, and workers seek to protect their return. Internal labour markets are the institutional framework for investment in enterprise–specific human capital. They see internal labour markets as determining wage and employment structures different from, but within the constraints set by, competitive market forces. Their account fits in easily with the transactions approach, which treats internal labour markets as providing an environment within which a number of transactions can be made but which would otherwise have been made (at greater cost) on the external labour market. Thus in Doeringer and Piore's argument there is some justification for treating internal labour markets as surrogate markets. The rest of this chapter examines this view in more detail.

Finally, one should not underestimate the key importance of treating specificity in production technology as a cause of skill specificity. This is also important for Becker's and Williamson's theories, although the former makes no explicit reference to technology, and the latter argues that his transactional theory of internal labour markets does not depend on technology. Becker's theory that the distribution of costs and returns of investment in training depends upon the degree of specificity or generality of skills is based on the assumption that the degree of specificity is independent of company policies on the distribution of training costs. Technological determination of training needs, if true, provides a strong reason for such independence. Williamson also, as will be seen shortly, takes over Doeringer and Piore's link between skill and technological specificity, although denying there is any causal link between these and internal labour market structure. The central importance of technology in their theories is easily shown if one considers how plausibly the causation could run from company personnel and training policies to skill specificity.

An employer preferring a stable workforce, for whatever reason, might adopt a pay structure rewarding long service. Skills within the organisation could evolve with the employer's changing skill requirements, so the end result could be the development of specific or non-transferable bundles of skills caused not by technology, but by long employment fostered by the linking of pay to length of service. Thus establishing a causal link between technical specificity and skills is fundamental to their theory. But in the following section it will be seen that it is really quite difficult. The weaker the influence of specific technology in relation to company personnel and training policies, the weaker is the case for treating internal labour markets as surrogate markets.

5.4. ARE INTERNAL LABOUR MARKETS MARKETS?

This section examines two problems arising out of Doeringer and Piore's analysis of specific skills, and the nature of the link between specificity and the bounds of the enterprise. It will be argued first that they slide too quickly over the relationship between specific technology and the bounds of the enterprise, and secondly, that the whole question of specific versus general skills runs into difficulties when one considers changes in the structure of firms. On the whole, neither Doeringer and Piore, nor their predecessors such as Kerr, really question the nature of boundaries around enterprise internal labour markets, and they tend to treat them as unproblematic. Thirdly, it will be argued that inter-group conflict may cause some seniority rules to be aimed at restricting management prerogative rather than protecting skills, and fourthly, that too little emphasis is placed upon the institutional determinants of the scope of internal and occupational labour markets.

(a) Specific skills and individual jobs

Doeringer and Piore slide too quickly from the level of skills at particular tasks associated with particular machines to that of the whole establishment. They do not really justify their presumption that the enterprise should form the boundary of an internal labour market. As they set out their argument, technological specificity tends to be related to individual pieces of equipment:

For example, the production of a pair of shoes requires some skilled operators and some skilled repairmen. Similar operating and repair skills are utilised in many labour markets, and it is generally possible to engage new operators as machine operators. But operators familiar with the indiosyncracies of the particular pieces of equipment can produce much faster and are also able to anticipate machine breakdown, thereby minimising machine downtime. Downtime is further reduced when the repair crew is also familiar with the equipment so that trouble can be quickly diagnosed and repaired. These skills are highly specific in character. (Doeringer and Piore 1971 p. 16)

This irreducible minimum of specificity they argue is further enhanced by the way in which line management and work groups continually find more efficient ways of operating the equipment and adapting it to their own specific needs.

Such a view relates specificity to individual pieces of equipment, and ties specific skills to the workers engaged on that equipment. Thus if specificity is to be a sufficient reason for not taking someone from the external labour market, it could equally be an obstacle to transfers from another department within the firm. Yet, internal transfers between departments have been extremely important in recent manpower adjustments in a number of different industries, such as the car industry (Marsden *et al.* 1985) and in the coal, steel and chemical industries in the UK, all of which have extensive internal labour markets.

By taking the scope of internal labour markets for granted, they overstress the importance of specific technology, which in the end is not a very convincing argument, and understress the role of institutional decision making, and the factors which determine this.

An alternative model, which maintains the idea of optimisation and which avoids this problem, has been put forward by Williamson (1975). He takes Doeringer and Piore's starting point of specific technology and jobs. But then he argues that the problem facing employers is not one of minimising costs of investment in training, but one of creating an environment in which workers will feel it in their interest not to exploit their short-term bargaining advantage over the employer because they hold a monopoly of knowledge about their particular jobs. In the short run, the employer is in a very weak position. The workers can withdraw their labour and can refuse to instruct new recruits, thus preventing him from substituting outside labour. Williamson argues that the offer of more stable employment and of internal labour market conditions creates a situation in which it is in the workers' own self-interest to promote the longer-term prosperity of the firm, and hence to adopt a cooperative attitude. Thus, Williamson reduces the dependence of Doeringer and Piore's argument on the link between technology and training, while maintaining the idea that internal labour markets are consistent with long-run cost minimisation. Nevertheless, Williamson still takes job specificity, or 'job idiosyncrasy' as he calls it, as his starting point for explaining internal labour markets, and he seems to have accepted the link between job idiosyncrasy and specific technology, otherwise an employer might consider designing jobs to make them more homogeneous as an alternative to developing an internal labour market.

As will be argued later, in common with Doeringer and Piore he overemphasises the particular characteristics of individual jobs, and ignores the impact of wider labour market institutions.

(b) Specific skills and enterprise structure

A general skill may become specific when an employer attains a monopsonistic position in the market for that skill. By the same token, a general skill could be treated as one for which there is competition among employers for that particular skill. For example, the British coal mining industry before the last war included many employers each seeking the same kinds of labour on their local labour markets. But with nationalisation in 1945 there emerged a single employer, and one very large internal labour market. Much the same would apply to the British steel industry, and although individual firms had their own internal labour markets before nationalisation, they were usually in a monopsonistic position on their own local labour markets. Similarly, in the English retail banks, it would seem that the main factor preventing the emergence of a competitive labour market for people with banking skills would be the tacit accord between the four main clearing banks not to seek to poach each other's staff.

These company reorganisations had the effect of creating new employing units within which a number of new manpower decisions could be taken, such as redeploying miners from exhausted pits to new ones to a greater extent than before without them having to change employer, and the development of industry-wide policies on training and manpower development. Administrative decisions displaced market transactions, but the reasons for this lay in the greater efficiency of productive units (for example for capital projects) and were not based on manpower and labour market considerations.

(c) Do the rules governing internal labour markets represent optimality?

Doeringer and Piore argue that the customary rules in internal labour markets grow out of practices established by a process of optimisation by employers and workers under conditions of job specificity. But some aspects of the inter-group bargaining raised by Williamson point to a different interpretation, in some cases at least. This might indeed be expected after the discussion of custom and practice in the preceding chapter.

Doeringer and Piore's model of custom reinforcing investment in training suggests a strong mutual benefit to employers and workers, but this is not always perceived in this way. Seniority rules in job allocation may reinforce investment in training, but they may also serve to restrict managerial prerogative by reducing the degree to which managers can use redeployment to a more pleasant or a higher grade job in order to reward cooperative workers. Both Gouldner (1954) and Crozier (1963) have shown that such seniority rules can be used in this way in conflictual relations between employers and employees. Under such circumstances, work groups may press for the introduction of seniority rules on job allocation irrespective of whether there is any increased skill content. Consequently, some internal labour markets could develop out of a gradual accumulation of seniority rules of this kind, and have little or no grounding in specific training. This would help to explain why in some manufacturing industries length of service should be quite high despite there being little in the way of length of service increments, and a comparatively short time needed for new recruits to reach experienced worker standard.

(d) The impact of higher level labour market institutions on internal labour markets

Fourthly, these internal labour market theories underplay the importance of other institutional factors behind the structure of labour markets, and to some extent fall victim to their own paradigm of an otherwise structureless labour market. The most important single factor left out of the picture is the systems of qualification or skill (as opposed simply to training) and the extent to which these are often external as well as internal to the enterprise. These were indeed at the heart of Kerr's analysis of craft labour markets, and although mentioned early in Doeringer and Piore's book were subsequently left out of the analysis, as they have been from most of the debate about segmentation (see Cain 1976).

Some of the most important illustrations of such skill systems are the apprenticeship-based skills in Britain and West Germany, and in the United States. While much of such training is undertaken on the employer's premises, the scope of the training and the rights which accompany its completion are backed up by rules established outside the enterprise. The methods of attainment of apprenticeship are very much a question of industry-wide collective bargaining in the UK. While the unions show a great deal of cooperation with the relevant employers' bodies on the actual content of the training, they are much more wary of any changes which might affect their degree of control over craft labour markets, such as relaxing the rules over the length of time an apprenticeship must last, and over the associated job demarcations, for example on who is entitled to use the tools of the trade. While this has clear safety reasons as concerns semi-skilled workers doing their own electrical maintenance for example, such a rationalisation does not hold when one considers the exclusion of former skilled men who have become technicians from carrying the tools of their old trade.

In West Germany, the apprenticeship system also extends well beyond the bounds of the enterprise, although much of the important action for its defence by skilled workers of course takes place within the enterprise. There the chambers of industry and commerce play a key role in supervising the general content and application of apprenticeship schemes, and the unions and employers collectively take a strong interest in this process. Kerr's example of a craft labour market also illustrates the importance of regulation from outside the enterprise in American labour markets.

In addition, the existence of craft labour markets can constrain the ability of employers to develop their own internal labour markets. For example, in the car industry at the moment, faced with a need for new skills for new technology, for increased flexibility of deployment of labour, and to create a work environment more conducive to good quality control, several European and North American producers have pursued a policy of encouraging internal labour markets and of offering improved employment security in return for greater job flexibility. In 1984, Ford US and General Motors both signed agreements offering greater employment security in exchange for concessions on job flexibility and seniority rules. In Britain, in contrast, such developments have been limited by the existing organisation of skilled jobs on craft labour markets. Workers on such markets wish to retain the transferability of their skills, and to maintain the restricted route of access through apprenticeships to craft jobs. This effectively blocks any possibility of significant upgrading for semi-skilled workers so that the employers can offer little by way of vertical mobility within the internal labour market (Marsden *et al.* 1985).

It might be argued that the apprenticeship systems of Britain and West Germany are to some exceptional, and so do not really affect the argument that the enterprise is at the centre of labour market structure. However, even in countries with more developed enterprise internal labour markets than those in Britain and Germany, such as France or Italy, questions as central to the functioning of internal labour markets as job grading and classification systems are only partly determined by individual enterprises.

In France, the state played a major role in the establishment of the Parodi system of wage grades after the last war. The Parodi system established a hierarchical set of job classifications related to the degree of skill required at each job level, starting from an index of 100 for unskilled workers. There are provisions linking it to transferable apprenticeship-type skills, such as the minimum grade at which skilled workers recruited to do a skilled job may be classified, but it is essentially a classification of jobs rather than individuals. One of the long-standing union complaints has been that highly trained workers recruited into a lowly classified job are not rewarded for their skills. This system is clearly therefore one related to a system of internal labour markets, yet it is one which transcends the level of the individual enterprise. The revision of the Parodi system in the French engineering industry in the 1970s was negotiated by the unions and the engineering employers' association at the industry level (Eyraud 1978). Hence, these constitute industry-wide forms of labour market regulation even when they do not create industry-wide opportunities for labour mobility.

The Italian case is more complex on account of the changes which took place in the middle 1970s, leading to a major decentralisation of bargaining, followed by a major shift back in the early 1980s with the sharp rise in unemployment. But there too a system of hierarchical job classifications was used, and one into which the principle of upgrading was built. Provisions for the recruitment of apprentice-type skills was not necessary as it had been in France, owing to the virtual absence of such training in Italy (see Giugni 1976). But in Italy also, the main framework of the classification system was established by national level industry-wide bargaining, as was the compression of the number of wage grades in industry collective agreements in the early 1970s, although a good deal of the pressure for this came from the rank and file membership in the factories and offices.

Thus in western European countries, even where there is a greater tendency to use internal labour markets, the grading systems and related pay rates are not solely the object of workplace custom and seniority rules but also of industry-wide arrangements often backed up by collective bargaining. Moreover, in Britain and Germany, where internal grading systems are used, perhaps because employers are less restricted by industry-wide agreements on such questions, they nevertheless have to fit them round existing systems of apprentice-trained skills. Thus in western European countries, it is much more difficult to base a theory of labour market structure purely on the personnel policies of enterprises, or on the impact of technological specificity upon the organisation of training within the enterprise.

The American literature might still be taken as providing a more limited explanation, perhaps of American conditions only—itself quite a considerable task. Would it be sufficient simply to drop the universalistic pretentions of their arguments? The answer must be negative, although in a different way for Doeringer and Piore as compared with radicals segmentation theorists, such as Edwards. Doeringer and Piore's argument is based upon the pressures on cost-minimising management when organising training under conditions of technological specificity. The European evidence shows that institutional conditions are extremely important, so that a revised argument by Doeringer and Piore would need to show which features in the institutional environment of American labour markets led firms to adopt such personnel and training policies. This would make their theory very different.

The problem is somewhat different for Edwards (1975) as he bases his argument upon the personnel strategies of large corporations. The fact that they might adopt different types of policy in the different institutional environment of western Europe would, at first sight, seem to be less of a challenge. However, his argument too was phrased in terms of their response to a technical environment, which enabled him to concentrate upon the central position of the enterprise in causing labour market structure. In any case, it could be suggested that his argument is not complete even for the United States, as his account of labour market structure leaves out the factors generating the type of craft internal labour market in the United States described by Kerr.

So far the emphasis has been upon skilled labour and its training, but the contribution of state secondary and higher education can also play a role, as has been argued by Maurice, Sellier and Silvestre (1982). This influence can be felt partly by the way the diplomas awarded can influence the range of jobs open to those people holding them, and partly by the content and ideology of the training itself. In the American literature, this would relate to the workers in the upper tier of the 'primary' labour market who possess general skills and have different patterns of labour mobility from the manual workers on enterprise internal labour markets. One of the examples most fully documented by their work was that of engineers in French and German manu-facturing firms. In the West German firms, the strength of the system of technical education gave the engineers also a strong status on account of their technical training. But in France, apart from those leaving the highly prestigious *Grandes Ecoles*, engineers tended to be more closely tied to the particular enterprise employing them, and with a less independently defined body of expertise. A similar situation to that of France can be found in Britain where engineers' training gives rise to an even weaker occupational identity, reflected perhaps in the number of industries in which tech-nical as well as administrative management is 'home grown', having grown up within the enterprise. This weak occu-pational identity was one of the reasons for the estab-lishment of the Finniston Inquiry in the UK in 1977 (Fin-niston 1980).

5.5. CONCLUSIONS

This chapter has examined theories which treat internal labour markets as a logical development within a com-petitive labour market, that is, as emerging out of the action of normal competition with employers seeking to minimise the costs of and workers seeking to defend their investment in training. By and large, the processes regulating internal labour markets in these theories, although formally different from normal competitive markets, fulfil the same functions under conditions in which open-market transactions would be less effective. Doeringer and Piore base their theory on investment in enterprise-specific skills, and Williamson bases his upon the more general framework of transaction costs. The uniqueness and idiosyncracy of individual machines was held to be the major cause of specific skills, such that internal labour markets emerge out of attempts by labour market actors to solve an economic problem subject to these technical constraints.

The model is one in which internal labour markets emerge out of an otherwise structureless competitive market, and as they fulfil mostly the same functions as normal market transactions, there is some justification, in theory at least, for treating them as internal 'markets'. The term 'internal labour market' is now part of the standard jargon, and probably cannot be changed. But how far are internal markets really markets in practice? Doeringer and Piore, and Williamson, would justify their analogy by the presumed causes of internal labour markets, and that they fulfil the functions of markets.

This chapter has argued that Doeringer and Piore's and Williamson's explanations run into a number of difficulties. Both take specificity (or 'idiosyncracy') as a datum, and do not fully consider how specific skills relate to the enterprise's structure, and in Doeringer and Piore's theory there is some problem in moving from job-specific to enterprise-specific skills. More important, it was argued that the seniority and other allocation rules could run counter to economic efficiency if they are instituted in order to restrict managerial prerogative. Finally, it was shown that national labour market institutions, often supported by collective bargaining, can also play an extremely important role in determining the structure of internal labour markets. This reduces the degree to which one can treat internal labour markets as surrogate markets as they are often not the result of skill formation under conditions of skill specificity. By comparison with the competitive labour markets of economic theory then, and despite the existence of a degree of competition between employees within internal labour markets for certain jobs, internal labour markets offer quite different transaction arrangements, and there is some doubt as to whether they fulfil the role of markets. But this may be to take a false view of labour markets outside the firm. As suggested in the last chapter, custom also plays an important role within these, one which involves more than freezing past economic relationships.

Two wider points should be raised in this connection. First, the importance of apprenticeships in establishing occupational labour markets for general skills suggests that such skills also may be largely dependent on an institutional base, rather than being a natural state of affairs. General skills also depend upon special transactional arrangements, a point implied by Kerr's treating craft markets as institutional markets. In the final chapter, it will be argued that one reason for this is that many occupational labour markets and general skills have many attributes of 'public goods', notably that they can be used by people who have not necessarily contributed to their cost. Although in theory the cost of training for general skills should fall upon the trainees, studies by Ryan (1980) on shipbuilding in the United States, by Noll et al (1984) on West German industry, and by IMS (1982) in the UK show that employers frequently bear much of the cost of such training, and are unable to recoup it from those they have trained.

Secondly, as will be argued in the final chapter, this parallel between general skills and public goods means that the occupational labour markets built on them may be difficult to maintain in practice unless protected by institutional rules, or by social consensus. Such markets, although enabling workers to change jobs while maintaining their skill levels, also often fall a long way short of the full competitive model. Taking greater cognisance of the importance of the institutional foundations of many inter-firm labour markets suggests that internal labour markets may indeed be considered as markets, but in a different sense from the one in which the question was originally posed.

NOTES

1. In subsequent work, Piore has devoted more attention to labour market stratification. The main focus of this chapter is, however, on Doeringer and Piore's work on internal labour markets as this has received much more attention from mainstream labour economists, and has become a part of the received wisdom on internal labour markets.

6 Social Norms and Macro Theories of Labour Market Structure

6.1. INTRODUCTION

The internal labour market theories of Doeringer and Piore, and Williamson, looked at in the previous chapter, started from the microscopic level, from the difficulties of management and training where jobs are very idiosyncratic. But another way of approaching the problem is to start from the product market pressures on employers, and examine the consequences for their labour policies. This has been the approach of some of the American labour market segmentation theorists, such as Edwards, and also of a group of French economists, including Aglietta, Boyer, and Mistral. In recent years, the most innovative work has come from the French group, and it is to their work that most this chapter will be devoted.

Why should these be covered in a book devoted to attempts by economists to take account of social and institutional influences on the labour market? The main reason is that just as Doeringer and Piore sought to explain internal labour markets as a logical development in a competitive market, the segmentation theorists seek to explain why labour markets have become divided into two or more broad segments: one of which is dominated by large enterprise internal labour markets, stable employment and high earnings, while the others lack such advantages. Some argue that the labour market falls into two broad segments, but the main issue here is the underlying assumption of the segmentation theories that there has been a move from a system of competitive labour markets in which money wages were flexible in response to demand changes, to one in which internal labour markets and administered wage and salary structures in large firms have profoundly altered the nature of the labour market. The consequence of this argument, if valid, is that the causes of wage inflexibility are to be found in these changes. Consequently, wage comparability and other norms restricting movements in relative pay, if effective, would owe their influence to these deeper underlying changes in the nature of the economy. This chapter challenges this view, arguing that the contrast between relative wage flexibility in the nineteenth century, and wage rigidity in the latter half of the twentieth is overstated. Although money wages in aggregate displayed a degree of cylicality in the nineteenth century, where suitable evidence can be found, these movements in response to demand were greatly attenuated at the industry and occupation level where established relativities between industries and between occupations appear to have been very influential. Because the evidence is more scattered, it has been necessary to go back to some of the main statistical series on pay, hence the somewhat different character of this chapter.

It also challenges another aspect of their theories, that the firm is at the centre of these processes. The automobile industry was one of the key industries in which many of these management changes were pioneered (thus the word 'Fordism'), but it will be argued that in the present restructuring in the industry, existing labour market institutions have been a major element in the choices management have made—which implies a more reciprocal relationship between companies' labour management policies and labour market structure than these theories allow for.

Before launching into a detailed analysis of the French group's theory, it is helpful to provide a brief outline of their argument, and how they account for the shift from competitive conditions in labour markets, and their relation to the American segmentation theorists.

The position of some of the American segmentation theorists is well summed up by Edwards (1973). He sets off from the change in the structure of the American economy with the emergence of giant corporations which changed the nature of competition in both product and labour markets, but recognises also that many of the smaller firms are not so much dying survivors of a more competitive age, but they work for the large firms, and are often very dependent on orders from a single large firm.

In common with Doeringer and Piore (1971), he retains the idea that the enterprise lies at the centre of the problem of labour market structure, and the personnel and sourcing policies of large corporations are, in broad terms, responsible for the formation of structure labour markets. The radicals' position is quite well illustrated by Edwards in the introduction to a collection of papers by the American segmentation theorists:

A consequence of the dualistic industrial structure was a corollary dualism in labour markets. This dualism constituted a clear *reversal* of those forces which, during the nineteenth century, had led to increasingly common, or shared, work experiences. In particular, the large oligopolistic corporations instituted a new system of labour management that was bureaucratic in form and emphasised the differentiation of jobs, rather than their homogenisation. Although proletarianisation continued, jobs in the capitalist sector became increasingly segmented. While these markets reflect (are a natural corollary of) divisions in the labour process, they have also institutionalised those divisions and hence perpetuated them. (Edwards 1975 p. xii)

The French group shares some of these ideas, but presents them in an alternative theoretical framework. It identifies two modes of regulation of the economic system, the 'competitive' and the 'monopolistic'. The competitive mode is supposed to have applied especially during the nineteenth century, the monopolistic mode having developed through the twentieth century at different rates in different countries. Although Aglietta's and Boyer and Mistral's main focus is on the economic system as a whole, changes in the nature of the labour market play an important part in the transition between the two modes of regulation, and will also be the main focus of this chapter. In labour market terms, the hallmark of the first is the flexibility of money wages over the economic cycle, and of the second the downward rigidity of money wages and the emergence of large scale employers with complex interlocking ownership relations.

The competitive mode of regulation has many of the

features of standard neo-classical labour markets, notably a multiplicity of individual employers and a labour market which makes use of lay-offs and re-engagements a viable strategy for employers to adjust to changing economic circumstances. Moreover, the flexibility of money wages over the cycle, although not stated explicitly, presumably entails an upward sloping labour supply curve, a standard component of neo-classical labour market analysis.

Monopolistic regulation of the labour market emerges out of competitive regulation as large firms develop their own internal labour markets, and provide greater security of income and employment to their employees, but partly at the expense of other workers in subcontractor firms. This accentuates labour market competition outside the larger firms, and thus Boyer (1980) argues that monopolistic regulation produces a form of labour market segmentation.

Aglietta, Boyer and Mistral argue that changes in the process of accumulation are the fundamental causes of the change of mode of regulation, and thus of the development of a segmented labour market structure. This appears to rest on two principal assumptions, namely that economies of scale linked to technical change are a major factor behind continued industrial development, and also that these lead to the development of larger scale production units which provide the scope and the need for the development of Taylorism and of internal labour markets.

Thus, if their theories of regulation are to be applied to the labour market, the main thrust would be that labour market structure emerges out of changes in the wage relation and in the pattern of accumulation, and that certain features of technical change which provide a basis for economies of scale, although not a cause of the accumulation process (which is to be found in the analysis of the nature of capital), are a major influence shaping the pattern of labour market organisation.

This chapter seeks to tease out the arguments of Aglietta, Boyer and Mistral, and to point out some of the deficiencies of the model in relation to evidence from different countries. Following the main thesis of this book, it will be argued that they pay insufficient attention to the institutional and 'social' forces underlying labour market organisation. It will be argued that existing institutional structures and market structures also exerted a major influence on the strategies of firms, and that although economies of scale and technology played an important part, even for firms with similar technical conditions, a wider range of manpower and labour market strategies are possible than envisaged by Aglietta, Boyer and Mistral.

It will also be argued that the evidence for money wage flexibility over the economic cycle in the nineteenth century does not fully support competitive regulation. Even though there is evidence of flexibility of aggregate money wages, there is little evidence of such flexibility in relative wages between branches or between occupations except for some exceptional occupations, which is surely what one would expect if labour individual branch and occupational labour markets were also competitive. Where major changes in occupational differentials occurred these were not cyclical in nature, and social custom and union pressure played an important part in labour market organisation from a much earlier date than suggested by the analysis of modes of regulation.

6.2. THEORIES OF REGULATION AND SEGMENTATION

In his view of recent theories of employment and unemployment, Aglietta (1978) argues that although the segmentation theories have some descriptive value, they cannot serve as 'theories' of unemployment and its distribution because segmentation is a historically specific pattern of labour market organisation, and as such it has to be set in the wider context of the organisation and regulation of the whole of the capitalist economy. In particular, it has to be set in the context of the regulation of the 'wage relationship' (rapport salarial). As a general statement, there is probably little in this with which any segmentation theorist would disagree. Further indication of the precise nature of Aglietta's critique can be found in his earlier work *Regulation et Crises du Capitalisme* (1976).

Aglietta's framework can be schematised as follows:

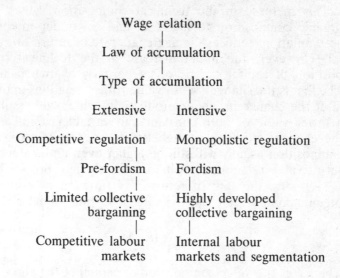

Wage relation
|
Law of accumulation
|
Type of accumulation

Extensive	Intensive
Competitive regulation	Monopolistic regulation
Pre-fordism	Fordism
Limited collective bargaining	Highly developed collective bargaining
Competitive labour markets	Internal labour markets and segmentation

An outline of Aglietta's theory of the transition between modes of regulation

Although the theory takes the wage relation and the extraction of surplus value as its starting point, the most interesting of Aglietta's observations on this can be left until after a brief discussion of the processes involved in the transition between modes of regulation. Discussion of the macro-dynamics of the model can be taken in two stages: the first deals with the problems raised by the tendency towards an increase in the organic composition of capital and its implications for the rate of return on capital; and the second deals with the relations between two key elements in the structure of the economic system, department I which broadly speaking produces capital goods, and department II which produces wage goods.

The fundamental problem of capital accumulation over time lies in the tendency for the organic composition of capital to increase, that is for the ratio of constant capital (fixed capital plus raw materials) to variable capital, or labour, to increase as a result of a labour-saving bias of technical change.

This increase in the technical composition causes the organic composition to increase, and so, under intensive accumulation, reduces the aggregate rate of return on capital. However, the initial increase in the technical composition of capital can be offset partially by two factors. The first is the changed set of value (price) relations in force after the change in labour productivity which will result in a lower value of both constant and variable capital after the change, although as Aglietta shows, the new organic composition usually will still be higher even under the new set of value relations than before the change (pp. 45–7).

Secondly, the rate of return is a function of both the organic composition and the rate of surplus value:

$$z = e/(k+1)$$

where k is the value composition of capital (C/V) and e the rate of surplus value (PL/V) (where C, V, and PL denote respectively constant and variable capital, and surplus value). It is clear that at the macro level, the effect of an increase in the value composition of capital can be offset by an increase in the rate of surplus value, leaving the aggregate rate of return on capital more or less unchanged.

Under extensive accumulation, the same possibilities exist but in addition because total value produced (measured in labour hours) can be expanded by extending the size of the labour force working under capitalist conditions, there is a further source of additional surplus value. However, as sources of additional labour power dry up, as in the United States with the ending of the Frontier and the slowing down of immigration, continued accumulation enters the intensive mode. The implications of this for patterns of work organisation and labour market structure will be spelled out more after examining the relation between the capital and wage goods sectors.

Relations between the capital and wage goods sectors

The dynamics of accumulation also depend upon the relations between the two departments of the economic system, producing respectively commodities used as constant capital (the capital goods sector), and commodities consumed in the renewal of variable capital (wage goods).

Aglietta locates the main impetus for capital accumulation in the capital goods sector, department I. Although not entirely clear from Aglietta's study, the main factors underlying this would seem to be the existence of economies of scale and of lower unit costs on newer vintages of capital equipment. Indeed, under the competitive mode of regulation, Aglietta suggests that one of the motors of accumulation lies in competition to invest in the newest vintages, and to expand output. The model is not dissimilar to Salter's (1966) vintage model of growth and technical change. Aglietta regards such investment as labour saving, and thus despite the cyclical elimination of old capital stock, there will nevertheless be a tendency for the organic composition of capital to increase. This provides a link to Aglietta's analysis of changing work relations as the labour-saving bias is associated with economies of scale in production units, and thus with the emergence of large scale organisations.

The transformation of the productive system, economising manpower, involves the collectivisation of labour through the use of large, indivisible means of production. (Aglietta 1976 p. 44)

The impact on the rate of return of an increasing organic composition of capital can be offset by two main factors. The first is the ability of firms producing capital goods in department I to find sufficiently large markets among firms producing wage goods in department II to enable them to take advantage of economies of scale and to maintain a high level of capacity utilisation. The higher the level of capacity utilisation of capital goods in department I, the lower is the value composition of the product, and since labour is a variable cost, the lower the organic composition. In the absence of sufficient markets in department II, an autonomous increase in investment and output by department I would soon be choked off as the rate of return, z, declined (p. 47). If economies of scale can be maintained, then the tendency for the organic composition to rise can be at least partly offset.

The second factor which can offset the rise in the organic composition is the reduction of the value of the labour input. This can be achieved by reducing the cost of reproduction of labour power through lower unit costs in department II. That increases relative surplus value. It also requires increased capital investment and thus changes in production methods in department II.

Balanced capital accumulation may take place if the output of department II is increasing fast enough to generate a demand for capital goods commensurate with the supply generated by internal accumulation within department I, but there is no inherent tendency towards an equilibrium growth path. Aglietta shows that the conditions for balanced accumulation in the two departments are fairly restrictive as the balancing of output and sales between the two department depends upon a fixed relation between the rates of growth of constant capital in both departments and their respective organic compositions (pp. 238–40). Hence, there is instability of accumulation within the capitalist system.

However, the central part of Aglietta's work has been to argue that two distinct patterns of regulations of the capitalist system can be identified in the economic development of the United States, and other industrialised countries, and that they can be understood through this framework.

Regulation and the wage relationship

Changes in the wage relationship are central to the transition between extensive and intensive accumulation. The key quantities within this relationship can be summarised as follows:

$$e = (t_v - t_n)/t_n$$

where e is the rate of surplus value, t_v the number of hours in the working day actually spent producing value, and t_n

the socially necessary time for reconstituting labour power. T is the actual length of the working day, and:

$$t_n < t_v < T.$$

As before, the equation describes a macro-economic relationship, although the working day might be thought of as a 'representative' working day, akin to Marshall's idea of a representative firm.

Absolute surplus value can be increased by extending capitalist relations to new sections of the labour force or by increasing the labour force. In the United States this was done by the extension of capitalist relations towards the whole of the Frontier, and by immigration. Such would be typical of the phase of 'extensive' accumulation. Another possibility is by extending the working day (raising T), thus the conflicts over the length of the working day in the early days of capitalist development.

In the phase of intensive accumulation, when the labour force under capitalist relations cannot easily be increased, there are two principal ways of increasing surplus value. The first consists of reducing the amount of the working day not actually worked, such time spent cleaning, between operations, moving around the plant, or waiting for materials, which were a major focus of Taylorism. These raise t_v towards T.

The second relies upon 'relative surplus value', that is increasing the rate of surplus value by reducing the socially necessary time for reconstituting labour power (reducing t_n). Whereas the variables T and t_n could be the object of action by individual firms, a reduction in t_n requires a cheapening of consumption goods, and hence requires a change in production techniques in the consumption goods sector.

Outside full employment, the unemployed or those in non-capitalist sectors of the economy can always undermine the individual or collective bargaining power of workers in the capitalist sector, reducing their ability to resist extension of the working day, or intensification of work rhythms. However, with near full employment, and where reserves of additional labour are exhausted, surplus value can be increased by raising relative surplus value, and hence reducing the socially necessary time for the reproduction of labour power t_n.

The problem of raising relative surplus value, once the possibilities for extending the labour force were restricted, lay at the heart of the transition between the competitive and the monopolistic modes of regulation. However, the particular solution discovered in the United States, which took the form of the innovations of Taylorism, and in particular of Fordism, were historically contingent. Competition to invest in the newest vintages of technology, and the link with the development of large scale production units were only part of the story. Of themselves, they did not entail the opening up of mass consumer goods markets, nor did they entail the development of the personnel practices, notably the stabilisation of money wages over the business cycle.

To summarise so far, Aglietta's argument is that the analysis of labour market structure has to be set within its proper macro-economic context, this being given on the one hand by the nature of the wage relationship, and on the other by the macro-economic constraints, and technological constraints upon the process of generating and accumulating surplus value. A crucial change occurred in the United States economy with the decline of extensive accumulation, and the development of intensive accumulation. The latter relies upon the balancing of two processes of intensification of work, and the cheapening of wage goods. Technical change and further investment in capital equipment in the wage goods sector enable the cheapening of wage goods, but this has to move at a rate sufficient to absorb the autonomously generated output from the capital goods sector, thus the potential instability of the process. Within Aglietta's model there are some important implicit assumptions concerning the nature of technical change associated with accumulation, and although these are not spelled out in detail, they need to be enumerated. First, an important part of the dynamic of accumulation in the capital goods sector would seem to derive from increasing returns scale, which may be contrasted with the assumption of diminishing returns used in general equilibrium theories (cf. Blaug's (1963) argument that much process innovation has been capital saving). Secondly, the increasing returns to scale appear to be linked in Aglietta's mind to increasing scale of organisational units—thus his reference to the collectivisation of work and the use of large indivisible production units. While these two assumptions may not amount to crude technological determinism, they are nevertheless strong assumptions, and without them it is hard to explain why there should be a more or less autonomous process of accumulation in the capital goods sector, and why the increasing scale of production and the associated forms of management, notably Taylorism, should play such a key role in the transition between forms of economic regulation.

The process of accumulation affects work organisation both by the increasing scale of organisation and, more important, by the continuous process of changing job requirements such that job analysis and job restructuring become a permanent aspect of industrial work, which thus extends Taylorism beyond its initial task of breaking down traditional craft jobs. The other important change associated with Fordism was the change in consumption patterns which made possible the expansion of demand for wage goods, but which required greater stability of income and job prospects for a considerable part of the labour force. Both of these are of major significance for labour market structure, and are examined more closely in the next section.

6.3. PATTERNS OF REGULATION OF THE CAPITALIST SYSTEM AND LABOUR MARKET STRUCTURE

The transition between the competitive and monopolistic modes of regulation was provoked by the transition from extensive to intensive accumulation. This affected both the organisation of capital, causing a 'centralisation' of capital, and that of the labour market. The process of centralisation involved changes in the financial relations between companies and the growth of relations of subcontracting in which one firm was dominant.

In the labour market, the corresponding changes arising out of the enhanced need to increased relative surplus value were twofold. The first consisted of increasing the intensity of work and increasing the scope of managerial prerogative, especially in the area of work organisation. The second lay in the cheapening of wage goods, but this required the development of a mass consumer market to provide the economies of scale necessary, and thus the extension of mass consumption to the working class. This would not have been possible under conditions of competitive regulation which entailed large fluctuations and a high degree of unpredictability in working class incomes, thus the importance of increased job security and income stability obtained by certain sections of the working class. The development of large financial and production units enabled employers to provide this kind of stability. The first of these changes has been mostly associated with Taylorism.

Taylor's main innovation for Aglietta had been to reduce the amount of non-work time during the working day, and thus to raise t_v nearer to T. This had been achieved primarily by breaking tasks down into simpler components and reallocating these mostly between less-trained workers. The move also represented a shift of control over work from skilled workers to management, but it did not involve any major change in the type of production equipment used.

Subsequent developments, included somewhat misleadingly by Aglietta under 'Fordism', extended the principles of Taylorist work organisation applying it to semi-automated production processes, which made great use of conveyor systems to transport materials within the factory, and of production lines. This required further changes in work organisation, notably the assignment of individual workers to work stations whose position was determined by the production line. These were important steps in the development of mass production on which mass consumption was to rest. Since maintenance of the growth of surplus value depends upon extracting more surplus value from the same aggregate labour force, it is necessary to sustain a continuous cheapening of wage goods (to increase relative surplus value) which requires continuous improvements in production methods, and thus continuous changes in work organisation. This, as will appear, is one of the sources of worker opposition to the monopolistic mode of regulation.

The increased productive potential of such methods required the extension of the demand for consumer goods. The early 1920s had seen an extension of this market to higher paid groups, but the extension of the market to working class households required greater stability and predictability of income than possible under the competitive mode of labour market organisation. According to Aglietta, this element of the system was provided by the development of collective bargaining in the late 1930s after the implementation of the Wagner Act and the establishment of the National Labour Relations Board. The fixing of wages in contracts which extended over several years reduced the amount of short-term fluctuation in workers' earnings, and the agreements also sought to regulate short-term variations in employment.

Such conditions could not be guaranteed by all firms because of the problem as to who should bear the cost of economic fluctuations. Herein lies Aglietta's analysis of labour market segmentation, which also ties in with his analysis of the centralisation of capital and with the analyses of Edwards and of Piore. Collective bargaining applies mostly in large firms, and the ones in a dominant relation to smaller suppliers. Moreover, the threat of unionisation led many large non-union firms to develop as favourable wage and employment conditions as those unionised, and thus greatly extended the impact of unionism. Nevertheless, the benefits of Fordism applied to a fraction, albeit an important one, of the American working class—the core labour force. Other sections remain excluded from both stable wages and employment, and from the realm of mass consumption. However, the extent to which these sections can provide all the flexibility needed in labour costs is limited. First, some continuity in the relation between large firms and their suppliers is necessary, especially if quality and stability of supply are to be maintained. Secondly, the smaller the proportion of the labour force in the core sector, the smaller is the mass market for consumer goods.

Thus some burden of adjustment has to fall upon the core labour force. First, in the short term, variability in core labour costs is introduced by the union-regulated system of seniority lay-offs and re-engagements. A second source of adjustment lies in the flexibility of work organisation. Employers have had the backing of the law in resisting strike action over questions of changes in work organisation (the Taft-Hartley Act excludes strike action over changes in work organisation introduced by the employer). However, evidence from the Future of the Automobile Project, and from Tolliday and Zeitlin (1982), suggests that Aglietta may have greatly overestimated the amount of flexibility of job boundaries and of redeployment of workers between jobs in major parts of United States industry, and of course the fact that the law makes certain provisions does not imply that they are effective. Evidence from the project also suggests that Aglietta's idea of a continuous process of radical change in work organisation (*un bouleversement continuel*) is mistaken, as such major changes in the car industry, the archetype of Fordism, have been infrequent although dramatic when they have occurred, as in the current changes in the industry (see Altshuler *et al.* 1984).

Aglietta claims some statistical support for his argument from Phelps Brown and Browne (1968). They showed that between 1860 and 1914 money wages (estimated annual earnings) had generally varied with the level of output, and the rate of accumulation of capital. In the years leading up to 1914 this cyclical tendency weakened with a slowing in the rate of increase in money wages as accumulation slowed or declined. This pattern, which is consistent with the competitive model of the labour market, weakened in the interwar period. After the Second World War the cyclical pattern disappeared to be replaced by a strong link between changes in wages and in prices. In this period, Aglietta argues that much of the burden of adjustment then fell upon the price level, thus one of the fundamental reasons for the post-war inflationary tendencies.

Several important questions need to be asked of Aglietta's theory. The first (section 6.4) is the extent to which his argument is supported by Phelps Brown and Browne's data for the United States, and how far the analysis is valid for the other countries they examined, notably Britain, France, Germany, and Sweden. In addition, how far does the subsequent statistical work of Boyer (1978) and of Boyer and Mistral (1983) on France bear out the analysis?

Secondly (section 6.5), one can question the role attributed to technical change, and the extent to which it constrains the range of strategies open to managements in dealing with their labour forces. A particularly important question is the extent to which the structure of markets and of institutions can exert a major influence. Such would seem to be suggested by Hannah's (for example 1980) work on patterns of vertical and horizontal integration of firms, and by some of the findings from the Future of the Automobile Project concerning the institutional constraints on management strategies in different countries. This then raises the question of the functionalism underlying Aglietta's approach to the analysis of systems of regulation in the role attributed to historically contingent phenomena.

A related set of questions concerns the plasticity of the American economic and social system at the time of the development of the 'monopolistic' mode of regulation, and the extent to which capital was free to shape the social and institutional structures appropriate to the monopolistic mode of regulation. The greater this plasticity, the more easily Aglietta can argue that his historical analysis offers a model of the transition between two ideal types of socio-economic organisation. If he can argue this, then the case for accepting analysis of these modes as a background to the segmentation debate is stronger.

The third question (section 6.6), raised especially in Chapter 4 of this book, is to what extent flexibility in the level of money wages identified by Aglietta, but also by Boyer and Mistral and other writers, with the competitive mode of regulation implies flexibility in relative prices between labour in different occupations, and in particular in different branches. For example, is Phelps Brown and Hopkins (1955)) evidence on the stability of skill differentials in the building industry throughout the latter part of the nine-teenth century up to the First World War at odds with the idea of a competitively regulated labour market? Other writers such as Clay (1928) also observed that the wage structure up to 1914 had displayed a good deal of stability, although Rowe's (1928) data suggest a slightly different picture if one compares workers in a number of different industries. Is the evidence of the stability of wage structure before 1914 sufficient to put into doubt some of the argu-ments about competitive regulation in the nineteenth cen-tury?

Finally (section 6.7), it has to be asked how far the discussion of labour market structure should be set within the framework provided by Aglietta and subsequently by Boyer and Mistral. These questions will be dealt with the the rest of this chapter.

6.4. LABOUR MARKETS AND PATTERNS OF MONEY WAGE FLEXIBILITY IN DIFFERENT COUNTRIES: PHELPS BROWN AND AGLIETTA

One of the central pieces of evidence used by Aglietta is based upon Phelps Brown and Browne's analysis (1968) of pay trends in the United States between 1860 and 1960. They observed that money earnings had responded to the state of the trade cycle between 1860 and 1890, but gradually ceased to do so over the next fifty years, and from the 1950s there was a steady upward trend in money wages. Phelps Brown and Browne explained these changes by the ease with which firms could raise prices in the latter period because of the belief that governments would seek to main-tain aggregate demand. Aglietta goes further and argues that there has been a change in the mode of regulation of the whole economy. However, his argument rests above all on the United States, and he did not make use of the data Phelps Brown and Browne had assembled on Britain, France, Germany and Sweden. This section examines how far such changes in the cyclical behaviour of money wages also took place in these countries, and whether they were accompanied by the same kinds of social and economic transformation noted by Aglietta in the United States.

(a) At the overall level, similar changes in earnings fluctuations (estimated annual earnings) indeed occurred in all five countries. In the period between 1860 and 1913 money wages increased in the positive phase of the business cycle, and decreased in the negative phase (Phelps Brown and Browne Figure 5), although the fluctuations in money wages were smaller in France than in the other countries. And in the period between 1945 and 1960, in all five countries, money wages rose continuously, and with relatively little fluctuation.

Some additional evidence that the pattern of labour market operation has changed since the close of the nineteenth century can be found in British analyses of the relationship between money wage changes and the rate of unemployment. These are best summarised by Lipsey's (1960) reworking of Phillips' (1958) analysis. The equation Lipsey obtained for the period 1862–1913 was:

$$\dot{W} = -1.21 + 6.45U^{-1} + 2.26U^{-2} - 0.19\dot{U} + 0.21\dot{P} \, .$$

In contrast, for the period 1923–39 and 1948–57, the equation was:

$$\dot{W} = 0.74 + 0.43U^{-1} + 11.18U^{-4} + 0.038\dot{U} + 0.69\dot{P}$$

where W, P, and U respectively denote wages, prices and the rate of unemployment, and the dot denotes the rate of increase.

The most notable differences between the equations for the two periods are the decline in the coefficient on the unemployment term and the tripling of the coefficient on the price term, indicating that after the First World War unemployment (indicating excess demand in Lipsey's model) had a smaller and the price level a much larger effect upon the rate of change of money wages. Lipsey's data stopped in 1957, but a number of subsequent models of inflation in the UK have given explicit recognition to the link between money wages and prices, as in the 'target real wage' models of inflation of Henry and Ormorod (1978), or Henry (1981). The equations of these models explicitly include a term designed to capture the effect of union wage demands to maintain real living standards.

For France, Boyer (1978) also found that the effect of price changes on money wages was relatively small in the late nineteenth century, but increased greatly in the inter-war period, notably on account of the introduction of indexation into a number of agreements. For the period between 1841 and 1913, he also found that the elasticity between percentage change in money wages and percentage change in the cost of living was 0.06, compared with 0.79 for that between 1920 and 1937, and 0.77 for that between 1947 and 1976 (Table 7).

(b) There were also some notable differences in the timing of the change in the behaviour of aggregate money wages between countries, and Aglietta's theory implies that these should correspond to changes in industrial organisation. It is to the latter that we shall look first. Broadly speaking, these occurred before the First World War in the United States, and in Germany in heavy industries, but during and after the war in Britain, and still later in France.

Changes in industrial concentration provide an imperfect indicator of the changes in industrial organisation described by Aglietta. These involved both centralisation of capital and increased concentration; nevertheless, in his analysis of the United States these were closely related, with increased concentration preceding increased centralisation.

By the First World War, the share of output of large manufacturing firms had progressed further in the United States than in Britain, and that it was only in the middle 1920s that Britain caught up (Prais 1976, Table 6.1).

Although plant sizes in manufacturing as a whole in Germany were smaller in the inter-war years than in Britain or the United States (Table 6.2), this was largely because of the number of small handicraft firms in light industries

Table 6.1: Shares (%) of the hundred largest enterprises in manufacturing net output in the United Kingdom and the United States 1910–70.

United Kingdom	1909 16[a]	1924 22[a]	1949 22	1958 32	1970 40/41
United States	1909 22	1929 25	1947 23	1958 30	1970 33

Notes: [a] approximate
Source: Prais (1976) Tables 1.1 and E.1.

Table 6.2: Median and quartile plant sizes in light and heavy industries, selected years 1925–61

	Light Industries			Heavy Industries		
	Britain	Germany	US	Britain	Germany	US
Lower Quartile						
1925–39	70	10	70	170	170	240
1958–61	70	30	60	320	250	240
Median						
1925–39	200	70	230	630	750	920
1958–61	220	120	190	1140	1140	1100
Upper Quartile						
1925–39	490	280	570	1800	3200	3100
1958–61	620	430	520	3600	4400	4000

Note: 1925-39: Britain 1935, Germany 1925, and United States 1939.
Source: Prais (1981) Table 3.4.

(including food, clothing, furniture making, etc.) (Prais 1981). In heavy industries (metals, engineering, cars, chemicals, etc.), Germany was much closer to the United States, with extremely large plants playing a very important role. In these industries a quarter of the labour force was employed in plants with over 3000 workers in Germany and the United States, as against 1800 workers in Britain.

In France, concentration also progressed more slowly than in Germany or the United States. As late as the 1960s, France lagged considerably behind with 21 per cent of workers in manufacturing in large establishments (with more than 1000 employees), as compared with over 30 per cent in Germany and the United States (J-P. Nioche 1969). About the time of the First World War, the proportion of large scale establishments increased sharply, as the percentage of workers in industrial establishments with more than 500 employees increased from 12.2 per cent in 1906 to 18.9 per cent in 1926, growing thereafter much more slowly, to reach only 25 per cent in 1954. But much of the increase even between 1906 and 1926 was due to the decline in employment in small establishments with ten or less employees (Didier and Malinvaud 1969). Their analysis of changes in the share of output of large scale enterprises also suggests a slow movement of concentration between 1910 and 1920, and acceleration of this during the 1920s, followed by a stagnation, and even a regression of their share in the 1930s and 1940s. Only from the mid-1950s did their share begin to increase again and then only slowly until the wave of mergers in the later 1960s (Gorgé and Tandé 1974).

This somewhat fragmentary evidence suggests that the changes in industrial structure and organisation which Aglietta associated with the emergence of monopolistic regulation developed first in the United States and Germany, but were slower to come in Britain and particularly in France. Aglietta argued that these changes caused the development of equivalent forms of labour market organisation. Thus his theory would predict that competitive regulation of the labour market should have declined first in the United States, and Germany, and should have done so only later in Britain and France. Thus one would expect the cyclicality of money wages (Aglietta's and Boyer's key indicator) to decline first in the United States and Germany and for this to be under way before 1914. In Britain and France, such changes would not be expected until the 1920s.

1860–1913

Between 1860 and 1913, the cyclical pattern of increases in money wages in boom periods and of decreases in recession weakens in the United States after about 1900, and in Germany and Sweden after 1890. Thereafter, money wage growth merely slowed in recessions. The cyclical pattern with decreases in money wages in recession was maintained throughout in Britain. In France, the cyclical changes in money wages were much smaller and almost never decreased, although the cyclicality persisted throughout the period. Thus far the comparisons would seem broadly to support Aglietta's argument.

Aglietta argues that the new monopolistic form of regulation began to develop in the United States in the 1890s and early 1900s with the development of the giant vertically integrated firms, and that this began to weaken the link between money wages and the business cycle. The dominant position of large scale enterprises, such as Krupp, in Germany's rapid industrialisation after 1870 would seem to lend further support to Aglietta's thesis, especially as these employers then played a major role in the organisation of the labour market, and in particular in the organisation of vocational training. Swedish industrialisation was similarly rapid, and there too employers could not count upon the availability of a large already trained skilled labour force.

The different behaviour of money wages in Britain and France is broadly consistent with Aglietta's argument, although it requires some qualifications. As already indicated, the parallel development large scale capitalist firms in these two countries had to await the 1920s. But the slower growth of concentration may have been heavily influenced by existing patterns of market organisation rather than by changes inherent in the process of accumulation, as suggested by Aglietta. For Britain, Hannah (1980) argues that this was the result of the prior existence of highly developed and highly efficient intermediate markets which vitiated the need for vertical integration. For France, Lévy-Leboyer (1980) argues that these developments were delayed until after the Second World War partly by the widespread existence of trading cartels and holding companies which, he argued, were an obstacle to more dynamic American forms of vertical integration.

In both Britain and France, the slower pace and initially higher level of industrialisation meant that the existing labour market structures could cope with the increased demand for skilled labour, the inadequacy of which pushed the large

German firms to organise their own training. The smaller growth in productivity between about 1900 and 1913 in the UK (Phelps Brown and Browne), and in France (Boyer), as contrasted with the other countries, suggests that a number of the changes in working practices and techniques which were taking place in the other countries were occuring much more slowly in Britain and France. However, in so far as the causes for different developments advanced by Hannah and Lévy-Leboyer are correct, they indicate the need for greater attention to the influence of structure of existing market institutions. Thus, up to 1914, patterns of wage behaviour and industrial organisation roughly correspond to Aglietta's thesis, as the slower pace of such reorganisation in Britain and France could account for the persistence of cyclical fluctuations in money wages.

Inter-war period

Changes in the inter-war period were more complex, and fit less convincingly into Aglietta's model. The indicators of concentration would suggest that fluctuations in money wages in the inter-war period should have been least in the United States and Germany where monopolistic regulation was most advanced, and greatest in Britain and France where it was least advanced.

The influence of the three main cycles whose three peaks came roughly in 1921, 1929 and 1937 was visible in the trends in money wages in all five countries. However, the largest variations occurred in the United States and Germany, and the smallest in Britain, which is the opposite of what Aglietta's analysis would have predicted for these countries. Only in Sweden and France did the behaviour of money wages correspond to that predicted for the inter-war period.

A counter-argument in defence of Aglietta's thesis might be that the first period (1919–23) was too greatly marked by the disruption following the 1914–18 war, and that the severity of the depression in the early 1930s was greater than that of the cycles of the late nineteenth century. However, Phelps Brown and Browne point out that to some extent the depth of the depression in some countries was itself the result of reactions in these countries to the crash: German and American employers pressed for and obtained large money wage reductions, whereas the strength of the union organisations in Britain and Sweden attenuated such pressures.

A second line of defence might be that Aglietta himself treated the inter-war period as one of transition in the United States, pointing out that the full development of monopolistic regulation of the labour market had to await Ford's new management methods not fully developed until the 1920s, and the labour legislation of the New Deal. However, his analysis of changes in industrial structure, and of money wage flexibility, suggested that these changes were already well under way before the First World War. Thus, even if Aglietta's argument is right for the United States, it has to be recognised that the processes he described may have been less general in the inter-war years than would have been necessary for them to dominate aggregate money wage movements.

A second paradox for Aglietta's and Boyer's argument is that the development of collective bargaining and of indexation agreements, which they associate with the rise of monopolistic regulation, were widely used in Britain and France, the two countries which on their indicators should have been closest to competitive regulation in the inter-war years. In both Britain and France, collective bargaining was fairly widespread before the First World War although it underwent a considerable extension during the war. Moreover, agreements linking wages to the price index spread fairly quickly during and after the war in these two countries.

Indeed, in Britain debates, interpretation of the changes in the behaviour of money wages has focused heavily on the increase in collective bargaining (Phelps Brown and Browne 1968, and Hines 1964), although these are not necessarily in contradiction with Aglietta's thesis. Moreover, there has been some tendency to link these changes between the late nineteenth century and the post First World War period to the spread of 'sliding-scale' (indexation) provisions in collective agreements. In the late nine-

teenth century in some industries these were linked to output prices (as in the coal mining industry), but in the early
1900s, and particularly during the First World War, partial
linking of wage scales to the cost of living became more
widespread (Rowe 1928, and Knowles and Robertson 1951).
The TUC supported them, and by 1925, according to
Knowles and Robertson, some 2.5 million workers in the
UK were covered by such agreements, although by 1933
the number had probably fallen below one million.

Boyer (1978) quotes similar developments in France,
notably the big increase in the number of collective agreements reached in the early 1920s, and their subsequent
decline into the early 1930s. France also saw a big increase
in agreements linking wages to the cost of living in the early
1920s.

Although this does not of itself refute Aglietta's and
Boyer's model, it nevertheless suggests that there is a great
deal more independence between the development of industrial organisation and labour market organisation than they
allow for, and that it is doubtful whether there is a single
dominant pattern of causation running from changes in
industrial organisation to changes in labour market organisation in the manner they suggest.

6.5. COMPANY MANPOWER MANAGEMENT STRATEGIES AND REGULATION

The model developed by Aglietta, and taken over to some
extent by Boyer and Mistral, makes fairly strong assumpions
about the scope for action open to company manpower
management. As shown earlier, Aglietta made strong
assumptions about the nature of the economies of scale
underlying accumulation process in the capital goods sector,
and about the continuous process of work reorganisation.
It is clear that such extensive reorganisation as envisaged
by Aglietta is likely to lead to the development of skills
which have only a limited market outside the worker's
current firm—indeed, Aglietta stresses the importance of
Taylorism and the attack by management on traditional

craft skills which had an extensive local labour market. The new skills are not transferable, or, in Becker's terms, are specific. In Chapter 5 we rejected the strong version of Doeringer and Piore's thesis that the presence of specific skills causes the development of internal labour markets, but it is still possible to maintain a weaker version, namely that firms are likely to develop internal labour markets when they depend upon specific skills developed within their own organisation. Another reason for using internal labour markets combined with higher than average pay is that it enhances managerial authority by making the threat of dismissal, management's ultimate sanction, more effective. Thus large capital-intensive firms under monopolistic regulation might develop their own internal labour markets and turn their backs to a large extent upon local labour markets. This would indeed be in line with the general idea of a move away from competitive market regulation, and is consistent with Boyer's (1980) suggested synthesis between theories of regulation and theories of segmentation.

What evidence is there that company manpower policies are constrained in this way? There are three main sources one can turn to, and each suggests weaknesses in Aglietta's and Boyer and Mistral's argument. The first relates to results of the Future of the Automobile Project (see Altshuler *et al.* 1984, and Marsden *et al.* 1985) concerning the scope for choice open to managements; the second refers back to comparative evidence on labour market structures and company organisation in western Europe; and the third relates to studies of job control in the car industry.

A crucial industry for Aglietta's argument would be the automobile industry, and indeed many of the managerial innovations he describes were first developed there. However, results from the Future of the Automobile Project suggest that management faces a variety of choices, notably in their approach to skills, training and local labour markets. The authors of the study argue that in the current crisis in the industry, in the manpower area, managements face a choice between two broad strategies: a 'neo-liberal' and a 'cooperative' strategy. The neo-liberal strategy involves a vigorous re-assertion of labour market discipline, using the

workers' fear of job loss as a means of rolling back bargaining advantages gained under more favourable
conditions. It also involves use of local labour markets
through lay-offs and new recruitment as a primary means
of adjusting the size and structure of the company's labour
force. In contrast, the cooperative strategy involves, after
initial manpower reductions, an offer of greater job security
in exchange for a more flexible attitude to technical change
and negotiations over job-related issues. The implicit offer
of greater job and income security means effectively that
the cooperative strategy entails the further development of
internal labour market conditions for at least the core labour
force, with the use of redeployment and retraining instead
of adjusting the skill structure of the workforce by adjusting
the mix of dismissals and recruitment. Effectively, therefore, the cooperative strategy entails a certain turning back
from use of local labour markets as the prime means of
achieving manpower adjustments.

Definition of these two options has been heavily
influenced by comparisons made often by the automobile
companies themselves with Japanese practices, but the logic
of the *quid pro quo* of greater job security for greater
flexibility has also arisen in a more piecemeal fashion from
experiments within the industry. Examples of policies typical of the cooperative strategy as tried in the United States
would be the development of employee involvement schemes in a number of Ford's American plants introduced
during the extensive manpower reductions and job reorganisation. This has involved a major change in Ford management's industrial relations policies, as for many years
it was strongly opposed to any such developments. More
dramatic, but perhaps of less fundamental significance, have
been the schemes for income and employment security in
the 1984 agreements negotiated by the UAW with both
Ford and General Motors. Similarly in West Germany,
much emphasis during the recent manpower adjustments
has been upon the avoidance of lay-offs and the use of
short-time working and of redeployment and retraining,
together with greater employee involvement in long-term
planning of the manpower side of technical changes. In

contrast to both the United States and West Germany, and also to Japan, is the UK car industry, which has also undergone very major changes in the last five years, including major increases in productivity, up to the standards of West German plants in some cases (based on comparisons made within General Motors and Ford, see Marsden *et al.* 1985), and on major investments in robotic techniques at BL and now at General Motors' Vauxhall plants. Despite an increased emphasis upon redeployment within the firm, and some changes in maintenance craft demarcations, there is little sign that the firms have turned their backs on their local labour markets. BL has gone the furthest towards breaking down traditional craft demarcations in the new technology area, but even there its management believe the new skills to be 75 per cent transferable, and management at both Ford and Vauxhall believe that there is little to be gained by dispensing with the apprenticeship-based craft system of organising maintenance and many other skills. This pattern of skill organisation is of course heavily geared to local labour markets. Maintaining such a pattern greatly limits the extent to which the firms can build extensive internal labour markets, reducing as it does the scope for upgrading of workers. Thus there would certainly seem to be evidence that companies have a degree of choice concerning their manpower strategies even in an industry with the same technology, size, and to a large extent, seeking to adapt to the same problem, and to some extent even having the same parent company.

The car industry would be one of the sectors which according to Aglietta's thesis should exhibit many of the characteristics of monopolistic regulation, so this diversity of response, and some of the reasons for it, namely existing patterns of labour market organisation, suggest a number of conclusions. First, Aglietta's thesis that the nature of the constraints upon accumulation in the capital goods sectors (i.e. economies of scale, labour saving, and large scale production units) generate similar manpower strategies is inadequate. Secondly, and more seriously, his contention that the theories of labour market structure need to be set in the context of modes of regulation, although suggesting useful additional insights, cannot be maintained. Labour market structure may be influenced by the type of phenomenon he describes, but it cannot be said to be wholly subordinate to it.

This last conclusion is given further support from studies of labour market and company organisation in western European countries, much of which has already been referred to in this book. First, the comparison of French and German manufacturing establishments by Maurice, Sellier and Silvestre (1982) illustrates the extent of differences in labour market and skill organisation in two advanced countries. Boyer (1978) has argued that monopolistic regulation had developed in France during the 1960s, although in terms of the relationship between employment changes and output, Boyer and Mistral (1979) suggested that West Germany remained within the competitive mode. However, that argument was based upon the coefficients in employment functions, and the macro-economic observations appear rather weak when set against the increasing evidence that the type of difference brought to light by Maurice, Sellier and Silvestre is a fairly long-standing phenomenon. Saunders and Marsden (1981) and Marsden (1982) extended some of this evidence also to Britain and Italy, and provided additional statistical support for their findings for other branches in France and Germany. This would also suggest that labour market organisation is fairly independent of the overall pattern of competitive or of monopolistic regulation, and that it does not necessarily change in response to the transition between the modes of regulation described by Aglietta and by Boyer and Mistral. This material also suggests that, although the idea of modes of regulation may be a useful one, it is doubtful that market organisation conforms to the typology these authors propose.

Finally, it could be argued that Aglietta, and Boyer and Mistral, greatly overestimate the extent to which management succeeded in breaking worker opposition with the introduction of Taylorism, and in doing so underestimate the extent to which pre-existing patterns of labour market and trade union organisation have been able to survive, and to shape the future. Comparing worker control over work organisation in the British and United States car industries, Tolliday and Zeitlin (1983) argue that workers very quickly succeeded in subverting the patterns of work organisation, and in particular the working of seniority rules, such that, by the 1960s, seniority districts were a serious obstacle to changes in work organisation. This would reinforce the argument stated earlier that Aglietta's and Boyer and Mistral's conception of technical change and accumulation under monopolistic regulation is mistaken. They saw it as requiring a continual upheaval, '*un bouleversement continuel*', of work organisation rather than changing in uneven bursts.

To conclude this section, Aglietta, Boyer and Mistral, although introducing an important new element to the debate about labour market structure, underestimate the range of strategies for labour force adjustment open to managements, and underestimate also the extent to which there are long-standing patterns of labour market organisation which are to a large extent independent of the pattern of regulation.

6.6. REGULATION AND FLEXIBILITY OF MONEY WAGES AND OF WAGE STRUCTURE

An important element of Aglietta's and of Boyer's view of the competitive mode of regulation is that of downwardly flexible money wages. Boyer, and Phelps Brown and Browne present impressive evidence that this was true of aggregate money wages in the nineteenth century, and that this gradually changed as the twentieth century progressed. However, Boyer's argument implies that money wage flexibility should be a characteristic not just of money wages in aggregate, but it should also be found at a more disaggregated level reflecting product and labour market changes at the industry and occupational level. Hence, the counterpart of the competitive mode of regulation should be a flexible wage structure as the labour markets for individual industries and individual occupations responded to business fluctuations. Indeed, Boyer (1978) seeks to show that this was the case in France in the nineteenth century.

It would seem then that, under competitive regulation, the wage levels of different groups are determined relatively independently of each other. Consequently, changes in wage differences between branches provide a form of macro-economic adjustment, just as do changes in the average level of wages. (Boyer 1978 p. 38)

But the impressive statistical evidence at the aggregate level is not reflected in the more fragmentary data at the industry and occupational levels. This section will examine some of the evidence on the flexibility of wage structure in the period crucial to Aglietta's and Boyer's argument, namely the late nineteenth and early twentieth centuries, for which there was clear evidence of aggregate money wage flexibility. It also looks briefly at the inter-war period, but this is of less interest because aggregate money wage flexibility was less clear. It deals with Britain, France, Germany and the United States, and will deal mostly with inter-industry differentials, but also in a more limited way with occupational differentials.

(a) Wage structure 1870 to 1913   Britain

Hicks (1955 and 1974) described the high degree of 'stickiness' of relative wages in Britain both before and after the First World War, and he pointed out that such variations in the occupational cum industrial wage structure as occurred in the late nineteenth century were due to large movements in a small number of trades which were sensitive to business fluctuations (Hicks 1974 p. 67). He attributed this to the establishment of standard union rates as early as the late nineteenth century. This is indeed supported by Bowley's (1900, Appendix I) analysis of average money wages in selected branches between 1840 and 1890. Except for mining, the rank order of industries remained little changed despite a 40 per cent increase in wages over the period, and despite cyclical fluctuations in money wages.

Aglietta's argument as applied to Britain implies that as the degree of concentration was increasing between 1909 and 1924, and as it had largely reached the United States level by 1924, the 1920s and 1930s should be an important transition period, and this should be reflected in the increasing stability of the wage structure. For skill differentials among manual workers, the evidence of Phelps Brown and Hopkins on seven centuries of building wages indicated a great deal of stability in the differential between skilled and unskilled building workers over the seven centuries up to the First World War, including the latter part of the nineteenth century. Knowles and Robertson (1951) found that the percentage differential in wage rates between skilled and unskilled workers in both the engineering and the construction industries changed very little between 1880 and 1914, and after the major disturbance of differentials during the war they were again very stable between 1920 and the late 1930s. Indeed, even the data on which Reder based his theory of cyclical variations in skill differentials are more accurately described as a sharp reduction during the 1914–18 war, followed by a fifteen-year period of stability before a long secular decline (Saunders and Marsden 1981).

France Material on the flexibility of industrial and occupational wage structure in France before 1920 is fragmentary, as has been stressed by Parodi's (1962) study of the reduction of wage differentials in France, Britain and the United States. Boyer (1978), using Kuczynski's series on indices of wages in mining, construction, metal working and textiles from 1789 to 1938, argues that the differential increases in wages between these four branches showed evidence of flexibility of wage structure. This was greatest between 1800 and 1850, less between 1850 and 1910, and still less pronounced between 1920 and 1939. However, some qualifications should be added. First, textiles showed the greatest deviation from the other three branches between 1800 and 1850, and it was at the time undergoing major changes in the organisation of production, which is indicative of long-term changes rather than a cyclical response to changing product and labour market conditions in the industry. Secondly, although Kuczynski's series give some evidence of independent cyclical changes in money wages between the branches in the earlier part of the period, Kuczynski (1955) gives no indication of the way in which he compiled his index, and only the most impressionistic description of his sources. Thus when, in the period between 1850 and 1910, his series suggests only half the increase observed by Simiand (1932) and Phelps Brown and Browne (1968), there is no means of tracing the difference. Nevertheless, the impression from the year-to-year changes is that in the latter part of the nineteenth century there is a discernible tendency for money wages in the four branches to move in unison, this being weaker in mining than in the other branches.

For 1870 onwards, Simiand (1932) provides fairly complete indices of daily wages of manual workers in five branches. Graphing these between 1870 and 1912 (based on Tables I Fm and 3 Pm) suggests that money wages in each branch rose and fell roughly in step, although the number of gaps in the series means that any such judgement must be tentative.

Germany Similar observations of a stable wage structure despite changes in aggregate money wages can also be found in Bry's (1960) study of wages in Germany between 1871 and 1945, particularly for the inter-war period. Inter-branch comparisons before 1914 are sketchy, but indicate some tendency for branch pay levels to move together over the economic cycle. Between 1871 and 1913, his series on wage rates and earnings in selected industries (Bry Chart 12) shows pay of miners, metal, railway, print and building workers responding to the same aggregate business cycles, with the exception of building workers between 1900 and 1913. Moreover, his data on cotton spinning wages show similar movements over much of the period (Bry Table A–9).

The United States For the United States between 1860 and 1890, rank correlations between industry annual earnings in 1860, 1870, 1880 and 1890 show that industries' earnings levels moved increasingly together. Using Long's (1960) series derived from the censuses, the correlations between

1860 and 1870, 1870 and 1880, and 1880 and 1890 are 0.73, 0.86 and 0.98 respectively. Some additional, but weaker, support can be derived from his other series on daily wages based on the Aldrich Report series which show a similar tendency (the correlations being 0.86, 0.81 and 0.96 respectively). This would indeed be consistent with Aglietta's contention that there was a gradual move away from competitive regulation towards the end of the century. However, year-on-year correlations for eighteen industries based on the Weeks Report series (Long 1960) show uniformly high values of 0.95 and above, with only two exceptions over the twenty years between 1860 and 1880 (Pearson correlations based on the series in Table A–3). Thus, for the United States also it seems that inter-industry wage differentials did not respond much to short-run variations in the economic conditions affecting individual industries.

This leaves something of a paradox. Under conditions of competitive regulation in the decades leading up to the First World War the high degree of flexibility in aggregate money wages was not reflected in corresponding responsiveness of money earnings to the conditions of individual industry labour markets. The stability of the inter-industry wage structure would only be consistent with the fully blown model of competitive regulation if either all industries shared the same global labour market for homogeneous labour, or alternatively if all their product markets were so closely interconnected that they fluctuated in unison. But both of these possibilities seem equally unlikely. Labour market skills were highly differentiated and transferable between industries to a limited extent only, and it is unlikely that the degree of substitutability between different categories was such as to even out labour demand fluctuations between industries and occupations. Product market conditions varied considerably between individual industries.

(c) Wage structure in the inter-war years

The inter-war years provide less of a critical test for the theory of regulation as applied to the labour market, as both Aglietta and Boyer see it as something of a transition period. Nevertheless, the depressions of 1920 and 1929 had a sharp effect upon the level of aggregate money earnings, and so again one might expect some evidence of flexibility in industry relative wages. However, the available series indicate that for all four countries the inter-industry wage structure was highly stable. Rank correlations between years were uniformly high in Britain (Department of Employment 1971 Table 9), Germany (Bry 1960 Table 28), and in the US (Cullen 1956). For France, again using Kuczynski's series, Boyer (1978) found a somewhat stronger tendency for the four branches (construction, metal working, mining and textiles) to move together. For skill differentials in wage rates in the inter-war period, in all four countries there was a reduction during the First World War, but they were mostly stable through the 1920s and early 1930s. In Britain and the US they began a long decline through the Second World War and into the 1950s, but showed little sign of cyclical fluctuations (Saunders and Marsden 1981). Moreover, neither Routh (1980) nor Knowles and Robertson (1951) found any tendency for skill differentials in Britain in the 1920s and 1930s to vary with changes in unemployment.

For Aglietta and Boyer, the inter-war years were a period of transition, with the United States and Germany more advanced than either Britain or France. Nevertheless, the apparent dominance of wage relativities over sectoral demand movements, implied by the high year-to-year correlations, even in this period, must cast some doubt on their model.

Thus, taking both periods together, one must conclude that the evidence of money wage flexibility at the aggregate level is not supported by equivalent flexibility of sectoral wages in response to sectoral demand movements, particularly in western Europe. This casts considerable doubt on Aglietta's and Boyer's interpretation of aggregate wage flexibility in the late nineteenth century as indicating a period of competitive labour markets free of the constraints on wage levels which emerged later. This is does not necessarily undermine their broader thesis about the shift from competitive to monopolistic regulation, but it suggests it needs qualification in the labour market. Their view of nineteenth century labour markets takes no account of the influence of the factors discussed in Chapter 4, such as the norms of customary and fair pay which Rowe and Clay felt were so important in Britain before the First World War. The pay structure the latter authors described was already in place when union membership represented a tenth or less of the labour force, but then working people have long had many ways of defending their working practices and their incomes other than trade unions. Their view also takes little account of the existing patterns of labour market organisation whose strength and potential influence on employers' strategies they underestimate.

6.7. CONCLUSIONS

The aim of this chapter has been to examine the theory of capitalist regulation developed by Aglietta, Boyer and Mistral as applied to labour markets. It was chosen in preference to the more familiar work on segmentation because it offered a more systematic framework for analysis of labour market structure. Their argument was that, under competitive regulation, labour markets worked in a way not dissimilar to the competitive labour markets of standard economic theory. Skills were such that employers could easily turn to their local labour markets for recruitment, and would lay off workers in recession. Changes in individual or collective bargaining power among workers were such that money wages would vary in relation to the demand for labour—thus the central argument of these authors concerning the flexibility of money wages over the economic cycle under competitive regulation.

Under monopolistic regulation, large firms internalise many functions of the labour market, partly as the result of the technical changes and the development of large scale units of production which implies a different organisation of skills, as provided by Taylorism, and partly under pressure from unions as a result of the growth of collective bargaining. This stabilisation of part of the labour force has the additional important consequence of providing greater stability of employment and income for the workers concerned, thus assisting the development of a mass market for consumer durables. The provision of more stable employment conditions and the development of internal labour markets limits the ability of firms to adjust to short-term economic fluctuations, and thus both Aglietta, and Boyer (1980), suggest that the lot of other sections of the labour force has been to provide a buffer. In this respect, there is a good deal of overlap with the thinking of Piore (1978 and 1980) on dualism as a response to uncertainty in product markets.

Azouvi's (1981) and Aglietta's (1978) critique of the segmentation theories is that they have neglected the macro-economic framework, and have sought to account for segmentation as if it were a general rather than a historically specific phenomenon. But their critique depends upon the validity of the macro-economic framework set forth. The main weaknesses in their model analysed in this chapter related to their views of technical change, of Taylorism, and of the nature of money wage flexibility.

First, their analysis of the labour process and labour market effects of the shift to monopolistic regulation rely heavily upon the effects of the technical change and economies of scale upon management strategies. Their argument is that technical and economic advantages of large scale organisations favour their development, and that these create the need for new patterns of work organisation different from those associated with the craft skills which had wide currency on local labour markets under competitive regulation. However, the managerial strategies can be considerably more varied than these authors allow, as is illustrated by some of the material from the Future of the Automobile Project. This study indicates both that past strategies of management have been influenced by the institutional structure of local labour markets in the countries in which the firms operate, and this has led to very different balance between use of internal and local labour markets in different countries. A corollary of this is the different development of Taylorism in different countries, it being for example less developed in Britain or France than in the United States. Indeed, Touraine's (1955) analysis of work organisation at the Renault car plant suggested that not only had Taylorist methods of work organisation not been fully extended throughout the firm, but it was not likely to be so either, as it was an intermediate pattern of organisation (his phase B).

The other main weakness in their hypothesis relates to the small degree of flexibility of relative wages at the time when aggregate money wages responded most to changes in general economic conditions. Boyer (1978) suggested that under competitive regulation money wages of workers in individual industries would be sensitive to changes in the demand for labour in those industries. As the demand for the product of individual industries varies, and does not necessarily fluctuate at the same time as in other industries, one would expect different industries to face different labour market conditions at any one time so that the inter-industry wage structure should be fairly flexible in the short run. It would also be flexible in the longer run if there were changes in skill composition, for example. But in the absence of such changes, one would expect short-run flexibility in the relative pay levels of different branches. However, except for the first part of the nineteenth century in France (similar data were not traced for the other countries), such flexibility appears to have been extremely limited in Britain, France, Germany and the United States both in the latter part of the nineteenth century and later. And Bry's (1960) analysis of Germany suggests that the variations in money wages occurred with a lag after changes in the level of activity, indicating considerable inertia in the labour market even under the period of supposed competitive regulation.

Thus it would appear that, although Aglietta and Boyer have pointed to a number of important developments in the organisation of labour markets and sketched possible relations with the macro-economic system, on the whole labour markets in the nineteenth century did not match up to the competitiveness and wage flexibility supposed by the competitive mode. It is a mistake to underestimate the importance even in the nineteenth century of social regulation of labour markets which may well help to account for some of the linkages in pay structure. Sydney and Beatrice Webb (1902) compiled an impressive list of methods of labour market reguation developed by trade unions, showing that joint regulation was already an important part of union activity in Britain by the end of the nineteenth century, and that it extended far beyond bargaining over wages. Union density then was low (about 10 per cent or less), but union action is only one form of working class action, and collective bargaining only one channel through which social forces influence labour markets. A number of examples of customary regulation of wages were given in Chapter 4. Phelps Brown and Browne's work on skill differentials over seven centuries suggests that ideas of customary differentials, even if they have some basis in economic reality, are extremely powerful and long lasting, and may be more powerful than short-run labour market pressures. In short, the main objection to the theory of regulation as a framework for understanding labour market structure is that the processes generating labour market structure are to a great extent independent of the system of regulation, and, one could argue, in some cases logically and historically prior to it.

7 Unions, Employers and Labour Market Organisation

7.1. INTRODUCTION

Trade unions and, to a much lesser extent, employers' associations are attributed a major role in labour market theory, but it is usually assumed, as in the examples in Chapter 2, that that labour is homogeneous, or that the union is representing workers of the same skill. There is an implicit assumption that the occupational structure of the labour force and the structure of the labour market determine the structure of trade union representation. This is also implicit in the more traditional approach to the economic analysis of collective bargaining which focuses on the elasticity of the demand for labour in which the demand curve relates to a particular category of labour.

The aim of this chapter is to question this assumption that the organisation of workers' and employers' representation is determined by labour market boundaries, and to develop two main arguments. The first seeks to show that the institutions representing workers and employers can influence the shape of labour markets as these bodies determine many of the rules regulating them, so that the relationship is a reciprocal one. Secondly, it seeks to show that in determining these rules, these institutions are not mere transmission belts for market and technical forces. Although pressures from markets and production methods influence the organisation of these institutions, there are also other factors which shape their structure and their powers, notably the struggle for bargaining advantage. The structure of representation and the division of powers between different levels of bargaining is often itself the outcome of negotiation. These too can influence the rules governing labour markets.

Two problems arise when one seeks to tie institutional organisation to labour market boundaries. The first is that in collective bargaining an employer or an employers' association usually faces a coalition of different occupational groups, each of which in this analysis might face a different demand elasticity and have different supply curves. The second, which will be the main subject of this chapter, is that in practice the relationship between collective bargaining and labour market organisation is a reciprocal one, and causation does not run in one direction only.

At first sight, this point may seem simple enough, and not much of a threat to standard partial equilibrium analysis of monopolistic unions bargaining with single large employers. In that analysis, both union organisation and the skill group can be taken as given in the short run, and it does not much matter which factor causes which, or whether both are caused by outside factors. But in the longer run it introduces another dimension to unions' and employers' action.

However, it becomes more important for the general theory of trade union action, and it matters particularly for theories which seek to explain how unions, and other forms of labour market collective organisation, might develop out of an otherwise competitive labour market. This was one of the methodological postulates mentioned in the first chapter, and encountered at a number of points in subsequent chapters, such as in the discussion of Alchian, and of Doeringer and Piore. If it can be shown that labour market actors can also exert a significant influence upon the shape of labour markets, then it is no longer valid to take a competitive market as the starting point for explaining the action of institutions upon labour markets.

This chapter starts by examining the action of unions and other forms of collective organisation in determining the boundaries of labour markets, and how they can affect the impact of technical change upon these boundaries. It will also look more generally at the role of institutional frameworks for labour markets, highlighting the important function of institutional rules. Bringing out the importance of such rules does not wholly demonstrate the reciprocal nature of the influence of institutional arrangements and labour market boundaries on each other. To explore this more fully, it is necessary to look more closely at the pattern of interaction between the parties involved. Dunlop's systems theory provides a famous model of how labour market rules are determined by employers, worker representatives and government agencies. It also has the advantage of considering the influence of many of the pressures that would be thought important by labour economists, such as technical and product market pressures. If Dunlop can show that these influences are the predominant ones shaping labour market rules, then the economist's approach to union action is largely justified, and one has to recognise that although such institutions are very important for policy analysis, they are to some extent only the channels through which market forces prevail. If, on the other hand, it can be shown that pressures from within an industrial relations system may also often prevail, for example, which derive from the structure of the main actors, then the case for treating institutional influences in their own right is much stronger.

The latter part of the chapter is devoted to an analysis of some evidence relating to this derived mainly from a comparison between French and German firms whose production methods, size and product markets were similar. This concludes that the institutional processes can indeed override technical and market constraints. The chapter ends with a short analysis of the way in which the bargaining relationship between the actors also influences their internal structure and organisation.

7.2. WORKERS' AND EMPLOYERS' ORGANISATIONS AND THE DEFINITION OF LABOUR MARKETS

The treatment of trade unions and employers' associations in economic theory has focused almost exclusively on wage and employment objectives and wage negotiations within a framework of occupational groups and labour markets whose boundaries have already been established, presumably by technical requirements for particular types of

skill. For example, in the recent attempts to provide a
micro-economic basis for studying union behaviour (see
Chapter 2), it was generally assumed that labour was homogeneous (except with respect to seniority) or that one was
dealing with a single skill group. In this section it is argued
that more attention needs to be given to the way in which
unions and employers' associations themselves shape the
boundaries of labour markets. If this is right, it then follows
that it is not satisfactory to treat collective bargaining as a
relationship of bilateral monopoly within pre-existing labour
markets, except in the short term. Trade union structure
and the levels at which bargaining takes place are generally
treated by economists as something which has little influence
on the outcome of negotiations, the main exception being,
in the UK literature, the empirical work on the impact on
wage levels of a worker's being covered by a local or by a
national agreement, but this has not given rise to much
theoretical discussion. But once one recognises the role of
bargaining and other forms of institutional regulation in
determining the scope and boundaries of many labour markets, the two questions of the structure of unions and
employers' associations (the structure of the actors) and of
the articulation of bargaining levels, and the way their
jurisdiction is divided up, become very important. This is
because the boundaries of labour markets and levels of
bargaining are not fixed in accordance with the interests of
one party only, but are themselves determined by bargaining.

To show the influence of bargaining and other institutions
on the boundaries of labour markets, it will first be shown
that, in the unionised sector, bargaining relationships maintain labour market boundaries, and that they also influence
their evolution. Technical change may often be important,
but there are other determining factors which may often
override the influence of technology.

To counter objections that the argument rests too heavily
upon unionised labour markets in whch bargaining is well
established, attention will also be focused on a less unionised
labour market, that for engineers. It will be shown that 'the
market for engineers' also depends upon a good deal of

institutional regulation, and it will be shown that one of the key diagnoses of the weakness of engineers in Britain, according to the Finniston report, is that there is no effective occupational labour market for professional engineers, and that one has to be created.

(a) Labour market boundaries in unionised markets

The maintenance of labour market boundaries by union action is perhaps most strongly illustrated by the behaviour of craft unionism in Britain with its emphasis upon 'job territories'. Put simply, the underlying principle is that the members of a particular craft have the exclusive right to undertake a particular set of tasks out of the whole set within an enterprise, and that this constitutes their 'job territory'. Sometimes specific tasks are referred to; sometimes the criterion of the type of material to be handled is used. Such groupings of work tasks into job territories are not inconsistent with high levels of technical competence, but the underlying principle is different. Such job territories have been documented in both Britain and the United States, and the boundaries around such labour markets are defended by demarcation principles. Indeed, among the first to use the term 'job territory' was Perlman (1928 especially pp. 273–5) in describing the principles of union organisation in the United States, and Kerr (1950 and 1954) writing on the balkanisation of labour markets, also in the United States. The latter author was among the first to spell out the importance of the distinction between craft and industrial labour markets. In Britain, although such demarcation principles are most typically strongly associated with craft jobs, and in particular with maintenance work, similar methods have been adopted by other unions for other occupational groups. Two main reasons stand out. First, the craft groups have been historically the strongest and most effectively organised groups within the labour movement, and they had already developed a method of job regulation which later unions could borrow. Secondly, if one group within a factory has appropriated a set of tasks into its exclusive job territory, other groups in the same factory will then feel under pressure to carve out their own areas of exclusive working in order to defend their supply of work. Moreover, a strong craft system among skilled labour means that individual employers can develop their own internal labour markets to only a limited extent because the access to the most skilled manual jobs is closed to those without apprenticeships.

In West Germany, where there is also a system in which access to skilled manual jobs is mostly by apprenticeship, and where such skills similarly have a form of craft market which extends across several firms, a different principle is used—that of *Leistung* or of technical competence based on training rather than of particular sets of tasks. Employers have greater flexibility in job design, and greater ease of adaptation to technical change because of the more abstract definition of skilled work, but the role of institutions in delimiting skilled labour markets is nevertheless strong. Two institutions play a central role: the chambers of industry and commerce whose training committees are essentially bipartite and so depend upon agreement between unions and employers, and the works councils, which regulate the passage to skilled work within the enterprise subject to individual workers passing the required examinations. Indeed, once workers have passed the necessary exams, they can go onto a waiting list for promotion, and the employer has to justify to the works council cases in which there is an excessive delay. This represents a considerable reduction of managerial prerogative in the definition of vacancies. Thus, the standards of competence required for access to skilled work, which define the skilled labour markets, are closely controlled by institutional rules. Moreover, such rules determine the boundaries between different types of skill. Because there is no tradition of craft unionism, and because of the greater control employers gained over training and over skilled work early in German industrialisation, German employers today have greater influence over the shaping of skills and thus of skilled labour markets than their British counterparts.

Nevertheless, a recent study by Streeck (1985) of the reform of apprentice training in the West German construction industry in the 1970s highlights the important role of relations between unions and employers' associations in reaching agreement on the private provision of funding of apprentice training in that branch, and the reorganisation of its specialisms. Streeck also stressed heavily the public good aspect of apprentice training, and the consequent need for private or public regulation, an argument to be taken up in Chapter 8.

In France, and Japan, the institutional shaping of skilled labour markets within enterprise internal labour markets is more notable still, and to some extent has already been discussed in the chapters on labour market structure. Both countries have sought to create skilled labour markets extending across several firms, in Japan in 1959 with the establishment of an apprenticeship-type examination (Dore 1973), and in France at various times this century (see Maurice, Sellier and Silvestre 1978). Nevertheless, in neither country has it really taken root, being undermined by the more attractive conditions in the large firms' internal labour markets in Japan, and both by the prevalence of internal labour markets for skilled jobs, and by the attractiveness of the general education stream in France and the consequent low esteem of vocational training. This again illustrates that, although technology and product and labour markets may be influential, there is no technical or economic necessity that skilled labour be organised on occupational or multi-employer labour markets. (In the same way in Chapter 5 it was argued that this necessity did not apply either to internal labour market organisation.) It also illustrates the capacity of the interests surrounding existing patterns of labour market organisation to undermine such initiatives.

In addition, existing institutional norms often help mould the evolution of skilled jobs and their markets in response to technical change. Some of the recent changes in British industry in response to the 'micro-electronics revolution' provide good examples. The Electrical, Electronic, Telecommunication and Plumbing Union (EETPU), which organises electricians, has been at the centre of these changes, and party to many of the agreements concerning who should work on the new electronically controlled equipment which straddles traditional job territories of both electrical and mechanical crafts. Into which skilled labour markets should the new tasks go, and, of course, which union's members should have access to them? For example, in the British car firm, Austin Rover, on the new assembly lines on which robotic equipment has been installed there have been a series of agreements on reducing the number of skilled trades involved in maintenance of the new equipment, and Austin Rover has currently negotiated a system of 'two trades response' so that maintenance of a particular piece of automated equipment is allocated to an electrician plus one mechanical craft. Previously, such work could have involved several different crafts depending on whose particular job territories individual tasks fell into. Willman and Winch (1984) stress that the idea of 'two trades response' is that while reducing the number of different crafts required to maintain a particular machine, it does not imply any change in the organisation of these crafts, as they retain their own apprenticeship provisions and craft traditions. Progress towards negotiating the introduction of 'multi-skilling' which gives a craftsman expertise in several disciplines has been much slower and much more strongly resisted by the unions.

The EETPU has been busy adapting its apprenticeship arrangements to ensure that it can increase the supply of suitably trained electricians quickly enough to meet the new demand and to avoid the danger of substitution by other crafts or other types of worker. It has also set up its own training school to enable some of its members to keep abreast of technical change. By this action, the EETPU is able to determine the evolution of the extent and type of work to fall within its members' labour market. It also maintains its members' exclusive right of access to this work (need for the union card). Similarly, in the printing industry, the recent agreement between the employers and the National Graphical Association which reduces apprenticeship requirements because of the now high degree of automation, divides up work of inputing material through word processors and automatic print setting equipment between NGA members and members of other print unions. Again this shapes the evolution of their particular labour market, and the fact that the work is divided between three different groups with quite different training illustrates that the technical nature of the work is not the determining factor in shaping these markets (although the technical changes have made this division possible). Other examples of similar changes in skill demarcations, and thus in the scope of individual craft labour markets, can be found in many other industries, such as British Steel and British Shipbuilders (see *Chronicle*, BJIR July 1984). It should, however, be stressed that while this has led to a big increase in flexibility of deployment of labour and in productivity in craft work in British industry, the basic craft principles of job territories have not changed. The territories have been redefined in the face of new technology, and in the realisation that their previous delineations made labour utilisation relatively inefficient when compared with Japanese and other countries' competition. Some of the most striking changes have occurred in those industries most exposed to foreign competition.

Do changes in other countries similarly illustrate institutional mechanisms reshaping labour markets? In the United States' automobile industry there have been parallels to the changes in the British car industry, notably in the relaxation of demarcation rules defining seniority districts. In France and Italy, employers have exerted considerable pressure to ease the rules governing their internal labour markets, notably by pressing for relaxation of certain rules on the use of labour, and by an increased use of subcontracting work to specialist firms, which involves pushing certain work back into external labour markets (see Freyssinet 1982). But in France too, the break-up of the national level negotiations on flexibility in 1984 illustrates the great difficulty of altering such rules. In West Germany, much of the reaction to pressures from technical change, and from the need to increase efficiency in the skill area, is handled through the chambers of industry and commerce, and the works councils.

While linkages between the wage levels set in different

labour markets have long been recognised in the establishment of wage rounds and of wage contours, which also usually require bargaining for their establishment and maintenance, the argument of the present section concerns more the way in which demand for labour and its supply are divided into different labour markets which are administered separately. While there may well be a number of labour markets which do not depend upon such arrangements, as argued in Chapter 8, it is likely that these are a minority, and in the next few paragraphs it will be shown that even in a weakly unionised labour market, that for engineers, the definition of the boundaries of the market, within which forces of supply and demand interact, still depends upon institutional administration, and that there is no naturally occurring market for that particular 'occupation'.

(b) The labour market for engineers

It might be thought that engineering skills would provide the technical basis on which a labour market for transferable skills would develop. Apart from a minimal need to certify the quality of people's training, one might expect such a market to flourish with only minimal institutional support. Moreover, in view of its potential scale in terms of the number of workers and employers standing to benefit, one might have expected there to be sufficient demand for the establishment of such a market. Yet the Finniston Report (Finniston 1980) was set up by the British government in 1979 in order to suggest remedies to the weakness of the engineering profession in Britain. After studying the British engineering profession compared with that in other countries it concluded that its weakness and unattractiveness to bright young recruits and to employers was because the profession lacked a strong labour market identity which strong professional regulation would have given it.

As the Finniston Report stressed, many countries have a system of registration for engineers. For example, in the United States, the Engineers' Council for Professional Development (ECPD), formed by the professional societies offers guidance to schools of engineering and accredits the degree courses of those meeting its standards on form and content. For non-academic training and experience (beyond an accredited degree) required for professional qualifications, the National Council of Engineering Examiners (NCEE) provides parallel guidelines. In addition, each state has its own machinery to test aspirant engineers, and generally applies NCEE tests, and accords recognition of the title of Professional Engineer. State registration is required in order to work as a consultant engineer, but not for employment in industry—although Finniston pointed out that there were moves in this direction, and that in any case many engineers chose to register for the recognition and status.

In West Germany, specialised engineering schools, the *Fachhochschule* and the *Technische Hochschule*, provide the diplomas of the middle level Ing. Grad, and the higher level Dipl. Ing, which serves the function of accreditation, and the schools are recognised as the sole qualifying agencies. These schools, it should be said, are part of the broader system of technical education in West Germany, which also provides the strength of the apprenticeship and the foremen's labour market status.

In France, the skills of engineers are developed and certified by the engineering schools (*Grandes Ecoles*), the top nine or ten Parisian ones forming something of a labour market apart. But there, the middle level ranks of engineers are much more weakly organised, with a high proportion of managers formed by experience and in-house training (*cadres autodidactes*, or *cadres maison*, Maurice, Sellier and Silvestre 1978). As the employment problems of the latter show, their labour market is much more weakly constituted.

The contrast with Britain is revealing. The Finniston Committee found that engineers had no clear social identity, and a survey they commissioned showed that about two-thirds of respondents thought engineers did manual work—no doubt because the occupational title extends from fitters and electricians such as 'telephone engineers', or 'heating engineers' to the designers and builders of bridges. While this might be the result of linguistic confusion in the wider community, within companies their enquiries also found that engineers had little clear professional identity, even though many might have university degrees in engineering, or have undertaken part-time education in the subject. This lack of professional recognition they suggested was also reflected in engineers' pay levels in industry, and in their poor degree of representation on company boards. In addition, the evidence to the Committee suggested that, in many cases, companies did not define engineering work and vacancies in their own organisations at all clearly, which added to their under-utilisation of engineering skills. For example, the Institution of Electrical Engineers reported:

A significant proportion of engineering graduates are engaged in work appropriate to technician engineers. This is sometimes because employers do not, or cannot, provide opportunities for the promotion of young engineers who have the capacity to undertake responsibilities appropriate to chartered engineers. In such cases the employers are not exploiting the full potential of their young engineers. (Finniston 1980 p. 58)

and the Institution of Mechanical Engineers reported:

We were, however, even more concerned by the charge that all too few job descriptions bear real comparison with the actual task—the successful candidate finds himself given work quite different from that which he is led to expect. At best, this suggests an inability on the part of personnel managers either to define a vacancy or to specify and recognise the type of engineer to match it. (Finniston 1980 p. 58)

The Report suggests that this indicates a lack of understanding by senior managers of what engineering work involves because many of them have no engineering training, but it is also a further indicator of the poor degree of awareness of engineering skills, and organisation of the occupation and its labour market. Another indicator of the weakness of the labour market for engineers that Finniston highlighted was the resulting difficulty of attracting the more able pupils into scientific subjects at school, and into engineering degrees at university.

The solution the committee put forward was to restructure the formal training leading to engineering qualifications, to introduce registration of engineers, to establish a special authority to oversee these arrangements, and to coordinate the activities of the large number of independent engineering institutions. Thus, although British companies might need the technical expertise engineers bring to their employers in other countries, Finniston argued they were not getting it because of the poor organisation, and the weak definition of the labour market for engineers. In a word, Finniston wanted to establish a market for engineering skills so that companies would recognise their need for them, and be able to call forth a supply of suitably able and qualified manpower.

To conclude, the example from unionised and less organised occupations illustrates that even where one might expect that a technical skill would provide a natural basis for the emergence of a corresponding market for a transferable skill, the absence of institutional regulation can give rise to under-utilisation of skills, poor rewards, and poor quality. Finniston contrasted the consequences of lack of such organisation in Britain with the effectiveness of the engineering profession in other countries where professional organisation of the labour market was much stronger.

These examples illustrate how the labour market boundaries of certain occupations are regulated, and also how a common technical basis does not necessarily give rise to an occupational labour market even though the number of workers and employers potentially benefiting would be large. The manual crafts also illustrate how the institutional framework can influence the dividing up of new tasks arising from new technology among existing crafts. This does suggest a considerable degree of independence of action by unions, and professional associations, over the evolution of the structure of labour markets, but before pursuing this further it is necessary to look at the problem in relation to the action of both unions and employers.

7.3. ACTORS AND LABOUR MARKET RULES

A well-known framework for examining the development of the rules governing worker–employer relations and those

governing labour market organisation is provided by Dunlop's (1958) industrial relations system theory. It covers
both procedural rules which govern the conduct of relations
between the parties, and substantive rules which govern
items including job classification, craft training, pay, and
health and safety rules. One of his prime interests was to
examine how these rules were influenced by the technical
context of production, the market context, and the overall
power context of an industrial relations system.

His concern with the technical and market contexts places
him fairly close to many labour economists. Hence, a central
reason for interest in Dunlop's systems theory is that it
would appear to provide a promising institutional framework for examining labour markets. Could one, for
example, use his model or a similar one to provide the
institutional mechanisms through which labour and product
market forces work in practice? If it could be shown that
the dominant influences on the rules generated within an
industrial relations system were indeed the technical and
market contexts, then it could be argued that much of the
institutionalist critique of current labour economics falls
short of its objective. It could then be said that institutional
rules are important in the labour markets of the real world,
but they do not necessarily lead to different outcomes from
those predicted by standard economic theory. This and the
next section therefore looks more closely at Dunlop's theory
of industrial relations systems, and in particular at some of
the evidence on the determinants of substantive rules.

Dunlop's theory of industrial relations systems provides
a framework within which the interaction of many of these
processes can be conceptualised. The key components of
such systems are the actors, namely workers and their organisations, managerial hierarchies, and government agencies.
The output of the system is procedural and substantive
rules. Finally, there is an ideology which 'binds the system
together'. Dunlop held that the influences shaping the rules
of an industrial relations system fell into three broad categories: the technical, the market or budgetary, and the power
contexts. The technical context covers such factors as technical determinants of work organisation, scheduling and

location. The market context covers such factors as variability or stability of markets and the degree of competition. These two sets of factors, Dunlop suggested, would affect mostly the substantive rules such as pay structures, the nature of remuneration and rules of the workplace. On the other hand, the power context expressed the locus and distribution of power in the wider society, and would shape especially the procedural rules of the system such as those for determining the scope of bargaining units, or the legitimacy of different pressure tactics.

Dunlop applied his theory in two case studies of industrial relations systems comparing rules in the bituminous coal mining and in the construction industries in different countries. In both branches, he saw the strongest influence on substantive rules as arising from the technical and the market contexts, which he illustrated in the mining industry by showing the similarity in different countries of rules governing accidents and safety, concessionary coal, housing and rents, wet and high temperature conditions, the measurement of the working day, tools and protective clothing, and hiring and lay-offs. In the construction industry, his examples covered rules governing travel time and bad weather working, tool allowances and lay-offs and hiring—substantive rules determined by technical conditions. Similarly, reflecting the market context, he showed the similarity of rules in different countries governing job classifications, wage levels, supplements, and piecework in mining, and apprenticeships and protection of standard conditions in the construction industry. These, he argued, reflected common responses to common problems posed by the technical and market contexts.

The biggest differences between the countries begin to emerge when he considers the rules concerning such questions as the status of the actors, the scope of the rules, and dispute settlement rules that reflect the different power contexts and different national industrial relations systems. This second set of rules is essentially procedural rather than substantive. On this point, Dunlop's case studies are less convincing as the examples of rules that he gives would seem to be more determined by the national power context than the national industrial relations system, especially in mining, but that is less relevant to our immediate concern.

More important in the present argument is the evidence of Maurice *et al.* (1984) that the contexts do not necessarily produce similar sets of substantive rules once these are examined in greater detail. Their evidence brings to light the independent influence of the actors upon important labour market rules where technical and market contexts are held constant.

7.4. THE INDEPENDENT INFLUENCE OF ACTORS ON LABOUR MARKET RULES

Maurice, Sellier and Silvestre (1984) re-examined Dunlop's notion of the relationship between rules and actors using data from their own comparison of French and German firms. Whereas Dunlop's case studies suggested that similar contextual constraints would give rise to similar substantive rules in different countries, their own comparison of France and Germany had shown the existence of pronounced differences in substantive rules between firms with similar technical and market contexts but situated in one or the other country. These concerned a number of differences.

First, there were bigger pay differentials between blue collar workers and their white collar and technical colleagues in the French firms than in the German ones, but the French firms also employed the white collar and technical staff in greater numbers, an observation which seems to run against the idea that the market contexts were dominating. The wage differential did not appear to correspond to differences in relative factor scarcities. But they also found, as mentioned in Chapter 5, that the rules defining skill were different, as in the German firms they were based on the acquisition of a technical qualification, whereas in the French firms they were based on promotion through job grades within the company. The relations between supervisors and workers were also different, with a greater number of hierarchical levels and less delegation in the French firms, and there were also different principles governing promotion and the provision of training within the enterprise. This led them to conclude that Dunlop had attached too much weight to technical and market contexts in determining substantive rules. But what of the reciprocal influence of the actors' organisation upon the substantive rules?

One of the key factors distinguishing the two countries is the strong system of technical training in West Germany which is strongly defended by the unions and supported by the employers (who bear most of the cost, see Noll *et al*. 1984). This gives rise to a wide diffusion of technical knowledge within the enterprise so that many decisions can be quite successfully delegated, hence the shorter hierarchy in the German firms. In the French firms, where much of training is dispensed by the employer in the form of in-house training as and when needed, skilled workers are much more dependent upon their hierarchical superiors. A good deal of the difference can be explained by differences between the national educational systems of the two countries and the demands they make of enterprise level training rather than by the market or technical contexts. The French secondary education system, rather than select at entry into different stages, allows large numbers to enter the prestigious stream to the *Baccalauréat*, but large numbers then drop out without completing the diploma. These then enter the labour market with no completed qualification and little professional training, and employers have to make up the deficit. Thus French workers are deprived of the strong professional organisation of German workers, and are tied more to company internal labour markets. The difference in training also affects pay differentials between white and blue collar workers. In Germany, the manual and clerical hierarchies are fairly independent, each having their own field of expertise, and there is a good deal of overlap in pay levels (a clerical worker earns about as much as a semi-skilled manual worker). But in France, the greater dependence of blue collar skills upon their position in the hierarchy within the enterprise, and the tighter links between hierarchical levels because of the lesser amount of delegation, means that there is a more continuous hierarchy.

There clerical staff earn more than skilled manual workers. The differences of job classification, which for Dunlop were also substantive rules determined by technical and market contexts, can also be explained by the different response of French and German employers to different education and training systems.

Thus there is an important independent institutional influence on the substantive rules which arises from the interplay of the actors' strategies. Having held the market and technical contexts constant, Maurice *et al*'s. results do not disprove Dunlop's argument about the influence of market and technical contexts, but they do illustrate that the influence is a reciprocal one, and not from one side only.

7.5. THE INFLUENCE OF MARKET AND TECHNICAL CONTEXTS ON THE ACTORS' INTERNAL ORGANISATION

Nevertheless, it would be wrong to leave the impression that the influence of market and technical contexts on the actors and the structure of their relations is negligible. It can be important, as is illustrated by some of Dunlop's own examples.

For instance, the most important influences Dunlop quotes among market factors concern mainly the state of product markets, such as their degree of competition or monopoly, the nature and frequency of market fluctuations, and how diversified they are. These factors also have profound influences upon the state of the labour market, and upon the organisation of the actors and the type of rules they develop for regulating the market. For example, a highly decentralised product market with a great deal of local variation is likely to require a good deal of decentralised rule making to adapt to local conditions, whereas one dominated by a few very large producers providing similar products, such as in English retail banking or in the United States automobile industry, may have much more centralised arrangements.

He also gives examples of the effect of market contexts upon the organisation of the actors; he points out that more diversified market and cost conditions within an industry will lead to more decentralised rule making and a more decentralised structure for the actors (p. 76). As concerns the impact of the technical context on the organisation of the actors, he suggests that this conditions the points of contact between the hierarchies of actors. For example, in supervision, a high degree of geographical spread of operations requires greater autonomy for supervisors. In addition, it can influence the degree to which one group may obtain a strategic advantage in bargaining (pp. 59–61).

The other main influence upon the organisation and powers of the actors that Dunlop highlighted derived from the wider set of rules either of the industrial relations system, or of the society as a whole. This shaped the 'status' of the actors, but this is of less relevance to this discussion.

While right to point out the influence of such factors upon the organisation of the actors, Dunlop has probably overstated it and he has underestimated the extent to which choice of bargaining level can arise out of an interaction between system-wide rules and actors' strategies, as is well illustrated in the French case by Sellier's (1961) analysis of the strategic considerations weighing in the struggle between unions and employers to establish bargaining at the level which put their bargaining partner at the greatest disadvantage.

7.6. ACTORS AND RULES—RULES STRUCTURING ACTORS

So far, it has been argued that the institutional actors in the labour market play an important role in shaping the boundaries of labour markets, and that when they do this they are not merely transmission belts for market and technical forces, nor do they develop merely as a reflection of these forces. This final section seeks to illustrate how the internal organisation of these actors is often influenced by their bargaining relationship with each other, and that their structure at any time is in large part a reflection of a continual jockeying for advantage in their bargaining relation. The law is often deemed to have been a major influence shaping union-employer relations in West Germany, so it is of some interest to show that, even in this case, the effective division of functions between institutions and the forms of bargaining activity are also subject to this struggle for advantage.

One important feature of the relationship between employers' and workers' organisations is how it is often structured so that the issues subject to joint regulation are divided between the jurisdiction of different institutions. These could be different levels of bargaining, or they could be institutions functioning according to different types of logic, as for example occurs in West Germany with the division between wage bargaining at the industry level, and co-decision making at the company and plant level. It can be shown that these divide up the areas of joint regulation in such a way that one side is inhibited from exploiting a bargaining advantage it might have in one area in its negotiations at another (Marsden 1978).

The West German case is interesting because the power relationships have been apparently of vital importance in shaping the system in practice despite the apparently central role of industrial relations law in establishing the basic rules. In West Germany, the areas of negotiation and consultation between workers and their employers are divided into three broad areas, notably bargaining over such issues as basic wage rates and conditions of employment, co-decision making over application of these agreements at plant and company level, and over such issues as lay-offs, training and job evaluation, and joint decision making on long-term plans for the enterprise. The first of these three, bargaining over basic wage rates and conditions, carries a right to strike or lock-out, and involves trade unions and employers' associations, usually at the industry–regional level. The second, that of co-decision making, falls within the competence of the company or plant level works council and the management board, and the parties have to reach agreement over the issues within their bailiwick. Issues dealt with at this level which are 'fleshing out' the industry agreement have legally to be settled within the terms of that agreement, and the other issues subject to co-decision making, such as redundancies and training, are similarly treated under a peace obligation. The third area which concerns long-term issues, such as investment strategy, is subject to joint decision making between shareholder and employee members of upper tier of the two-tier board structure, the supervisory board. But at this level the shareholder representatives have a built-in majority enabling them to win any straight confrontation.

One might expect workers' representatives to try to use a bargaining advantage in one set of issues as leverage in discussions of another area. For example, they might try to back up negotiations on grading in the works council by pressure from industry level negotiations. But the division between each of these levels is such that the employee side can pursue a cooperative strategy quite successfully, but not a conflictual one. The unions, which bear the right to strike, are excluded as collective organisations from the works council's dealings with the employer, and would find it very difficult to exert pressure from outside to back up negotiations in progress between the works council and management. Moreover, the works council is unable to use its greater day-to-day contact with rank and file members in order to mobilise them for collective action in support of the union's negotiations. Neither can it link up with other works councils to refuse agreement with the employers over a particular question subject to co-decision making to support the union in its negotiations given their peace obligation, and the obligation to reach agreement. Similarly, neither the union nor the works council can bring pressure tactics to bear on the supervisory board, nor can they use their position on the board to support their dealing at the other levels. Thus employee representation is divided up between three main sets of issues dealt with by different institutions, and subject to different kinds of procedural rules.

German unions have been acutely aware of the strategic weakness this imposes on them, and have tried different policies to break down the divisions between these different levels, and in particular to break down their exclusion as collective bodies from the workplace, notably by developing a network of shop stewards, by building up individual union membership of works councils, and by attempting to develop direct union–company bargaining through the *Betriebsnahe Tarifpolitik*. The latter policy was soon abandoned because the employers refused to accept clauses making this possible in the industry-level wage agreements, and they never accepted that union shop stewards should displace the monopoly of representation accorded to the works council. Also, works councils have learned how to use wildcat strikes to avoid the peace obligation, although its use remains much more limited than in Britain and many other countries.

Although the basic structure of representation was determined by legislation, this should not obscure the intense pressure brought on the political process by employers and unions at times to change these institutions, for example over the extension of codetermination in the middle 1970s. But a key factor in making the institutions work the way they have has been the employers' determination to remain within the legally based institutions, and not to give way to decentralising pressures as did their counterparts in Britain and in Italy from the early 1960s. Thus it is fair to argue that even the apparently legalistic structure of employee representation in West Germany has been very much shaped by the conflicts between workers and employers, and if worker representation in West Germany is divided between these largely watertight institutions it is in no small measure due to the way in which employers have made the legal framework effective.

The contrast with Great Britain is particularly interesting because of the importance of mutual agreement between British workers' and employers' representatives, as opposed to legislation, for the establishment of the basic ground rules. In Britain the clauses of recognition and procedure agreements play a central role in this process of dividing up the areas of representation. These specify the areas of competence recognised to unions and to management, the types of issue that can be raised, and under what circumstances (e.g. whether they were subject to bargaining, consultation, or information only), the procedures by which recognised grievances can be handled, and the powers of shop stewards and union officials. Here the organisation of representation can be determined by bargaining, and will be subject to the power relations between the actors, and the functions given to them under existing institutions.

In this case, the structure of employee representation and its subsequent development reflected the outcome of conflicts, and of the desire of the employers' side to ensure that measures of joint regulation that were conceded under pressure from the workforce in the 1960s and 1970s were structured in such a way as to stabilise the areas of joint control, and to slow further encroachments into management's area of control.

A number of conclusions can be drawn which bear on how the actors can shape issues and rules with a degree of independence of the market and technical contexts. First, the dividing of issues dealt with at different institutional levels did not reflect inherent characteristics of the issues themselves, and they did not fall naturally into discrete categories such that one would expect certain issues always to be dealt with at the industry level and others at the company and the plant levels. Indeed, they were clustered differently in Britain, France and West Germany (Marsden 1978). A subsequent comparison of bargaining in the British and French engineering industries by Eyraud (1983) confirms this as many job- and skill-related issues were dealt with at the work group level in Britain, and at the plant level in France. An important factor explaining this difference lies in the structure and organisation of work groups and their power relations with management.

Secondly, the actors can influence the level many issues such as training, upgrading, labour utilisation and other employment conditions are dealt with. The level of negotiation can be very important in determining the working of labour market boundaries within the enterprise, for example. In Britain, the pattern of job control associated with the organisation of skilled work on the basis of job territories requires a high degree of job level representation. Shifting day-to-day regulation to a higher level would make enforcement of such rules more difficult. One of the criticisms of the Fawley productivity agreements was that they shifted job regulation from the work group to be the plant level, and from the shop stewards to union officials, weakening the workers' capacity to mobilise support around their customary rules. In contrast, the determination of grading and job boundaries at the level of the works council in West Germany leaves much less opportunity for job level regulation, and such questions have to be debated using the more abstract formulation of grievances appropriate to this level. These are not the only factors responsible for the different organisation of skilled work in Britain and West Germany, but they illustrate how the level of negotiation can affect job regulation. The relationship with other levels of negotiation can affect the factors brought to bear in any particular negotiation.

Another example of how a shift in bargaining level and the pattern of representation can affect skill utilisation can be found in the British and West Germany motor industries, although the focus is more on internal labour market conditions. In the British motor industry, the companies in which the development of shop floor bargaining seemed to have had the most damaging effect upon productivity, notably, BL, Talbot and Vauxhall, were those in which management had made the most piecemeal concessions bargaining with stewards in order to keep production moving. In contrast, Ford UK, although it had a much weaker performance than its sister plants in West Germany, never made as many concessions on issues over which shop stewards could bargain. It succeeded for example in maintaining a system of pay grades which facilitated job mobility within the plant, whereas the more complex pay structures of the other firms, partly conceded under pressure from the shop floor, inhibited the range of jobs between which people could be moved without affecting their earnings, and thus necessitating further bargaining. In the recovery in the British car industry, the management has been very aware of the cost of its past concessions. The German system of employee representation made it easier for the employers to resist shop floor pressures in the 1960s and 1970s, but they could easily have let their control slip had the German unions been more successful in pressing for shop stewards, or for direct negotiations between unions and individual companies. No doubt one factor behind the German employers' greater ease of deploying labour within the factory is in part the technical training system, but also important is the more centralised system of employee representation within the plant and enterprise so that these questions are dealt with in a less particularistic way with more attention to general principles such as production efficiency.

In so far as these institutional structures are affected by employers' desire to maintain their area of managerial prerogative, their success or failure in this is also likely to affect the development of particular labour markets. Finally, it should again be stressed that the purpose of this argument is not to deny the importance of labour markets and of labour market pressures on firms, but rather to stress the equal footing on which the institutions should be placed in our understanding and our theoretical models of labour markets.

7.7. CONCLUSIONS

This chapter has dealt with the fifth of the problems outlined in the introduction facing economists trying to bring a wider range of institutional and social factors into their analysis. This case concerned the nature of the labour market actors, and the assumptions that collective bargaining and trade union action were conterminous with the boundaries of individual labour markets. Making this assumption has facilitated the analysis of trade union action in wage bargaining, and in trade union objectives (as examined in

Chapter 2). This strategy involved maintaining broadly the conceptual space of labour markets while attributing the normal actors of the theory with different types of institutional structure. This involved grouping individual workers into unions and employers into employers' associations taking the bounds of the particular labour markets as given.

It was argued that although this might be valid for a short-run analysis, the delimitation of labour markets was not independent of the actors, and that the same workers' and employers' organisations which were involved in determining wage rates could also be involved in determining the scope of the labour markets on which they were acting. It was suggested that one had to treat labour markets as institutionally bounded phenomena, and not as determined solely by technical influences on the demand for labour and the economics of training. This point was illustrated for both unionised and non-unionised markets, showing that institutional regulation was as necessary to the non-unionised market for engineers.

This question was pursued through Dunlop's systems analysis which sought to establish a framework in which employers' and workers' representatives bargain to establish procedural and substantive rules subject to pressures from the market, technical and power contexts in which they operate. Attention was focused on the market and technical contexts because these were closest to the variables in economic models, and if he could show that these contexts exercised a determining influence on labour market rules, then it could be argued that actors do not really have a significant independent influence upon the rules defining labour markets, and their working.

In fact, evidence from the comparisons of France and West Germany (Maurice *et al.* 1984) showed that they did have some independent influence, confirming the view that the relations between actors and labour market boundaries were reciprocal. The chapter closed with further consideration of the dynamics of the relations between labour market actors, as to some extent their organisation is shaped by the outcome of their bargaining relation. This affects the powers of representatives, the issues open to bargaining, and the levels at which they may be handled. This structuring can also affect the important aspects of the working of labour markets, such as the deployment of labour between jobs and between parts of the plant, vital for the working on internal labour market.

To conclude, the boundaries of many labour markets are fixed by institutional rules determined by the main actors, and there is a reciprocal influence between these as the actors help shape labour markets, and the labour markets contribute to shaping the actors. This suggests that it is mistaken to try to explain trade union action and objectives in terms of models which start out from the hypothesis of a given skill group or from homogeneous labour, and then ask what services or functions unions would have to fulfil if people were to join them. The same point applies to the traditional monopoly model of trade unions, which is only valid in the short run when its labour market boundaries can be assumed to be fixed for the particular group it is representing. In the longer run, the boundaries and organisation of labour markets, as well as the levels at which the actors negotiate, are variable and may themselves be the object of negotiation.

The next chapter begins by exploring why labour markets, even fairly competitive occupational markets, might be institutional phenomena and dependent upon a strong institutional underpinning.

8 An Alternative Approach to Labour Markets

8.1. INTRODUCTION

The theme of this book has been the attempts by economists to analyse the influence of normative and institutional forces on labour markets in such a way as to maintain broadly the conceptual framework of micro-economic theory. The various strategies used by economists share a number of common features, notably, the idea that in the long run competitive conditions are the norm, and that the development of institutions should be understood as a response by the actors of microeconomic theory to certain market failures, or that social norms could be influential, but only within the limits set by long-run competitive forces. This chapter argues that this perspective should be revised, that stable multi-employer labour markets, especially for skilled labour, are themselves institutional phenomena, and that unless certain conditions are met, the higher the degree of skill involved, the more the natural long-run pattern for labour markets is that of internal labour markets rather than occupational markets. The fact that employers commonly bear much of the cost of training even for transferable skills and experience generates pressures towards the internalisation of labour markets, which means that without institutional support, occupational markets tend to be unstable.

This argument seeks to show why, even within the terms of standard economic theory, labour markets are on the whole so imperfect, why relative wages so rarely behave in the way theory would predict, and why occupational labour markets so often are characterised by quite wide dispersions of earnings between firms within the same locality. It also seeks to shed further light on Marshall's question as to why the market for labour differed so much from that for other goods. It is hoped that it also provides a basis from which

economists can work more easily with sociologists and industrial relations specialists, as is illustrated later by a brief
discussion of three recent research projects, each of which
sets out recognising the institutional nature of labour
markets, and cross disciplinary boundaries in their analysis.

Labour markets, and especially those for skilled labour,
are institutional phenomena in that they depend upon an
institutional underpinning. Such a contention may seem
uncontroversial for internal labour markets, but this chapter
will argue that the same also applies to the multi-employer
markets for skilled labour, which should, along with casual
and unskilled markets, be those most closely resembling the
competitive markets of economic theory. It will be argued
that, in practice, occupational labour markets can be very
difficult to maintain, and have an inherent tendency to
break down, unless there is some institutional framework,
because they are like 'public goods'. Indeed, because of
these tendencies, one might expect company internal labour
markets to be the natural state of affairs, and that, if
anything, one should have to explain how occupational
markets sometimes emerge when employers have developed
their own internal labour markets. The main force of the
argument relates to skilled labour, but it applies, albeit less
strongly, to semi-skilled labour where the same tension
exists between internalisation and inter-firm mobility. It was
shown in Chapters 5 and 7 that internal labour markets and
occupational labour markets were, to a considerable extent,
alternative ways of organising labour markets, even where
technology, product markets, and firm size were comparable.

If the argument is right, then a number of points follow,
two of the most important being that at any time the number
of occupational markets will be limited, remaining skill
requirements being met usually by internal labour markets,
and that firms will usually fall back on their own internal
markets if occupational markets fail or are not available.
Consequently, the scope for competitive pressures within
the labour market is greatly reduced. Competitive pressures
from product markets overall will often be important, but

their ability to bring the relative pay of a particular occupation into line, or to eliminate a particular inefficient labour practice will be greatly blunted. The force of the Marshallian long run is also reduced because inadequacy of occupational markets increases the set up costs for new entrants to an industry, who would have to develop much of their skilled labour force from a much lower level. It also greatly enhances the scope for the action of customary and group pressures within the workplace, and between firms.

This book has not sought to provide a new stylised fact to describe the pressures of institutions and of social norms on labour markets. The public good argument about the potential instability of occupational markets, to be developed shortly, is contingent upon a significant degree of employer finance of training. The argument itself is not multi-disciplinary, but seeks to show that even from the reference point of mainstream economic theory, there are strong theoretical reasons for doubting the general applicability of any non-institutional model of labour markets. It therefore rounds off the empirical and conceptual analysis of the preceding chapters. However, the implications drawn below from the public good argument should not be seen as the building blocks for a new deductive multi-disciplinary theory because they are based on assumptions close to those of mainstream labour market theory examined in earlier chapters. To treat them this way would do injustice to the research findings from industrial relations and sociology. The chapter closes with a brief account of three institutionally grounded studies of labour markets crossing disciplinary boundaries, and an examination of the sort of methodological criteria that might be applied to models of labour market behaviour which take account of the influences specially studied within industrial relations and industrial sociology.

8.2. OCCUPATIONAL LABOUR MARKETS AND TRANSFERABLE SKILLS AS PUBLIC GOODS

Much public discussion, and much academic debate often

treats the competitive labour market as if it were the norm, if not in reality then in an ideal world. Labour markets characterised by local monopolies, by lack of information or by custom are generally treated as deviations from the competitive norm, and a source of 'rigidities'. This section offers a reason why occupational labour markets, which are the norm of theory, should themselves be recognised as institutional creations, and far from being the natural state of the labour market are in fact fairly unstable unless backed up by a high degree of institutional regulation. Thus instead of trying to explain, as do Doeringer and Piore, and Williamson, how it is that internal labour markets and other labour market institutions emerge from a system of competitive labour markets, one should explain how occupational labour markets for transferable skills develop. In doing so, one becomes aware of their fragility.

For the present discussion three main types of labour market can be distinguished: occupational labour markets for transferable skills, internal labour markets for non-transferable skills, and unskilled or casual labour markets. Semi-skilled labour markets provide an important intermediate case, displaying both inter-firm mobility, with weak institutional regulation, and pressures towards internalisation. The full argument is developed first for skilled occupational markets, and is then extended to deal with semi-skilled markets.

To understand the emergence of occupational labour markets, and the transferable skills they distribute, it is illuminating to look at both as public goods. These are goods or services such that if one member of a group uses them, it is not feasible to exclude other members from using them. This is sometimes referred to as the condition of non-excludability. Clearly, one important limitation of the analogy is the common condition of employment that an employee should not work simultaneously for another employer. A second characteristic is that once the good is supplied to some members of a group, it can be supplied at no extra cost to the others. This is the condition of 'jointness of supply'. The classic textbook example of this is the warning to shipping provided by lighthouses (for a discussion of the limitations of this example see R. H. Coase 1974). A further characteristic sometimes cited is that use of the good by one member does not diminish its availability to other members. Again, if the last two conditions were wholly applicable, skill shortages would not arise. Nevertheless, as will be argued shortly, some aspects even of this condition are relevent. Examples of public goods are the services provided by the state for defence, law and order, or for the road network. Public goods need not be provided by the state, although the difficulty of confining the benefits to those charged for them has often been used as an argument for state intervention. They can also be provided by private associations, as Streeck (1985) has argued occurs between unions and employers' associations and the chambers of industry and commerce in West Germany. The following paragraphs look first at the characteristics of occupational labour markets that make them available collectively, and then at the advantages accruing from them, and the problems raised by the difficulties of meeting their costs.

Occupational labour markets have a number of key features. First, there is the establishment of standards of the mix of skills and the level of attainment offered by people trained in a particular occupation. Secondly, there is some standardisation of the form of training. And thirdly, there is some standardisation in job slots or job descriptions across organisations. Together these help assure a high degree of transferability of skills which is the prime characteristic of occupational labour markets. An employer recruiting from such a market needs to know what sort of training or experience has been obtained by workers, and what standard has been reached. Anyone can claim to have some electrical knowledge, but employers seeking electricians need to know what kind of training potential recruits have received, and how well they have mastered this. Similarly, someone wishing to become an electrician needs to know what kind of training employers will expect, and what areas of competence need to be acquired. In order to be able to hire such workers, employers using occupational markets need fairly standardised job slots into which such workers can fit. Use of non-standard jobs either requires additional training, or leads to the under-utilisation of the skills for which employers are paying. Moreover, as skills are maintained by practice, having made their initial investment in training, skilled workers have an incentive to seek jobs which enable them to maintain their skills. There are, however, also a number of drawbacks to be discussed in a later section.

Among the benefits likely to flow from occupational labour markets are that once standardisation has been established employers can draw on this pool, and workers can seek the relevant training in order to gain access. This can be especially important for small employers giving them the ability to them to expand their labour forces rapidly to meet increased demand without delays for additional training. Benefits for workers include ease of job changing without loss of skills acquired and of pay. Not all job changes are motivated by increased pay, and many are related to change in personal circumstances, a dislike of colleagues, or poor prospects for the firm, for example.

Society may benefit through a better allocation of skilled resources as workers are able to move in response to the changing structure of demand of different firms. It is also easier to lay people off if they expect to find a similar job elsewhere, which enables employers more easily to treat skilled labour as a variable rather than an overhead cost. Finally, the presence of occupational labour markets reduces one of the barriers to entry to product markets by new firms which can obtain ready-trained skilled labour.

These features of occupational labour markets make them very akin to public goods. In an economy in which labour has the right to change employer freely, the standardisation of skills means that firms cannot easily be deprived of access to the market. Moreover, once the system of standardised skills is established, in the long run its use by other employers may even enhance it, spreading some of the fixed costs of regulation more widely.

A necessary condition for a viable occupational market is an adequate supply of suitably skilled workers, and of suitably defined job slots. Transferable skills may be hired by any employer who so wishes, which meets the non-excludability criterion from the employers' side. In contrast, access from the workers' side is often restricted, for example by age restrictions for candidates for apprenticeships. On the criterion of being available at no extra cost, and that use by one person does not diminish availability to others, the position is less clear, and depends upon the elasticity of supply of suitably trained labour. Given the time required for training, in the short run there is a fixed supply of transferable skills, and if one firm takes on a large number of skilled recruits, this diminishes the supply available to other firms. But in the longer run, if supply is fairly elastic then they come closer to being public goods on these criteria.

In looking at the costs of occupational labour markets, and the implications of their funding, it is useful to divide them into the cost of establishing and the difficulty of maintaining such markets. Particularly in the first case, the problem of free-riders threatens the stability of occupational markets. Before looking at these, it is necessary to look first at why employers commonly bear much of the cost of training for transferable skills.

8.3. THE DISTRIBUTION OF COSTS OF TRANSFERABLE TRAINING

In theory, in a regime of competitive markets, trainees learning transferable skills would bear the whole cost of their training (Becker 1975). Once they are fully trained, the employer is unable to recoup the cost of training by paying them less than the value of their output because they can easily move to another employer who will. In the absence of public intervention, a common way for trainees to pay for their training has been to accept a special trainee rate below the value of their output. The special rates paid to apprentices in Britain and West Germany are good examples of this. There are, however, a number of reasons why employers may often be faced with inappropriate wage structures, and so bear the whole or a significant part of such costs.

First, skilled workers may fear that employers will substitute cheaper trainee labour for their own if special discounts are available. In a pure competitive equilibrium this would not be a problem because the marginal substitutability of trainee for skilled labour would equal the employment cost of trainees relative to skilled workers. But if, because of their bargaining power, or some other reason, skilled workers had succeeded in increasing their wage, then they might fear substitution. Their response could then be to seek to increase trainee wages in order to limit substitution from this source, which would prevent employers from passing the cost of transferable training onto trainees.

A second and related reason is the fear among skilled workers that trainees may be used as a source of cheap labour as employers offer apprenticeships which involve only a small training component, as often occurred in Britain in the 1930s (Ryan 1986). There is also evidence that they are a source of cheap labour in parts of the small firm sector in West Germany (Casey 1986). To counter such actions, skilled workers could either insist on a degree of institutional supervision of training, thereby forcing the employer to meet the cost of training, or raise trainee rates, and thus limit substitution.

Finally, for trainees to agree to such rates, they want to be sure that there will be a market for their skills, in other words, that there will be suitable job vacancies so they can use their skills fully.

Skilled workers are more likely to accept special trainee rates if the fear of cheap trainee labour or of substitution can be allayed, for example by institutional provisions regulating the quality of training. The institutional guarantees offered by the apprenticeship systems in Britain and West Germany help explain why significant discounts on youth employment are to be found these countries, but only to be a much lesser degree in France, Italy, and Belgium, countries whose industry relies more of school based training and experience (see Marsden and Ryan 1986).

Nevertheless, studies of British and West German apprentice training show that, despite the existence of special apprentice rates of pay, a great many employers incur substantial net costs in providing apprentice training. In Britain, a four-year engineering apprenticeship in 1981–82 was estimated to cost a typical employer about £18,500, or about two-and-a-half times the gross annual earnings of a skilled engineering workers. The net cost, after allowing for the value of the apprentice's output, was about £12,000 (IMS 1982). In West Germany, the Federal Institute for Vocational Training estimated that the standard three year apprenticeship in 1980 cost an employer about 60,000 DM, or about twice the gross annual earnings of a skilled worker. The net cost was about 37,500 DM (Noll *et al.* 1983). A similar study ten years earlier produced broadly similar conclusions (Edding 1974). Ryan (1980) has shown that some US employers also bear a large part of the cost of training for transferable skills.

Public funding, as in the provision of school-based training or of subsidies, offers an important alternative to private provision, but it does not escape these problems. Vocational training in state run establishments often fails to provide the work experience (often itself transferable) which has to be gained in the firm, and which is nevertheless costly to provide. Germe (1986) has highlighted this problem in France, where the state plays a major role in formal school-based vocational training, but the unwillingness of firms to provide such experience to qualified young workers (with the CAP) has been a major problem for youth employment. Thus it would seem that state finance of formal training leaves a substantial need for firm-based training. Skilled workers in France may be unwilling to accept a special induction wage rate for such workers because of the difficulty of controlling potential substitution by employers (Marsden and Ryan 1986). Although subsidies could undoubtedly help offset some of the costs incurred by employers, the problem of possible substitution effects again may provoke resistance by skilled workers, especially if the employer depends upon them for the provision of training.

The argument is a *contingent* and not a *necessary* one, and depends upon the existence either of non-compensating wage differentials (which do not correspond to differences in productivity or in working conditions), or of a degree of mutual distrust between skilled workers and their employers. However, the problems giving rise to employer funding are widespread in modern economies, except where institutional provisions make special trainee and induction rates more acceptable to those concerned, although even then employers commonly bear a significant part of the cost.

8.4. COSTS OF ESTABLISHING OCCUPATIONAL LABOUR MARKETS

The establishment of occupational markets involves a considerable investment by both employers and workers. Although conceptually separate from the costs of establishing an occupational market, an adequate pool of skilled labour is a necessary precondition for such a market, so the two sets of costs will be examined together. The costs of training can have a critical impact in the early stages, and may explain some of the difficulties of setting up such markets. To reap the benefits of occupational markets standardised training has to be set in motion. Thus workers have to be persuaded to invest in the requisite training, and employers, to design their jobs in such a way that there are appropriately designed jobs for these workers to go to.

In the absence of industry-wide coordination, establishment of such a market will start from a position in which employers have mostly developed their own in-house training provisions to supplement the training already received in schools. The first employers participating in the occupational market may then face the problem of preventing non-participating employers from poaching the labour trained to new standards. If this were widespread, then poaching would quickly undermine the establishment of the new occupational market causing a reversion to in-house training and the development of payment systems and other fringe benefits designed to discourage labour turnover. Although the attractiveness of such poaching would be reduced by the non-standardised job slots of such employers, it is not difficult to envisage cases in which the costs of external recruitment of a certified skill might be less than that of loss of market share owing to internal training bottlenecks.

A similiar problem could arise with the skills engendered by new technology. The first firms to invest in this have to train their own staff, who will then be available when other firms begin to adopt the same technology. One might expect this to lay the foundations of new occupational labour markets for example in electronics and programming skills but for the reaction of those firms which first installed the new equipment and trained their staff. These will be under heavy pressure, in the absence of suitable occupational markets, to devise ways of limiting labour turnover, among the most effective of which may be to encourage the development of their own internal labour markets. Length of service increments may help reduce labour turnover. In addition, firms can spread the training over a number of jobs, and arrange this in such a way that workers build up their skills. The avoids providing a big lump of transferable training at the beginning, and thus reduces the opportunities for other firms to poach. Such measures then greatly diminish the possibilities for establishing a standardised skill and an occupational market, and once a number of firms have opted for development of their internal markets, they may be unwilling to unscramble them. Clearly these problems are sometimes overcome and occupational markets are established, but there are many cases in which such attempts have failed, such as the repeated attempts to establish a West German style apprenticeship system in France, and the current attempts to standardise engineers' qualifications in Britain in order to establish an engineering profession discussed in Chapter 7.

8.5. THE DIFFICULTY OF MAINTAINING VIABLE OCCUPATIONAL MARKETS

(a) Pressures to dilute training standards

In addition to the set-up costs, the maintenance of occupational markets involves a number of costs, and can be undermined by free riders, notably by dilution of standards. Among employers there may be a temptation to provide less than the full amount of training. Under the old system of time served apprenticeship in Britain, which involved no examinations, employers could use apprentices as cheap labour, and apprentices could put in less than the required amount of study. So long as the apprentices got their craftsman's card at the end they could gain access to that particular market. Training to externally set standards with a provision for day release and greater college training for apprentices as under the new engineering apprenticeship system helps to raise and to standardise the quality of new craftsmen entering that particular occupational market, but it also raises the cost.

(b) The loss of flexibility due to standardised skill norms

There are other forces eroding skill norms in occupational markets arising from the difficulty of adapting these to technical change, and from the practice of incorporating them into systems of administrative or negotiated rules. For example, it can be difficult to adapt jobs whose contents are standardised across a large number of firms to the slow but cumulative changes in technology and work methods. This can encourage employers to seek their own individual solutions.

If all the adaptation is done at plant or company level, which is often quicker and cheaper in the short run, the general standard is gradually eroded, and firms lose their original ease of recruitment of skilled labour from outside, and the skilled workers lose the transferability of their skills. Collective regulation may take time, and involve complex bargaining, which increases the likelihood that some employers will seek to bypass the occupational market and seek their own private adaptation. It is thus not surprising to observe in Britain, and to a lesser extent in West Germany, that technical change should provoke an increase in the disputes over job demarcations. Skilled workers are often suspicious of such piecemeal adaptation to individual employers' skill requirements because it threatens their occupational market.

(c) Loss of confidence and fear of shortages

Another factor undermining occupational markets is employers' fear of cyclical skill shortages and their effect upon their ability to retain their own skilled labour. This may induce them to devise ways of tying such skilled workers to their firm, for example by specially designed payment systems, or by organising training and jobs in such a way that the most transferable portion of their training is provided to more senior workers who might by then be tied to the company by other commitments. Where standardised training is tightly regulated this may not be possible, but in other cases it might be, as in Ryan's (1984) example of welding in which training was phased in such a way that only more senior workers got the more marketable types of training. Osterman's (1982) study also provides examples of employers using internalisation as a way of reducing labour turnover in labour markets which would otherwise have functioned as unregulated occupational markets. In Britain, the near collapse of the apprenticeship system in the current recession may further reduce employers' faith in occupational markets for skilled manual labour.

(d) The bargaining power of workers with transferable skills

The additional bargaining power of such workers derives from two main sources. First, they can use the threat of short-term disruption to the firm's production by threatening to leave when labour and product demand are high, when market share is most easily lost if demand is not met. Secondly, their occupational identity, having undergone similar training, and doing similar work, provides a useful basis for collective organisation. To counter this, employers may seek to tie such workers to the firm, or to devise alternative training methods. Again Osterman (1982) gives an example of employers providing limited amounts of training in computer programming to established members of their workforce as an alternative to recruiting programmers with transferable skills.

8.6. OVERVIEW OF THE INSTABILITY OF OCCUPATIONAL MARKETS

The cost of training argument, in so far as it depends upon non-compensating differentials giving rise to pressures for substitution, suggests that deviations from the trainee and skilled wage differentials of competitive equilibrium will generate pressures on employers either to internalise their skilled labour force, or to invest in the establishment of institutional regulation of the occupational market and so provide the guarantees that make the trainee discount acceptable to their skilled work force. The pressures work towards internal markets, or institutional markets, but not towards a reassertion of unregulated competitive markets. This differs strongly from the views of Hicks and Marshall concerning the dominance of competitive forces in the long run.

Secondly, a number of other factors causing instability in unregulated occupational markets have been highlighted, particularly in relation to pressures to internalise in order to reduce the rigidity of work allocation associated with transferable skills, to increase predictability of skilled labour supply over the economic cycle, and to reduce the bargaining power arising from transferable skills.

Institutional regulation can reduce these problems in several ways. It can oversee the quality of training, thus reducing the danger that employers will use trainees as cheap labour, and that trainees will not study. It can also maintain uniform standards. It can control some aspects of the free-rider problem by establishing a framework by which training costs can be shared either among employers, as in the case of the British training board levies, or with trainees, by use of special trainee rates.

Finally, it can increase the amount of trust between employers and workers, thus increasing the acceptability of special trainee rates to trainees and to existing skilled workers. The effect of such trust can be seen in West Germany, where training levies on employers are not used, but there is a widespread belief among employers in their responsibility to train (Edding Commisssion, 1974), surely an important factor behind the high levels of apprentice training there.

It could be objected that *unregulated* occupational markets flourish for a number of skilled and semi-skilled occupations. However, the same pressures towards internalisation can be seen in these cases. Osterman's (1982) study covered secretaries and computer programmers in the United States. The costs of training, and of enterprise specific experience, particularly important among programmers as each organisation has its own system, he argues, have led firms to seek ways of stabilising their programming workforce (because of training costs, and because of unpredictable supply over the business cycle). Hence some employers provide more limited and less transferable training to their own established staff, and so internalise the occupation. Similarly with secretaries, he observed that firms created internal market conditions for a core of their secretarial workforce on whom they could depend, and then used a secondary market for general typists. Osterman argued that the employers pursued a strategy of dividing the workforce in this occupation between an internal labour market, and a secondary labour market for which subcontracting could be used. This individual solution renders such occupational markets less stable.

Internal and casual labour markets
The other major type of multi-employer market is that for unskilled and casual labour, and comparison with transferable skills and their markets reveals further the extent to which occupational markets may be considered public goods. Casual markets can work with relatively little regulation because of the small degree of investment in skill that

is required and the low technical specification of vacancies. The cost of the market organisation is low because little is required in the way of skill certification beyond broad educational qualifications. Nevertheless even in such markets one should not overlook the importance of informal information networks, running through contacts held by the firm's current employees, which reduce the scope of competition.

For skilled labour, the main alternative to establishment of occupational markets is the provision of training within company internal labour markets. Such markets are private goods in the sense that employers have exclusive use of their own internal labour markets for filling certain vacancies, this being reinforced by the design of training and of pay and job progression structures so as to discourage internally trained workers from leaving. Moreover, many of the skills are also likely to be of limited transferability because they are tailored to the firm's needs. In addition, where some of the skills involved may have a market outside, employers are not bound by external rules which prevent their organising skill acquisition in such a way as to reduce transferability. In such markets, employers gain possible flexibility in being able to tailor skills to their own individual requirements, and in ensuring a return on their investment in training by reducing the possibilities of poaching by other employers. But they lose the main advantages an occupational labour market as they cannot then take on and lay off labour as they need it, and have to treat their skilled labour as an overhead cost, a quasi-fixed factor.

The argument so far has been that the establishment of an adequate institutional basis for the funding of occupational labour markets and of transferable skills is a necessary condition for the development of a stable occupational labour market. If trainees do not bear the full cost of transferable skills, as they do not in practice even for apprenticeships in Britain and West Germany, then the need to protect the market from free-riders is very great to prevent it degenerating into a series of company internal labour markets. Moreover, even if trainees do bear the full cost,

as Becker argued, there still needs to be some standardisation of training and of job slots in firms, although
some of the pressures undermining the occupational market
may in that case be weaker. Thus even though it may be
possible to find some occupational markets which do not
face these funding problems, the pressures on the mass
markets for transferable skills are great, and are such that
without institutional support, or a strong consensus among
employers as in West Germany, they are unstable and likely
to break up into a number of internal labour markets.

Finally, the discussion so far may leave the impression
that if a satisfactory solution could be found to the funding
of occupational markets and of transferable skills, then
the economy could function with a large number of stable
occupational markets. Clearly, extensive public support
could substantially reinforce existing occupational markets
by easing the free-rider pressures. But first, much engineering training in Britain takes place in publicly funded
universities, and this has created only a weakly organised
occupational labour market (Finniston 1980). Usually, a
considerable amount of work experience is needed to complement this, which helps explain why so many engineers in
British firms are established on internal labour markets
(Mace 1979). Secondly, it is not so obvious that public
support could lead to the establishment of a whole set of
new occupational markets in an economy in which there
are already a number of well developed labour market
institutions. Under such conditions, many workers and firms
will already have invested considerable amounts in existing
systems of skill formation, and in organising internal labour
markets. Even though individual employers might be prepared to write off their previous investment, they could still
face very substantial transition costs from opposition from
and loss of morale among their existing employees. Sudden
introduction of external recruitment for certain skilled or
more senior jobs would affect the prospects for promotion
or up-grading of the firm's existing employees. It is notable
that efforts by the public authorities in both France and
Japan to introduce apprenticeship systems, with markets for
transferable skills, have failed. Thus devising an adequate

solution to the funding of occupational markets and of training for transferable skills may be a necessary, but not a sufficient condition for the establishment of occupational markets, and the difficulties in this domain are a continual source of break-down for existing occupational markets.

The next section seeks to trace out some of the implications for our understanding of labour markets.

8.7. SOME IMPLICATIONS FOR LABOUR MARKET THEORY

The argument so far has sought to show that occupational labour markets are analogous to public goods because it is often difficult to exclude those who are not prepared to contribute to their funding, especially when setting up such a market. It has also sought to show that for skilled labour, the main alternative form of organisation is that of enterprise internal labour markets. This section seeks to trace out some of the implications of this for the study of labour markets.

(a) Occupational labour markets in an economy will be limited in number, and confined to more qualified sections of the labour force. This follows from the costs of establishing such markets. The main benefit stems from the need for an organised occupational market in order to facilitate the private provision of training, and for workers to invest in training.

Although similarity of equipment used in different firms undoubtedly facilitates the development of transferable skills and the establishment of occupational markets, it was shown in Chapter 5 that it was not a sufficient condition. Whether there will be an occupational market turns on the benefits to be achieved by organising certain skills in such a way that they are transferable, and whether a method of funding the necessary investment can be found.

(b) Because the number of such markets in an economy will generally be limited, employers using occupational markets will mostly also have provision for some kind of internal market for other skills needed. Thus for skilled labour, firms will either have only internal labour markets, or they will use a mixture of internal and occupational markets.

This also helps explain the pattern of segmentation within primary labour markets noted by Doeringer and Piore. Job ladders, they argued were to be found for semi-skilled and skilled workers up to a certain level. Above this level, they observed that skills became transferable. Piore suggested that this could be because of the inherent nature of the activities involved using more abstract skills. But it could equally be that below a certain level of skill it is often not worth organising an occupational market.

(c) The 'public good' argument used above implies that Becker's model of training in competitive occupational markets rests on a knife edge. Deviations from the wage relativities of the competitive equilibrium, rather than set in motion forces restoring that equilibrium, could as easily trigger off actions preventing employers from passing the cost of transferable training to trainees, and so lead towards the further development of internal labour markets. If correct, this argument implies that the Hicks-Marshall long-run competitive equilibrium may not be achieved, and that instead, a system of internal labour markets would come to predominate, reducing labour market competition, and hence further weakening the forces working for a restoration of the long-run equilibrium.

(d) The break-down of institutional regulation of occupational markets does not lead to the re-establishment of competitive markets which are free of institutional interference. Instead, it leads back to dependence on enterprise internal labour markets. This follows from the costs of establishment of occupational markets and their nature as public goods. This turns the analytical method used by Doeringer and Piore, Williamson and others on its head as they sought to explain the existence of internal labour markets by explaining how they could develop in a system of predominantly competitive labour markets. Instead of seeking to explain the emergence of 'specific' and 'idiosyncratic' skills, they should have focused on the emergence of transferable skills and occupational markets. The same point can be made against the device used by other economists to account for the emergence of institutions in otherwise atomistic labour markets discussed in Chapter 2. At stake is the methodological principle of the logical priority of competitive labour markets in explanations of labour market behaviour.

(e) Occupational labour markets will generally be confined to higher paid groups. This stems from the link between occupational markets and training. Such groups will be higher paid especially if workers have to bear some proportion of the cost – perhaps in the form of lower trainee rates of pay as suggested by Becker. This might be reduced by the extent to which public resources are used extensively, or to which employers bear the cost.

(f) Following the Marshall rules, the market power of workers in occupational markets is often greater than that of their fellow workers confined to an internal labour market. First, the elasticity of supply of workers on an occupational market is likely to be greater than that of those on an internal labour market (supply of cooperant factors of production). Workers on occupational markets can always work at the same skill level elsewhere if their current employer goes out of business, and during a strike, can often work free-lance. Neither opportunity is so readily available to skilled workers on internal markets, hence their lesser elasticity to supply. Secondly, substitution for skilled workers on an occupational market will often be less easy than for similar workers on an internal market, because of the organisation of occupational markets around standardised job descriptions, which give employers less control over job design than in an internal market. The two remaining Marshall rules could apply equally to either type of skilled group.

This has two consequences: it contributes to frequent higher pay of workers on occupational markets; and it suggests that there is a strong incentive for groups on such markets to use their organisation to exploit their bargaining advantage.

(g) The possibilities for monopolistic bargaining arising from the lesser elasticity of demand for workers on occupational markets may induce employers to adopt policies to counter potential mobility. This can be done by raising the cost of quitting, for example, by linking higher pay, and access to more pleasant jobs in the company to length of service.

(h) As many firms will have recruited only a limited number of their workers from occupational markets, with the remainder on internal markets or recruited from unskilled markets, competitive pressures from their local labour markets will be limited. This gives management greater flexibility in the design of jobs, pay and grading structures, subject to the constraints set by groups on occupational markets and unskilled markets. For the remaining groups, labour market pressures will be fairly weak.

The pressure of competitive forces within this framework might then be thought of as acting on certain points within the firm's organisation of its labour force, such as unit costs, and on the rates of pay offered to those recruited externally, but apart from these, competitive market pressures may have little sway. Thus labour market competition may have little influence on internal pay and grading structures. One of the problems of the 'margin of indeterminacy' left by market forces discussed in Chapter 4 was that it was seen in terms of the prices of individual categories of labour. In addition, no substantial justification for the existence of such a margin was offered. The present argument is that market forces have little influence on wages beyond the constraints on unit costs and on those points at which the firm must recruit. Thus many employers determine their wage and grading structures with respect to their organisational objectives, such as facilitating flexible deployment of manpower within the firm, subject to intra-organisational pressures such as work-group politics, and the constraints on pay and grading set by the firm's points of contact with local labour markets.

(i) Occupational labour markets depend upon institutional structures supporting them to regulate standards and to adapt them to a changing environment. Once employers and workers are organised to achieve this, it is unlikely that these structures will be confined to questions of labour market administration. On both sides, a coalition of interests is set up that can be used for other purposes, as for example happened with the growth of collective bargaining by the craft unions, and as has happened more recently with the professional associations in the British National Health Service which have assumed more of a collective bargaining role as a larger number of their members have become salaried. For example, this happened with the British Medical Association. Moreover, the need to maintain the coalition of interests may introduce additional considerations, such as fairness. These institutions can also be a vehicle for the influence of group norms on labour markets, such as those discussed in Chapters 3 and 4.

(j) Because of the considerable freedom employers have with respect to market pressures in the design of their organisations, there is no reason to expect labour market pressures alone to reduce inter-country differences in internal pay and grading structures such as might have been the case if use of similar technologies generated similar skill requirements and thus similar labour market structures. This is quite consistent with competitive pressures on unit costs leading firms to look very closely at the labour management practices of competing firms in other countries, as happens at the moment very extensively in the car industry, but there are many different ways of changing organisational structures in order to cut unit costs.

(k) One important consequence of attributing a more central role to institutions within labour markets is to give more weight to questions of comparability and fairness of wage comparisons. The language of collective bargaining which is used to build support for a particular group's pay claim focuses on shared norms.

The importance of institutional underpinnings of occupational markets provides a mechanism through which workers' and employers' ideas of fairness can prevail. It also provides a medium within which it is often necessary, if one group is to press its pay claim, to elicit the support of other groups. The claims on other groups' support are based on the understanding that there is a mutually accepted idea of fairness. This may itself be subject to debate, and to dispute by other groups, and claims may sometimes be made opportunistically, but the underlying mode of thought is one of criteria and comparisons which all the groups concerned would accept as fair. Otherwise the argument would have no force.

(l) Finally, what of the degree of competition on occupational labour markets? There is a good deal of evidence that even on occupational labour markets wages do not behave in the manner predicted by competitive theory. Mackay *et al.* (1971) for example found evidence of persistent differences in earnings levels for the same occupation between firms in the same local labour markets, and only a weak tendency for the lower paying firms to experience higher rates of turnover (for other examples see Marsden 1984). To some extent, even on occupational markets, mobility with transferable skills is only potential, and so it is quite consistent for workers with such skills to have high lengths of service, although on average, one would expect their turnover rates to be more sensitive to the state of the local labour market and earnings opportunities elsewhere than for workers with non-transferable skills. Varying the pay of craft workers in response to cyclical changes in a firm's local labour market would disrupt internal relativities within the firm. It is usually difficult to negotiate such changes in unionised firms, but one should not underestimate the difficulty even in non-unionised firms if they have established pay structures. Thus firms employing workers with transferable skills may well seek other methods of retaining them, which if widespread will reduce the fluidity of the occupational market. This could help explain why many employers wishing to overcome skill shortages prefer other policies, such as additional training, or reducing wastage, to altering the wage they offer compared to other firms (Hunter *et al* 1978).

8.8. ILLUSTRATIONS OF MULTI-DISCIPLINARY RESEARCH ON LABOUR MARKETS

The implications of the public good argument open up

economic analysis of labour markets to some of the institutional and social influences examined in earlier chapters,
but there is no presentation of an alternative cross-disciplinary theory of labour markets. As mentioned earlier, the
aim of this book has not been to produce an alternative set
of 'stylised facts', but one may nevertheless ask what cross-
disciplinary study of labour markets would be like. The next
section takes three related pieces of research, two of which
are still in progress. They are presented primarily as illustrations of studies which set off from a recognition of the
institutional nature of labour markets, and which have
adopted a strong cross-disciplinery orientation. The first,
already discussed in Chapters 5 and 7, is the comparison of
wage structure in French and German manufacturing firms;
the second, a project on labour force adjustment and economic change in Britain and France (Eyraud *et al.* 1984);
and the third, a study of youth employment in European
countries.

(a) Wage structure in France and Germany

Maurice *et al* (1978) sought to explain why it was that
French firms appeared to pay a higher differential to white
collar and technical staff while at the same time employing
them in greater proportion given establishments of similar
size, using similar production techniques, and producing
similar products. They sought to explain this discrepancy
with economic theory by further examining the organisation
of skilled work and training, collective workplace
regulation, and the authority structure in matched plants in
the two countries. Their argument was discussed in some
detail in Chapter 7, but it is perhaps worth recalling their
method.

In their study, using a comparative typology based on
French and German firms, they sought to identify those
features of the French and German systems of education
and training, their organisation of skilled work, their authority hierarchies, and of their systems of industrial relations
which acted together to give rise to the pattern of wage
differentials and employment structures described earlier in
this book. Their model was not one in which there was

a single causal mechanism responsible for a single set of observations, but one in which the patterns of wages and employment in the two countries were shown to form a consistent part in the articulation of the four processes mentioned. The study required getting behind the aggregative categories of official statistics by combining analysis of these with their own plant level studies.

(b) Labour force adjustment and industrial change in Britain and France

This study[1] sets off from the hypothesis that two distinct models of labour market adjustment can be identified, one in Britain and the other France. In Britain, greater use is made of occupational labour markets, while in France, there is greater recourse to enterprise internal labour markets, particularly as concerns skilled industrial workers. The justification for these two models of adjustment is based in previous work by the main researchers, Eyraud, Marsden, and Silvestre, including evidence on wage structure, internal mobility indicators, employment functions, training systems, and on collective bargaining in these two countries.

Although reliance on internal or on occupational labour markets is to some extent a question of degree, preponderant use of one kind of market limits recourse to the other. Workers with transferable skills are often reluctant to dilute their transferability, while those with non-transferable skills are usually opposed to external recruitment to jobs which would limit their chances of upgrading.

In Britain, even though well organised occupational markets for manual workers are mostly the preserve of craftsmen, organisation of these jobs on a craft basis restricts the upgrading opportunities of lesser skilled workers, and reduces the potential for employers to develop internal labour markets. In contrast, in France, the weaker occupational markets for skilled workers, impose a greater need on employers to develop their own vocational training provisions, but at the same time give them greater scope for organising internal upgrading within the enterprise.

The implications for adjustment to economic change are that the occupational market model enables employers to recruit from and to lay-off to their local labour markets, whereas the enterprise internal market model makes recruitment of skilled labour more prolonged (because of the need to upgrade people), and gives rise to greater opposition to redundancies because skills are less easily transferred to other firms. In contrast, job structures which are standardised across several firms can make adjustment to incremental technical change more difficult than in enterprise internal markets, so what the French employers lose by difficulty of laying people off, they gain by greater ease of deployment between and revision of job categories. Hence, one element in the research is to test this idea.

The labour market model also affects the content of collective bargaining, and of union action. In the occupational model, union action would focus a lot on job related matters because these affect the workers' basis for organisation, whereas in the enterprise model, the workers will not have established occupational criteria as a basis for collective action, and Eyraud (1983) has argued that this favours organisation at the enterprise, and at the branch levels. A second area of the research then is to examine how far it is true that technical change and the need for greater workforce flexibility is provoking negotiations on job related issues in Britain, but attempts to alter the broad framework of work rules in France. One could contrast the British 'flexibility agreements' of the last three years, which deal extensively with job demarcations and deployment of workers between jobs at plant and company level, with the national level negotiations in France, which have dealt with working time, and reducing employment protection in a general way. Nevertheless, in both countries, progress towards agreement has been small.

Finally, linking these two strands of the research is the idea that national training systems, and the national, or industry-wide organisation of labour markets shape the options open to employers as between use of occupational or internal labour markets, a choice discussed in Chapter 5 above. A prime test of the relevance of such models to analysis of labour markets is the extent to which they shape the response to economic change, as in the current recession, of employers, workers union, and the public authorities.

(c) Youth employment in some European countries

In this study[2] of the distribution of youth employment between industries, the authors found a price effect on youth employment in Britain, Germany, and the Netherlands, but none in Belgium, France and Italy. The analysis has so far been confined to male manual workers in industry, and the relative pay variable compared young males under 21 to those aged 21 and over (Marsden and Ryan, 1986).

The authors explain the different impact of youth relative pay on youth employment shares in terms of the institutional structure of labour markets in the six countries. In Britain, Germany, and the Netherlands, apprenticeship systems provide special access channels for young workers. The presence of such channels makes it easier for skilled workers to influence employers' use of young trainees, and in particular to monitor potential substitution, and so may make them more willing to accept payment of special lower rates to young trainees. In Belgium, France, and Italy, young workers often enter the labour market with school-based qualifications needing to complement these with practical experience on-the-job. The absence of a clearly defined trainee status, combined with possession of skills gained off-the-job, increase the potential for substitution, compared with that associated with apprentices. The dangers of substitution are enhanced by the greater prevalence of enterprise internal labour markets as skills are more dependent upon the enterprise. Consequently, skilled adults, much better represented in union negotiations than young workers, may seek to reduce the threat of substitution by insisting that such young workers receive the full rate for the job. As a consequence, employers in Belgium, France, and Italy are reluctant to take on young workers and to provide experience. Squeezed out of skilled work, young workers mostly get unskilled jobs in unattractive sectors of employment.

The differential between young and adult males affects

youth employment in Britain, Germany, and the Netherlands because the access channels cause many young males to be potential substitutes for adult males. In contrast, in Belgium, France and Italy, near exclusion from paths leading to skilled jobs, means that the effective differential for young males may be with regard to adult women and minorities in 'secondary jobs', a hypothesis to be tested in later research.

To sum up, the institutional structure affects youth employment through its impact upon the acceptability or otherwise of a discount on youth employment; by determining access to certain kinds of job, and by its influence upon the potential patterns of substitution between youths and other workers.

Of these examples, the first is the most thoroughly multi-disciplinary, and the other two more modest. Nevertheless, each in its way raises problems for the evaluation of explanations it puts forward. To tackle these questions, both of the two current studies demand use of data from several different sources, and gathered using different research methods, including statistical, documentary work, and interviews with companies and with unions. This raises a number of problems for evaluation of the results.

8.9. CRITERIA FOR EVALUATING EXPLANATIONS

Each of the three disciplines has its own broad consensus as to what count as valid research methods, and what sorts of evidence count for the refutation of a particular hypothesis, although there may be real disagreement on the weight to attach to particular evidence. The problem now is to assess how far these can be used for hypotheses which span two or more disciplines. As Popper (1959) pointed out, an empirical test bears on a single proposition by convention only, but in fact the whole network of propositions, and subsidiary statements needed to relate theory to potential observations is in question. There are no such conventions for cross-disciplinary work.

Research methods are closely related to theory and to previous knowledge within each discipline. This is because one needs a reason for relating a particular set of observations, actual or potential, to a given hypothesis. For example, in trying to estimate demand elasticities for young workers' labour, in order to overcome the identification problem if the supply elasticity is positive, the demand and supply relations should be estimated similtaneously, but this is very difficult on existing data. The usual practice has been to make crude but simple assumptions about the supply elasticities (that supply is elastic at prevailing wage rates, or alternatively that it is highly inelastic), and to judge these against other econometric evidence on labour supply elasticities (OECD 1984). Using these assumptions it is possible to give an economic meaning to an otherwise uninterpreted statistical relationship, and thus to relate it to other economic knowledge.

Industrial sociology also has its consensus on research methods, although it is perhaps less widely accepted than in economics because of the more pronounced cleavage between different schools of theory. Much of its work relies on the construction of typologies, and of classifying forms of behaviour and beliefs according to ideal types which may be derived a priori from a particular theory, or may be based on observations, or a mixture of both. Case study work is also often situated in relation to other work and theory by means of ideal types. Joan Woodward's classification of types of production technique from the point of view of their influence upon work organisation is an example of one very influential typology (for example, it was used by Maurice *et al.* (1978) in constructing their sample of firms). The emphasis upon ideal types does not preclude statistical analysis, and the development of factor analysis has proved very popular as a multivariate technique helpful for the construction and testing of typologies. As in economics, it is mostly the accumulation of counter-evidence, rather than individual studies, which brings down particular hypotheses, although there have been some notable exceptions, such as the 'Affluent Worker' study (Goldthorpe *et al*. 1968). But as in economics, the evidence usually bears on the subsidiary propositions involved in making theoretical predictions and rarely on the core propositions and concepts of sociological theory. The criteria of evidence have been mostly developed for testing limited statements, and so as in economics, are ill-adapted to areas of research which fall outside the usual scope of sociological theory.

Industrial relations is in something of an intermediate position in not having a strong body of theory of its own, except to say that the process of rule making has been a major focus of interest, and has led to the development of analytical methods for studying this. Although influential, the work of Dunlop, and of Flanders has not provided the central core of theory equivalent to those in economics and sociology.

Theory plays an important role in generalising research findings, and in relating the findings of one study to those of another, and it is by tracing out the logical implications of such theories that we can set out the events which would constitute the potential falsifiers of a hypothesis. Although as noted earlier, there is an important degree of convention in this decision.

In cross-disciplinary work, these discipline-based criteria of evidence apply less well, and there is no established convention as to which propositions make up the theoretical core, and which are subject to test. Moreover, it is difficult to judge which adaptations of theory made in order to account for a set of observations are to be counted as *ad hoc* explanations, and which are an enrichment of theory.

In contrast, the core of theory in economics and in sociology helps to make clear which are key propositions in a hypothesis, and which might be *ad hoc* adjustments, that is, additional assumptions or ideas introduced into a model and which are meant to accommodate some anomalous set of observations. The attempts by economists to broaden the scope of economics reviewed in the earlier chapters by and large avoided such *ad hoc* adjustments seeking instead to amend the core theory in some way, or alternatively to show that the problem could be redefined to make it tractable.

Clearly, if we are to follow Popper's idea that the empirical content of one theory compared to another depends upon its greater chance of falsification, then it is desirable to restrict the introduction of new elements on *ad hoc* basis as this reduces the theory's empirical content. For example, the way in which Phillips (1958) introduced the formation of employers' associations in the 1890s as a possible reason why the Phillips curve fitted the data for those years less well has been widely criticised for recourse to an observation which had little to do with his main explanation of the curve (shifts in labour demand). In contrast, the charge of making *ad hoc* adjustments is less clear in Hines (1964) study when he devises an indicator of trade union militancy and uses that to explain variations in wage inflation in the UK. Although there remain a number of unanswered questions in Hines' article concerning the relations between the independent variables, and how he reconciles cost push pressures with competitive pressures, he does go to considerable lengths to explain his key variable (changes in trade union membership density) and its relation to wage increases.

This problem is posed even more acutely by cross-disciplinary research. It is necessary to introduce new mixtures of variables to explain certain phenomena representing processes normally within the conventional domain of different disciplines. At present, one has to deal with two or even three separate cores of concepts, and corresponding differences in the nature of evidence used. It is, therefore, extremely difficult to formulate clearly testable hypotheses in advance, and it is not clear what types of adjustment to the research object remain consistent with a fair degree of rigour. As suggested, the strict exclusion of *ad hoc* adjustments could very easily make such research impossible, and so would not be a helpful criterion. In addition, Friedman's criterion of simplicity, given the differences between the core concepts of the relevant disciplines would also be hard to apply because it is not clear what the criterion of simplicity would be.

One possibility, which is close to that used by historians

is that of consistency between different kinds of evidence, and this has played an important role in the three examples of cross-disciplinary studies outlined above. This need not be confined to explaining singular historical patterns or events, although there is a sense in which all empirical social science is historically specific in that studies are carried out on economic and social behaviour which takes place in a particular society and a particular institutional setting. Theory plays a valuable role in defining the conditions for generalisation from such observations. So there needs to be also a degree of consistency in theory, requiring possible adaptation of the core concepts of the disciplines involved. The limitations of the attempts to analyse the impact of institutional and normative pressures on labour markets covered in this book were mainly judged in terms of consistency with evidence and empirically supported theory from sociology and industrial relations. Clearly the additional consistency required makes cross-disciplinary research and policy analysis very difficult. Could the criterion of consistency be extended to be used as a guide for the construction of explanations which straddle conventional disciplinary boundaries?

For example, one test of econometric evidence that employers treated skilled and semi-skilled labour as substitutes depending on their relative wages (as in Nissim 1984), would be to examine behaviour at the enterprise level. Between which categories of skilled and semi-skilled labour did substitution occur (the statistical categories in the industry-wide data used econometric research are extremely broad). Was there substitution of semi-skilled for craft labour, which would appear to contradict some institutional evidence discussed earlier in this book, or was substitution between skills on the borderline between skilled and semi-skilled work? If the change occurred in new firms, how did they get round some of the likely union pressures? Similarly, Marsden and Ryan's (1986) econometric results that youth relative pay appears to affect youth employment in Britain, West Germany, and the Netherlands, but not in Belgium, France, and Italy, requires, in addition to further statistical work, closer analysis of training systems and of employers' recruitment practices in these countries. Econometric work often makes assumptions about the general pattern of behaviour of individual workers and employers, but this is rarely investigated directly, despite the contrary expectation from enterprise level research that substitution in response to fairly small changes in relative wages would be unlikely in the short-run. This path was taken by Maurice *et al.* (1978), and was a principal reason for combining comparisons based on aggregate statistics with plant level analyses.

The study by Maurice *et al.* (1978) remains at the stage of attempting to describe historically specific patterns of social and economic organisation, and to trace some of the interactions. Maurice *et al.* went further than Eyraud *et al.* (1984) or Marsden and Ryan (1986) in developing a special conceptual framework. But in none of these cases have the conditions of generalisation to other countries been described, and consequently, it is hard to judge what would be the implications of inconsistent findings from other countries, or from other historical periods. To demand a cross-disciplinary general theory is to ask too much, particularly as the record of general theory in economics, and to some extent also in industrial relations and industrial sociology, has been that it closes disciplines off to research findings from other disciplines. In the immediate future what seems to be needed is more confrontation between empirical findings from the different disciplines, and more open discussion of the theoretical models underlying them, treating them less as competing explanations than as potentially complementary to each other. By doing this, and trying to define the areas of empirical disagreement more clearly, it may be possible to move towards a labour economics which is more sensitive to industrial relations and industrial sociology, and an industrial sociology and industrial relations more aware of the pressures of labour markets on the behaviour of workers, unions and management.

Finally, a great deal of use has been made at various points in this book of comparative research, and this has often highlighted the influence of national institutional frameworks on labour market behaviour. One of the causes of this increasing awareness has been the process of European integration. The immense difficulty of such integration has been a stimulus to the research, not least as an input into social and economic policy discussion. It has been realised that the patterns of social and economic organisation of the member countries of the European Community are proving to be a much more serious obstacle to European integration, and even to policy harmonisation and creation of Europe-wide markets than was anticipated. Even such a practical step as the harmonisation of educational diplomas in order to facilitate labour mobility between countries has proved extremely difficult. Although there has been some measure of convergence between the countries during the forty years of rapid economic change since the last war, many fundamental differences remain, and show little sign of weakening. Durkheim observed that sociology grew out of the failure during the French Revolution of attempts to organise society according to the ideal of reason of the Enlightenment. In a more modest way, many of the concerns reflected in this book have been stimulated by the realisation that differences of social and economic organisation between European countries are likely to persist despite the slow progress towards European economic and political integration.

NOTES

1. See Eyraud *et al.* (1984). Project funded jointly by the Economic and Social Research Council and the Centre National de la Recherche Scientifique.
2. Funded by the Rowntree Trust.

References

Aglietta M. (1976) (*Régulation et Crises du Capitalisme*, Calmann-Lévy, Paris.
——(1978) 'Panorama sur les théories de l'emploi', *Revue économique*, No. 1, January.
Alchian A., and Demsetz H. (1972) 'Production, information costs, and economic organisation', *American Economic Review*, December pp. 777–95.
Altshuler A., Anderson M., Jones D., Roos D., and Womack J. (1984) *The Future of the Automobile: the report of the MIT International Automobile Project*, George Allen and Unwin, London.
Arrow K. (1963) *Social choice and individual values*. Yale University Press, New Haven, Conn.
Arrow K. (1972) *Models of job discrimination*, in Pascal A. H. (ed.).
Arrow K. (1973) 'Higher education as a filter', *Journal of Public Economics*, No. 2. pp. 193–216.
Azariadis C. (1981) 'Implicit contracts and related topics: a survey', in Hornstein Z *et al.* (ed.).
Azariadis C., and Stiglitz J. (1983) 'Implicit contracts and fixed price equilibria', *Quarterly Journal of Economics*, Vol. 98, 1983 Supplement, pp. 1–22.
Azouvi A. (1981) 'Théorie et Pseudo-théorie: le dualisme du marché du travail', *Critiques d'Economie Politique* New series, No. 15–16, April–June.
Bakke E. W. (ed.) (1954) *Labour mobility and economic opportunity*, MIT Press, Cambridge, Mass.
Batstone E., Boraston I., and Frenkel S. (1977) *Shop stewards in action*, Basil Blackwell, Oxford.
Becker G. S. (1971) *The economics of discrimination*, second edn, (first edn. 1957), University of Chicago Press, Chicago.
——(1975) *Human capital: a theoretical and empirical analysis, with special reference to education*, second edn, University of Chicago Press, Chicago.
Best S. (1984) *And now for something completely different: a report on personnel management in Sumitomo Metal Industries, Japan*, British Steel Corporation, London.
Blackburn, R. M., and Mann M. (1975) 'Ideology in the non-skilled working class', in Bulmer ed.

——(1979) *The working class in the labour market*, Macmillan, London.

Blaug, M. (1963) 'A Survey of the Theory of Process Innovations', *Econmica*, February, pp. 13–32.

Bloch M. (1939) *La Société Féodale*, Albin Michel, Paris.

Booth A. (1984) 'A public choice model of trade union behaviour and membership', *Economic Journal*, Vol. 94 No. 376, December, pp. 883–98.

Bosch G., and Lichte R. (1981) 'Die Funktionsweise informeller Senioritätsrechte (am Beispiel einer betrieblichen Fallstudie) ', in Dohse *et al.*

Bowers J., Deaton D., and Turk J. (1982) *Labour hoarding in British industry*. Basil Blackwell, Oxford.

Bowley A. L. (1900) *Wages in the United Kingdom in the Nineteenth Century*, Cambridge University Press, Cambridge.

Boyer, R. (1980) 'Rapport Salarial et Analyses en Terme de Régulation: une mise en rapport avec les théories de la segmentation du marché du travail'. Note prepared for *Les journées d'économie du travail*, LEST, Aix-en-Provence, March.

——(1978) Les Salaires en Longue Période', *Economie et Statistique*, No. 103, September.

Boyer R., and Mistral J. (1983) *Accumulation, Inflation et Crises du Capitalisme*, 2nd edn, Presses Universitaires de France, Paris.

Brown W. A. (1973) *Piecework Bargaining*, Heinemann, London.

Brown, W. A., and Sisson K. (1975) 'The Use of Comparison in Workplace Wage Determination'. *British Journal of Industrial Relations*. Vol. 13 No. 1 March, pp. 23–53.

Bry G. (1960) *Wages in Germany 1871–1945*, National Bureau of Economic Research, Princeton University Press, New Haven, Conn.

Bulmer M. (ed.) (1975) *Working-class images of society*, Routledge & Kegan Paul, London.

Cain G. (1976) 'The challenge of segmented labour market theories to orthodox theory: a survey', *Journal of Economic Literature*.

Cairnes J. E. (1874) *Political Economy*, Harper, New York.

Cartter A. M. (1959) *Theory of wages and employment*, Richard Urwin, Illinois.

Casey B. (1986) 'The dual apprenticeship system and the recruitment and retention of young persons in West Germany', *British Journal of Industrial Relations*, Vol. 24 No. 1, March, pp. 63–82.

Chandler A. and Daems H. (1980) 'Managerial hierarchies: comparative perspectives on the rise of the modern industrial enterprise', Harvard University Press, Cambridge, Mass.

Chiplin B. and Sloane P. (1974) 'Sexual discrimination in the labour market', *British Journal of Industrial Relations*, Vol. XII No. 3, November.

'Chronicle: Industrial relations in the UK', *British Journal of Industrial Relations*, every issue.

Clay H. (1928) *The Problem of Industrial Relations*, Macmillan, London.

Coase R. (1937) 'The nature of the firm', *Economica* November, pp. 386–405.

Coase R. H. (1974) 'The lighthouse in economics', *Journal of Law and Economics*, October.

Cole G. D. H. (1923) *Workshop Organisation*, Hutchinson, London.

Cousins J. and Brown R. (1975) 'Patterns of paradox: shipbuilding workers' images of society', in Bulmer (ed.).

Crozier M. (1963) *Le Phénomène Bureaucratique*, Seuil, Paris.

Cullen D. E. (1956) 'The Inter-industry Wage Structure 1899–1950'. *American Economic Review*, No. 3, June, pp. 353–69.

Department of Employment (1971) *British Labour Statistics Historical Abstract 1880–1968*, HMSO, London.

Daubigney J. P. and Silvestre J. J. (1972) 'Comparaison de la hiérarchie des salaires entre l'Allemagne et la France, mimeo, *Laboratoire d'Economie et de Sociologie du Travail*, Aix-en-Provence.

Delamotte Y. (1971) *Les partenaires sociaux face aux problèmes de productivité et d'emploi*, Organisation for Economic Cooperation and Development, Paris.

Dertouzos J., and Pencavel J. (1981) 'Wage and employment determination under trade unionism: the International Typographical Union', *Journal of Political Economy*, Vol. 89 No. 6, pp. 1162–81.

Didier M., and Malinvaud E. (1969) 'La Concentration de l'Industrie s'est-elle accentuée depuis le Début du Siècle?, *Economie et Statistique*, No. 2, June, pp. 3–10.

Doeringer P. B., and Piore M. J. (1971) *Internal Labor Markets and Manpower Analysis*, Heath, Lexington, Mass.

Dohse K., Jürgens U., and Russig H. (eds.) (1981) *Statussicherung im Industriebetrieb: alternative Regelungssätze im internationalen Vergleich*, Campus Verlag, Frankfurt.

Dore R. (1973) *British factory, Japanese factory: the origins of national diversity in industrial relations*, George Allen and Unwin, London.

Dunlop J. T. (1944) *Wage determination under trade unions*, Macmillan, New York.

Dunlop J. T. (1958) *Industrial relations systems*, Holt, New York.

Dunlop J. T. (1966) 'Job vacancy measures and economic analysis', in *The measurement and interpretation of job vacancies*, National Bureau of Economic Research.

Edding (1974) *Sachverständigungskommission Kosten und Finanzierung der beruflichen Bildung: Abschlussbericht*, Bielefeld.

Edwards R. C. (1975) 'The socialisation of production in the firm and labour market structure', in Edward *et al.* (eds.).

Edwards R. C., Reich M., and Gordon D. M. (1975) *Labor market segmentation*, Lexington Books, Lexington, Mass.

Eicher J.-C., and Lévy-Garboua L. (eds.) (1979) *Economique de l'éducation*, Editions Economica, Paris.

Elliott R. F., and Fallick J. (1981) *Incomes Policy, Inflation, and Relative Pay*, Macmillan, London.

Eyraud F. (1978) 'La fin des classifications Parodi', *Sociologie du Travail*, July–September, No. 3, pp. 259–79.

Eyraud F. (1983) 'The Principles of Union Action in the Engineering Industries in Great Britain and France: towards a neo-institutional analysis of industrial relations', *British Journal of Industrial Relations*, Vol. XXI No. 3, November, pp. 358–78.

Eyraud F., Marsden D. W., and Silvestre J. J. (1984) 'Labour force adjustment and industrial change in Britain and France', *Research project funded by the Economic and Social Research Council, and the Centre National de la Recherche Scientifique.*

Finniston M. (1980) *Engineering our future*. Report of the Committee of Inquiry into the Engineering Profession, Cmnd 7794, HMSO, London.

Flanders A. (1964) *The Fawley Productivity Agreements: a case study of management and collective bargaining*, Faber and Faber, London.

Flanders A. (1968) 'Collective Bargaining: a theoretical analysis', *British Journal of Industrial Relations*, March, pp. 1–26.

Freeman R. and Medoff J. (1979) 'The two faces of unionism', *The Public Interest*. No. 57, Fall, pp. 69–93.

Freyssinet J. (1982) *Politiques d'emploi des grands groupes français*, Presses Universitaires de Grenoble, Grenoble.

Friedman M. (1953) *Essays in positive economics*, University of Chicago Press, Chicago.

Gallie D. (1978) *In Search of the New Working Class: automation and social integration within the capitalist enterprise*, Cambridge University Press, Cambridge.

Germe J. F. (1986) 'Employment policies and the entry of young people into the labour market in France', *Brtish Journal of Industrial Relations*, Vol. 24 No. 1, March, pp. 29–42.

Giugni G. (1976) *Aprenticeships in Italy*, European Commission Social Policy Series, Brussels.

Goldthorpe J. H., Lockwood D., Bechhofer F., and Platt J. (1968) *The Affluent Worker*, Cambridge University Press, Cambridge.

Goodrich C. (1920) *The Frontier of Control: a study in British workshop relations*, Bell and Sons, London.

Gordon D. M., Edwards R., and Reich M. (1982) 'Segmented work, divided workers: The historical transformation of labor in the United States', Cambridge University Press, Cambridge.

Gorgé J. P., and Tandé A. (1974) 'Concentrations d'Entreprises: ralentissement en 1973, *Economie et Statistique* No. 58, July–August, pp. 49–60.

Gouldner A. (1954) *Patterns of Industrial Bureaucracy*, Free Press, Glencoe.

Hannah L. (1980) 'Visible and Invisible Hands in Great Britain', in Chandler and Daems (ed.).

Henry S. G. B., and Ormorod P. (1978) 'Incomes Policy and Wage Inflation: empirical evidence for the UK 1961–1977', *National Institute Economic Review*, August, pp. 31–9.

——(1981) 'Incomes policy and aggregate pay', in Elliott R. and Fallick L. (ed.).

Hicks J. R. (1955) 'The Economic Foundations of Wages Policy', *Economic Journal*, No. 259 Vol. LXV September, pp. 389–404.

——(1974) *The Crisis in Keynesian Economics*, Basil Blackwell, Oxford.

Hines A. G. (1964) 'Trade Unions and Wage Inflation in the United Kingdom 1893–1961', *Review of Economic Studies*, Vol. 31, pp. 221–51.

Hobsbawm E. J. (1964) 'Custom, Wages, and Workload', in E. J. Hobsbawm *Labouring Men*, Wiedenfeld and Nicholson, London.

Hornstein Z., Grice J., and Webb A. (eds.) (1981) *The economics of the labour market*, HMSO, London.

Hunter L. (1978) *Labour shortages and manpower policy*, Manpower Services Commission, HMSO, London.

Institute of Manpower Studies (1982) *Evaluation of Apprentice Support Awards*, IMS, University of Sussex.

Kerr C. (1950) 'Labour markets: their character and consequences', *American Economic Review*, Vol. 20, May, pp. 278–91.

——(1954) 'The balkanisation of labour markets', in Bakke (ed.).

Keynes J. M. (1936) *The General Theory of Employment Interest and Money*, Macmillan, London.

Knowles K. J. C., and Robertson D. J. (1951) 'Differences between the wages of skilled and unskilled workers 1880–1950', *Bulletin of the Oxford Institute of Statistics*, April, pp. 109–27.

Kolm S. C. (1969) 'Notes sur la division du travail', *Revue Economique*, March, pp. 337–50.

Kuczynski J. (1955) *Die Geschichte der Lage der Arbeiter in Frankreich 1789–1830, und seit 1830*, (2nd Edn.), Tribune-Verlag, Berlin.

Leroy M. *La Coutume Ouvrière*.

Lester R. A. (1952) 'A Range Theory of Wage Differentials', *Industrial and Labor Relations Review*, Vol. 5 No. 4, July, pp. 483–500.

Lévy-Garboua L. (1972) *Une analyse économique de la distribution des revenus individuels*. Thèse de Doctorat de Sciences Economiques, Université de Paris 1, December.

Lévy-Garboua L. (1979) 'Education, origine sociale et distribution des gains', in Eicher J,-C. and Lévy-Garboua L. (ed.).

Lévy-Leboyer M. (1980) 'The Large Corporation in Modern France', in Chandler A. and Daems H. (ed.).

Lipsey R. (1960) 'The Relation between Unemployment and the Rate of Change of Money Wage Rates in the United Kingdom 1862–1957, a further analysis', *Economica*, February.

Long C. (1960) *Wages and Earnings in the United States 1860–1890*, National Bureau of Economic Research, Princeton University Press, New Haven, Conn.

Mace J. (1979) 'Internal labour markets for engineers in British industry', *British Journal of Industrial Relations*, Vol. 17 No. 1, March, pp. 50–63.

Machlup F. (1946) 'Marginal analysis and empirical research', *American Economic Review*, Vol. 36, pp. 547–54.

Mackay D. I., Boddy D., Brack J., Diack J. A., and Jones N. (1971) *Labour Markets Under Different Employment Conditions*, George Allen and Unwin, London.

Marsden D. W. (1976) *Critique de l'analyse économique des faits sociaux: le cas de la recherche sur le marché du travail*, mimeo, Laboratoire d'Economie et de Sociologie du Travail, Aix-en-Provence.

———(1978) *Industrial Democracy and Industrial Control in West Germany, France and Great Britain*, Research Paper No. 4, Department of Employment, London.

———(1980) 'Industrial Democracy, Job Regulation and Internal Labour Markets', in Diefenbacher H. and Nutzinger H. G. (ed.) *Mitbestimmung: Probleme und Perspektiven der empirischen Forschung*, Campus Verlag, Frankfurt.

———(1982) 'Collective bargaining and industrial adjustment in Britain, Germany, France and Italy', paper presented to the Centre for Labour Economics, LSE, forthcoming in Shepherd G. and Duchêne F. (eds.) *The management of industrial change in Europe*, Frances Pinter, 1986.

———(1984) 'Homo Economicus and the labour market', in P. J. Wiles and G. Routh (eds.) *Economics in disarray*, Basil Blackwell, Oxford.

Marsden D. W., Morris T., William P., and Wood S. (1985) *The Car Industry: labour relations and industrial adjustment*, Tavistock, London.

Marsden D. W., and Ryan P. (1986) 'Where do young workers work? Youth employment by industry in various European economies', *British Journal of Industrial Relations*, Vol. 24 No. 1, March, pp. 83–102.

Marsh A. (1965) *Industrial Relations in the Engineering Industry*, Pergamon Press, Oxford.

Marshall A. (1920) *Principles of Economics*, Eighth edn, Macmillan, London.

Maurice M., Sellier F., and Silvestre J. J. (1978) 'Production de la hiérarchie dans l'entreprise: recherche d'un effet sociétal France-Allemagne', *Laboratoire d'Economie et de Sociologie du Travail*, Aix-en-Provence, (later published as Maurice M. et al. (1982).

———(1982) *Politique d'Education et Organisation Industrielle en France et en Allemagne*, Presses Universitaires de France, Paris.

———(1984) 'Rules, contexts, and actors: observations based on a comparison between France and Germany', *British Journal of Industrial Relations*, Vol. 25 No. 3, November, pp. 346–64.

Maurice M., Sorge A., and Warner M. (1979) 'Societal differences in organising manufacturing units. A comparison of France, West Germany and Great Britain', *International Institute of Management*, working paper IIM/79–15, Berlin.

Mill J. S. (1871) *Principles of Political Economy*, Parker, London.

Mincer J. (1962) 'On-the-job training: costs, returns, and some implications', *Journal of Political Economy*, Supplement, October, pp. 50–79.

Mincer J. (1974) *Schooling, experience and earnings*, National Bureau of Economic Research, New York.

Morel C. (1977) 'Les stratégies de négociation dans l'entreprise', *Sociologie du Travail* October–December, pp. 362–82.

——(1979) 'Le droit coutumier social dans l'entreprise', *Droit Social* No. 7–8, July–August, pp. 279–86.

——(1981) *La grève froide: stratégies syndicales et pouvoir patronale*, Les Editions de l'Organisation, Paris.

Mottez B. (1966) *Systèmes de salaire et politiques patronales: essai sur l'évolution des pratiques et des idéologies patronales*, Centre National de la Recherche Scientifique, Paris.

Nagel E. (1963) 'Assumptions in economic theory', *American Economic Review*, Vol. 53 No. 2, pp. 211–19.

Nioche J. P. (1969) 'Taille des établissements industriels dans sept pays développés', *Collections de l'INSEE*, Entreprises E1–1969, Institut National de la Statistique et des Etudés Economiques, Paris.

Nissim J. (1984) 'The price responsiveness of the demand for labour by skill: British mechanical engineering 1963–1978, *Economic Journal*, Vol. 94 No. 379, December, pp. 812–25.

Noll I., Beicht U., Boll G., Malcher W., and Wiederhold-Fritz S. (1984) *Nettokosten der betrieblichen Berufsbildung*, Schriften zur Berufsbildungsforschung, Band 63, Beuth Verlag GMBH, Berlin.

OECD (Organisation for Economic Cooperation and Development) (1984) *Employment Outlook*, September, Organisation for Economic Cooperation and Development, Paris.

Okun A. (1981) *Prices and quantities: a macroeconomic analysis*, Basil Blackwell, Oxford.

Olson M. (1971) *The logic of collective action*, Harvard University Press, Cambridge, Mass.

Osterman, P. (1982) 'Employment structures within firms', *British Journal of Industrial Relations*, Vol XX No. 3, November, pp. 349–361.

Osterman P. (ed.) (1984) *Internal labour markets*, MIT Press, Cambridge, Mass.

Oswald A. (1982) 'The microeconomic theory of the trade union', *Economic Journal*, Vol. 92 No. 367, September, pp. 576–95.

——(1983) 'The economic theory of trade unions: an introductory survey', Commissioned for the *Social Science Research Council* Labour Economics Study Group Conference, Hull University, July, revised as *Centre for Labour Economics* Discussion Paper No. 211, Feb. 1985, London School of Economics.

Oswald A., and Turnbull P. 'Pay and employment determination in Britain: what are labour contracts really like? ', *Centre for Labour Economics* Seminar on Unemployment, December 7 1984.

Parodi M. (1962) *Croissance Economique et Nivellement Hiérarchique des Salaires Ouvriers*, Editions Marcel Rivière, Paris.

Pascal A. H. (ed.) (1972) *Racial discrimination in economic life*, Lexington Books, Lexington, Mass.

Perlman S. (1928) *A theory of the labour movement*, Augustus Kelly, New York.

Phelps Brown E. H., and Browne M. (1968) *A Century of Pay*, Macmillan, London.

Phelps Brown E H., and Hopkins S. (1955) 'Seven centuries of building wages', *Economica*, Vol. 22 No. 87, August, pp. 195–206.

Phelps Brown E. H. (1977) *The inequality of pay*, Oxford University Press, Oxford.

Phillips A. W. (1958) 'The relationship between unemployment and the rate of change of money wages in the UK 1861–1957', *Economica*, Vol. 25, pp. 283–99.

Pigou A. C. (1921) *The Economics of Welfare*, 1st edn., Macmillan, London.

Piore M. J. (1973a) 'On the technological foundations of economic dualism', *MIT Dept. of Economics Discussion Paper*, No. 110, May.

——(1973b) Notes for a theory of labour market stratification. In *Edwards et al. eds.* (1973).

——(1978) 'Dualism in the labour market: a response to uncertainty and flux', *Revue Economique*, No. 1, January, pp. 26–48.

——(1980) 'Economic fluctuation, job security, and labour market duality in Italy, France, and the United States', *Politics and Society*, Vol. 9 No. 4, pp. 379–407.

Popitz H., Bahrdt H. P., Jures E. A., and Kesting H. (1957) *Das Gesellschaftsbild des Arbeiters: soziologische Untersuchüngen in der Hüttenindustrie*, J. C. B. Mohr (Paul Siebeck), Tübingen.

Popper K. (1959) *The logic of scientific discovery*, Routledge and Kegan Paul, London.

Prais S. (1976) *The Evolution of Giant Firms in Britain*, Cambridge University Press, Cambridge.

Prais S. J. (1981) *Productivity and industrial structure: a statistical study of manufacturing industry in Britain, Germany, and the United States*, Cambridge University Press, Cambridge.

Pratten C. F. (1976) *Labour productivity differentials within international companies*, Cambridge University Press, Cambridge.

Reynolds L. G. (1951) *The Structure of Labor Markets*, Harper and Brothers, New York.

Reynolds L. G., and Taft C. (1956) *The Evolution of Wage Structure*, Yale University Press, New Haven, Conn.

Routh G. (1980) *Occupation and Pay in Great Britain 1906–1979*, Macmillan, London.

Rowe J. W. E. (1928) *Wages in Practice and Theory*, Routledge and Kegan Paul, London.

Ryan, P. (1980) 'The costs of job training for a transferable skill', *British Journal of Industrial Relations*, Vol. 18 No. 3, November, pp. 334–51.

——(1981) 'Segmentation, duality, and the internal labour market', in Wilkinson (ed.), pp. 3–20.

——(1984) 'Job training, employment practices, and the large enterprise: the case of costly transferable skills', in Osterman (ed.), pp. 191–229.

——(1986) 'Trade unions and the pay of young workers', Forthcoming in Junankar P. N. (ed.) *From school to the dole queue?*, Macmillan, London.

Salter, W. E. G. (1966) *Productivity and Technical Change*, Second edn., Cambridge University Press, Cambridge.

Saunders C. T., and Marsden D. W. (1981) *Pay Inequalities in the European Community*, Butterworths, Sevenoaks.

Schumann M., Gerlach F., Gschlösll A., and Milhoffer P. (1971) *Am Beispiel der Septemberstreiks -Anfang der Rekonstruktionsperiode der Arbeiterklasse?* Europäische Verlagsanstalt, Frankfurt a/M.

Sellier F. (1961) *Stratégie de la lutte sociale*, Editions Ouvrières, Paris.

Simiand F. (1932) *Le Salaire: l'Evolution Sociale de la Monnaie: essai de théorie expérimentale du salaire*, Librairie Félix Alcan, Paris.

Slichter S. (1950) 'Notes on the structure of wages', *Review of Economics and Statistics*, vol. XXXII No. 1, February.

Sorge A. and Warner M. (1978a) 'The societal and organisational context of industrial relations: a comparison of Great Britain and West Germany', Working Paper, 78–53, International Institute of Management, Berlin.

——(1978b) 'Manpower training, manufacturing organisation and work roles in Great Britain and West Germany', Working Paper, pp. 78–96, International Institute of Management, Berlin.

Spence M. (1973) 'Job market signalling', *Quarterly Journal of Economics*, Vol. 77, pp. 355–74.

Stiglitz J. (1973) 'Approaches to the economics of discrimination', *American Economic Review*, Vol. 63 No. 2, May, pp. 287–95.

——(1984) 'Theories of wage rigidity', paper presented to the Centre for Labour Economics, London School of Economics, April.

Streeck W. (1985) *Die Reform der beruflichen Bildung in der West-deutschen Bauwirtschaft 1969–82*, Internationales Institut für Management und Verwaltung, Berlin.

Streeck W., and Hoff A. (eds.) (1983) 'Workforce restructuring, manpower management and industrial relations in the world automobile industry', Vol. 2 Case studies, International Institute of Management, Berlin.

Sutton J. (1981) 'Comment on Azariadis', in Hornstein *et al.* (ed.).

Thompson E. P. (1968) *The Making of the English Working Class*, Second Edn., Penguin Books, Harmondsworth.

Tolliday S., and Zeitlin J. (1982) 'Shop Floor Bargaining, Contract Unionism, and Job control: an Anglo-American comparison', Kings College Research Centre, Cambridge, paper prepared for the session on Mass Production Unionism in Britain and America, AHA convention, Washington D.C., December.

Touraine A. (1955) *L'évolution du travail ouvrier aux usines Renault*, Editions du CNRS, Paris.

——(1966) *La conscience ouvrière*, Seuil, Paris.

——(1965) *La Sociologie de l'Action* , Seuil, Paris.

Tressel R. (1955) *The ragged trousered philanthropists*, Lawrence and Wishart, London (page reference to Panther edition).

Webb S. and Webb B. (1902) *Industrial Democracy*, Longmans, London.

Wiles P., and Routh G. (eds.) (1984) *Economics in disarray*, Basil Blackwell, Oxford.

Wilkinson F. (ed.) (1981) *The dynamics of labour market segmentation*, Academic Press, London.

Williamson O. (1975) *Markets and hierarchies: analysis and antitrust implications*, Free Press, Glencoe.

William P. (1982) *Fairness, collective bargaining and incomes policy*, Oxford University Press, Oxford.

Willman P., and Winch G. (1984) *Innovation and management control: labour relations at BL cars*, Cambridge University Press, Cambridge.

Wood A. (1978) *A Theory of Pay*, Cambridge University Press, Cambridge.

Wootton B. (1955) *The Social Foundations of Wage Policy*, Unwin University Books (second edn. 1962), London.

Index